Teaching Young Adult Literature

Teaching Young Adult Literature

Developing Students as World Citizens

Thomas W. Bean
University of Nevada, Las Vegas

Judith Dunkerly-Bean
Innovations International Charter School of Nevada

Helen J. Harper
University of Nevada, Las Vegas

Los Angeles | London | New Delhi
Singapore | Washington DC

Los Angeles | London | New Delhi
Singapore | Washington DC

FOR INFORMATION:

SAGE Publications, Inc.
2455 Teller Road
Thousand Oaks, California 91320
E-mail: order@sagepub.com

SAGE Publications Ltd.
1 Oliver's Yard
55 City Road
London EC1Y 1SP
United Kingdom

SAGE Publications India Pvt. Ltd.
B 1/I 1 Mohan Cooperative Industrial Area
Mathura Road, New Delhi 110 044
India

SAGE Publications Asia-Pacific Pte. Ltd.
3 Church Street
#10-04 Samsung Hub
Singapore 049483

Acquisitions Editor: Diane McDaniel
Editorial Assistant: Megan Koraly
Production Editor: Libby Larson
Copy Editor: Sheree Van Vreede
Typesetter: C&M Digitals (P) Ltd.
Proofreader: Wendy Jo Dymond
Indexer: Jean Casalegno
Cover Designer: Gail Buschman
Marketing Manager: Terra Schultz
Permissions Editor: Adele Hutchinson

Printed in the United States of America

Library of Congress Cataloging-in-Publication Data

Bean, Thomas W.

Teaching Young Adult Literature : Developing Students as World Citizens / Thomas W. Bean, University of Nevada-Las Vegas ; Judith Dunkerly-Bean, Innovations International Charter School of Nevada; Helen J. Harper, University of Nevada-Las Vegas.

pages cm
Includes bibliographical references and index.

ISBN 978-1-4129-5684-0 (pbk. : acid-free paper)

1. Young adult literature—Study and teaching.
2. Teenagers—Books and

reading—United States. I. Dunkerly-Bean, Judith.
II. Harper, Helen J., 1957- III. Title.

PN1008.8.B38 2014
809′.892830712—dc23   2012040732

This book is printed on acid-free paper.

13 14 15 16 17 10 9 8 7 6 5 4 3 2 1

BRIEF CONTENTS

Detailed Contents

FOREWORD

Navigating the field of young adult literature can be a difficult journey filled with much angst, just like adolescence. There are many twists, turns, and road-blocks along the way. There is so much literature being published in so many genres that the numerous issues and ideas being written about can become overwhelming. It is a relief to find a resource that serves as a guide for the journey. Thomas Bean, Judith Dunkerly-Bean, and Helen Harper's book, *Teaching Young Adult Literature,* does a great job of helping readers navigate their way. Whether undergraduates, postgraduates, teachers, or librarians, this book provides a plethora of ideas and activities to help readers delve deeper into young adult literature as the authors integrate the Common Core Standards seamlessly.

Bean, Dunkerly-Bean, and Harper have a wealth of knowledge of titles including classics, current favorites, new titles to explore, and a few hidden gems as well. Their selection of books includes the genres of realistic fiction, mystery, humor, graphic novels, poetry, contemporary texts, and so much more. Adolescent readers with varied interests will find a book or text that will engage them in reading.

Not only that, but with so much technology being used and explored in class-rooms across the globe, it is nice to have a resource that includes an abundance of websites, apps, and other resources that could be used in conjunction with the literature presented in the book. The example found in Chapter 8 is but one illustration of allowing readers the option to examine the uses of technology in the classroom, and to be critical examiners of what might be beneficial for their own students.

The vignettes peppered throughout the book help provide practical ways that young adult literature is and can be used in the classroom. One example is in Chapter 10's discussion of comics. The vignette discusses how a teacher's activity allows the students the opportunity to research the history of superhero characters found in comic books. With all the new films with such characters as

Batman, Spiderman, and the Avengers, this is an excellent chance for students to delve deeper into the history of these characters. Taking meaningful characters they know about currently, and finding their origins, furthers their engagement in reading.

This book serves as a strong resource that will help current and future teachers reach readers with very diverse needs. I am confident that this will be a well-used resource for all teachers and educators.

May your students be turning the pages in their books and buzzing with ideas.

Happy reading,

Dr. Matthew D. Zbaracki
Australian Catholic University

PREFACE

Young adult literature is dynamic, wide ranging, and engaging for readers between the ages of 12 and 18. Young adult literature offers readers insights into their own lives, identities, and life trajectories.

Teaching Young Adult Literature is aimed at preservice and inservice educators who will be teaching contemporary young adult literature. In writing this text, we sought to encompass multiple genres and interests, highlighting key titles and providing teaching strategies aimed at increasing students' critical literacy practices, as well as more traditional reader response interpretations of young adult literature. With the advent of Common Core Standards, we aimed to make the text consistent with the goals set forward in this important document.

With respect to Common Core Standards, we agree with scholars Richard Beach, Amanda Haertling Thein, and Allen Webb (2012), who note,

> Literature allows students to imaginatively step into alternative worlds, both like their own as well as far-distant, and gain understanding of self and others in rich social, cultural, and historical contexts. From this perspective what matters most about the study of literature is not the memorization of different genres or forms or gaining passing familiarity with a canon of cultural monuments. Instead, you can select works that will address issues in their lives and the broader world. (p. 137)

Young adult literature can play a profound role in developing students as world citizens able to navigate an increasingly permeable global world linked by the Internet across nation-states and vast geographic boundaries. Becoming familiar with diversity, diasporas, and the struggles of adolescents in a variety of contexts can broadens students' sense that we are increasingly living at the nexus of the local and global in our classrooms (Harper, Bean, & Dunkerly, 2010). Thus, we sought to include, in addition to established genres, an array of titles that encompass international, global young adult literature.

ORGANIZATION

Teaching Young Adult Literature is divided into three major sections:

Part I: Foundations for the Teaching of Young Adult Literature

The four chapters in this introductory section address the following topics: adolescent life, the texts available for teaching a history of young adult literature, aspects of teaching with young adult literature, and teaching young adult literature relevant for exceptional learners.

Part II: Established and Emerging Genres of Young Adult Literature

The eight chapters in the genre study section address the following established and emerging genres: realistic fiction, romance, and mystery; science fiction, fantasy, and horror; historical fiction; short stories, poetry, and humor; nonfiction, biographies, informational, and self-help books; comics, manga, graphic novels, zines, and street (urban) literature; postmodern forms of young adult literature; and global and multicultural literature for young adults.

Part III: Critical Issues in Young Adult Literature

The four chapters in this final section consider the following topics: boys books/girls books—gender and sexuality in young adult literature; young adult literature and critical content area literacy; censorship; and technology and the future of young adult literature. In our own work with young adult literature in our classes, we find each of these major areas important in developing a strong foundation in young adult literature and related pedagogical practices.

FEATURES AND BENEFITS

Major features within Part I and throughout the book designed to assist instructors teaching these courses include

- Learning objectives
- Common Core Standards related to each chapter's content
- Classroom vignettes of teachers' classrooms and related young adult literature
- Professional Reflection and Discussion activities aimed at furthering a critical understanding of each chapter's content
- Specific young adult literature titles and synopses, as well as resources to locate high-quality young adult literature
- Resources that support unit and lesson planning with young adult literature and related teaching approaches and strategies
- Small group activities aimed at deeper understanding of chapter content
- Discussion questions to assess and ensure students' understanding of chapter content
- Recommended readings from professional sources that extend understanding and application of chapter content
- Recommended young adult literature
- Recommended films
- Recommended websites
- References

Additional features in Part II and related genre chapters (5–12) include

- Defining characteristics of each genre
- Criteria for selecting high-quality young adult literature related to each genre
- Multimedia Text Sets integrating young adult literature and multimodal resources including music and video clips

Part III is aimed at exploring key issues in young adult literature (e.g., gender and sexuality, critical content area literacy, censorship, and technology) and at offering strategies and solutions to address these issues.

INSTRUCTOR TEACHING SITE

A password-protected site, available at www.sagepub.com/bean, features author-provided resources that have been designed to help you plan and teach your course. These resources include an extensive test bank, chapter-specific PowerPoint presentations, a sample syllabus discussion questions, and Web resources.

REFERENCES

Beach, R., Thein, A. H., & Webb, A. (2012). *Teaching to exceed the English Language Arts Common Core Standards: A literacy practices approach for 6–12 classrooms.* New York, NY: Routledge.

Harper, H., Bean, T. W., & Dunkerly, J. (2010). Cosmopolitanism, globalization and the field of adolescent literacy. *Canadian and International Education, 38*(2), 1–13.

ACKNOWLEDGMENTS

We would like to thank our editor, Diane McDaniel, and her editorial assistant, Megan Koraly, for their work on this book. We would also like to thank the students in our classes who have been able to discover a rich array of young adult literature that engages their students in thoughtful consideration of a host of contemporary issues.

Special thanks to those who helped review our book:

Cathy Collins Block, Texas Christian University

Manya Chappell, Mississippi State University

Jacquelyn Culpepper, Mercer University

Linda Kay Davis, Austin Peay State University

Margaret Phillips Dillner, University of Delaware

Suzanne Fondrie, University of Wisconsin–Oshkosh

John T. Ikeda Franklin, Pittsburgh State University

A. Waller Hastings, West Liberty University

Judith A. Hayn, University of Arkansas–Little Rock

Lisa A. Hazlett, The University of South Dakota

Beverly J. Hearn, University of Tennessee at Martin

Holly Johnson, University of Cincinnati

Melanie A. Kimball, University at Buffalo, State University of New York

Karen Mae Lafferty, Morehead State University

Mark Letcher, University of Oklahoma

Barbara Stein Martin, University of North Texas

Andrea Neptune, Sierra College

Donna L. Pasternak, University of Wisconsin–Milwaukee

Buzz R. Pounds, Lewis University

Robert G. Prickett, Winthrop University

Barbara J. Ray, Northeastern State University

Maurine Richardson, The University of South Dakota

Lynda Robinson, Cameron University

Marilyn Russell, University of Cincinnati

James A. Salzman, Cleveland State University

Roxanne Myers Spencer, Western Kentucky University

Janice Marcuccilli Strop, Cardinal Stritch University

Anne R. Thomson, The University of Michigan–Dearborn

Karen Laurd Towers, Saint Mary's of Minnesota–Winona

Warren B. Westcott, Tennessee State University

Daha J. Wilber, Montclair State University

Sue E. Williams, Olivet Nazarene University

ABOUT THE AUTHORS

 **Thomas W. Bean, PhD,** is a professor of literacy and reading in the Teaching and Learning Department, College of Education, University of Nevada, Las Vegas. Tom earned his PhD at Arizona State University and is considered a leading scholar in content area literacy and the infusion of multicultural and global young adult literature in the classroom. His work has been published in *The ALAN Review, Reading Research Quarterly,* and *Journal of Adolescent & Adult Literacy.* Along with co-author Dr. Judith Dunkerly-Bean, he served as co-editor of the International Reading Association's *Journal of Adolescent & Adult Literacy.* Tom is the senior author of the widely used text, *Content Area Literacy: An Integrated Approach* (now in its 10th ed.). He can be contacted at beant1@unlv.nevada.edu.

 **Judith Dunkerly-Bean, PhD,** a literacy specialist and award-winning classroom teacher, has served as a faculty member at the University of Nevada, Las Vegas, where she has taught university courses in literacy methods including children's and young adult literature. Her research focuses on the intersection of human rights, social justice, and critical literacy through a cosmopolitan framework. Her work has been published in several journals, including *Current Issues in Comparative Education and Language and Literacy.* Along with co-author Dr. Thomas Bean, Dr. Dunkerly-Bean served as the associate editor for the International Reading Association's *Journal of Adolescent and Adult Literacy.* She currently teaches at Innovations International Charter School of Nevada. She can be contacted at judith_bean@iicsn.org.

Helen J. Harper, PhD, was a professor of cultural studies and English education in the Curriculum and Instruction Department, College of Education, University of Nevada, Las Vegas. Helen earned her PhD at the University of Toronto, Ontario Institute for the Study of Education (OISE). She was a widely published scholar and co-editor of the International Reading Association journal *Journal of Adolescent & Adult Literacy.* Her research was published in major journals and handbooks in the field including the *Handbook of Research on Teaching the English Language Arts* (3rd ed.). Dr. Harper's research in critical literacy included the books *Wild Words/Dangerous Desires* and *Advocacy Research in Literacy Education: Seeking Higher Ground.*

PART I

Foundations for the Teaching of Young Adult Literature

Chapter 1

An Introduction to Adolescent Life, Texts, and Teaching

Adolescent life is often viewed as a tumultuous time of physical, cognitive, social, and psychological development (Latrobe & Drury, 2009). For example, as early as 1904, G. Stanley Hall, often referred to as the "father of adolescence" commented: "Adolescence is a time of storm and stress." But more contemporary views suggest that adolescents are much more complex, less homogenized, and actually very diverse (Lesko, 2001). Indeed, according to recent demographics, the adolescent population is growing and immigration accounts for much of that growth with the fastest growing group largely Hispanic (Bean & Harper, 2011; Campano & Ghiso, 2011).

In this and the chapters that follow, we explore the dynamic nature of **young adult literature**, and the current and possible use of young adult literature in contemporary English classrooms as well as in other content subjects. We define *young adult literature* as literary works (usually fiction but not always) intended for readers between the ages of 12 and 18.

Each chapter in the book provides specific leaning objectives, and discussion questions based on the learning objectives are located at the end of each chapter to deepen your knowledge of young adult literature and related teaching practices.

We begin this chapter by going into an urban, middle school English/Language Arts classroom where young adult literature figures prominently. This is a real classroom and a real teacher facing difficult but not uncommon pedagogical challenges. The remainder of the chapter provides a rationale for the book and a consideration of the changing nature of adolescent life, texts, and teaching in relation to young adult literature.

Learning Objectives

- Understand the importance of adolescents reading across a broad range of young adult literature for pleasure and information on a variety of issues.

- Consider and be able to discuss the changing nature of young adult literature including online communication technologies.

- Develop an initial understanding of the relationship between students' ethnic and cultural diversity and available young adult literature that engages students' interests.

- Know how to use online lesson planning resources to create engaging young adult literature lessons.

- Begin creating a database of young adult literature.

Vignette: Ashley's Middle School English Class

As a way to begin thinking about young adult literature in the classroom, we follow Ashley Norton into her middle school English/Language Arts classroom. Ashley is a young teacher, intelligent, dedicated, and relatively new to the profession. She is currently working on her master's degree while teaching full time. Her school is located in a high-density, urban area in the southwestern United States. A large number of students at her school live in poverty, and there is a substantial population of second-language learners. Indeed, 65% of the students are English language learners with the majority speaking Spanish as their first language. Many students struggle with literacy in both English and their native language. All of the students in Ashley's class are functioning below grade level, although there is considerable variation. The students' reading levels (in English) range from second to sixth grade.

The school itself is an attractive oasis in a depressing sea of casinos, small bars, and older strip malls in decline. The faculty is dedicated to creative and engaging teaching, fostered by a principal who supports their ongoing professional development and, in particular, the use of multimedia technology. The school operates using a middle school philosophy and organization. This allows Ashley to work in a core team with science and social science teachers, co-planning a **thematic unit** centered on social justice.

The students in Ashley's English Language Arts class had recently completed their reading and discussion of Walter Dean Myers's young adult novel *Monster* (1999).

The novel takes the reader into a county jail as the main character, Steve Harmon, a 16-year-old African American, goes on trial as an accomplice in a convenience store robbery and murder. Throughout the novel, Steve's guilt or innocence remains a question. The novel format features time-bending, shifts in scenes, voice and font, and a variety of text **genres.** For example, the author includes diary entries, court transcripts, and photo images to forward the plot. The novel, like many contemporary young adult books, appealed to Ashley's students.

With help, her students were able to read and engage the novel with success. In class discussions, the students addressed the stereotyping of delinquent teens, especially minority teens, in popular and school culture.

As a culminating activity, Ashley's students created *Body Biographies* (Bean, Readence, & Baldwin, 2012; Smagorinsky & O'Donnell-Allen, 1998) depicting Steve's struggles. Body biographies involve tracing the outline of a life-sized human body on butcher paper, on which collage-like images culled from magazines, the Internet, and the like, along with key quotes are positioned to capture themes and character elements in a novel. Once they completed their body biographies, students in Ashley's class conducted a "gallery walk" during which time students presented (in English with occasional code-switching to Spanish) their biographies and talked about the particular elements they included. Figure 1.1 displays an example **Body Biography.**

FIGURE 1.1   Body Biography

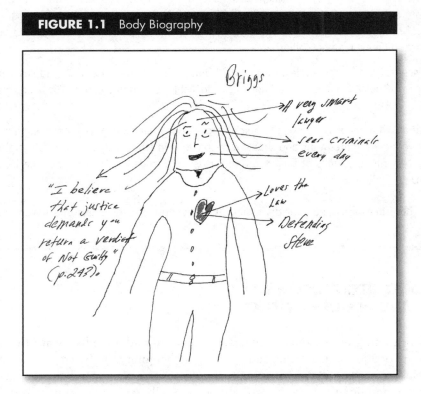

Body biographies represent one of many ways to engage students in the reading and discussion of young adult literature. As this text progresses, we introduce a wide array of strategies for readers to consider. For now, we simply want to introduce the possibility of using contemporary young adult literature in

English Language Arts classrooms, including Ashley's, and to begin to think more deeply about our individual and collective notions of text, teens, and teaching. To initiate such thinking, Activity 1.1 asks you to discuss the following questions and, of course, to add your own.

ACTIVITY 1.1: Professional Reflection and Discussion

Discuss the following questions individually and then in small groups.
Record your answers.

1. **Text:** What is the difference between "text" and "book"? What texts were evident in the students' experience of *Monster* in Ashley's classroom? What counts as "legitimate" text in many of today's classrooms? What counts as school literature? What texts are used to evaluate students' reading ability?

2. **Adolescents:** Who is the adolescent reader? What is the usual image of the adolescent reader in schools? From what we know, how do Ashley's students confirm or belie this image?

3. **Teaching:** What needs to be done to help improve adolescents' literacy? What is contemporary young adult literature, and should it be included in school curriculum? What might be the benefits and limits of this literature for Ashley's students? How might it be best taught?

Consider these questions and your discussion as you continue to read this and upcoming chapters.

YOUNG ADULT LITERATURE AND THE CHANGING NATURE OF TEXT

As beginning or seasoned teachers, readers are undoubtedly aware that the nature of adolescents, texts, and teaching is changing rapidly. These new times include emerging communication technologies and the incumbent changes in textual and linguistic practices—what is generally referred to as new literacies (Bean, 2010; Kist, 2010; Knobel & Lankshear, 2008)—are demanding new approaches to the teaching of literacy. Many adolescents are comfortable users of the new technologies, and they are engaging with multiple forms of text including print-based novels, nonfiction books, and magazines, but increasingly,

reader experiences the Apaches' deep connection to nature and belief in the importance of trust.

Traditionally intended for readers between the ages of 12 and 18 (Latrobe & Drury, 2009), young adult literature has evolved over the years to encompass postmodern features where a single novel or work may include elements of a play, a diary, poetry, images, and other media. The boundaries of what constitutes "text" are blurring. Young adult literature is flourishing because it, like its young adult audience, is dynamic and interesting. Young adult literature can be read simply for the window it offers on a topic, but it can illuminate content area concepts and events in history, mathematics, science, English, and other content areas. In addition, paired with classical canonical texts including Shakespeare, young adult literature can form a powerful bridge for students to read and appreciate parallel themes in the classics and contemporary literature. The resources available to assist your lesson and unit development in English classes have never been better. In Activity 1.2, you can explore one of the many resources available that make planning powerful young adult literature lessons manageable.

Contemporary young adult literature can be paired with the classics.

ACTIVITY 1.2: Professional Reflection and Discussion

ReadWriteThink is a co-sponsored online project supported by the National Council of Teachers of English and the International Reading Association. This site offers a huge array of carefully crafted lesson plans that include young adult literature and other topics. The site is easily searchable and includes links to journal articles, lists of student objectives, and instructional plans directly linked to key standards. In this activity, you have an opportunity to examine a specific lesson plan for the high-interest young adult novel *The Bully* (Langan, 2007) developed by Kathleen Benson Quinn (2009).

1. **ReadWriteThink:** Go to the URL for the lesson plan on this novel (www.readwritethink.org/lessons/lesson_view.asp?id=390).

2. Examine the lesson plan and its related links, including the synopsis of *The Bully*.

3. Discuss how you would use this teaching resource with another teacher or class member in a Think-Pair-Share fashion.

This activity foreshadows a wide array of resources, many of them online, that can support your teaching with young adult literature. Planning for teaching young adult literature also means thinking about multiple forms of text including films, podcasts, television, and other media-based resources.

TEACHING WITH YOUNG ADULT LITERATURE

Because young adult literature has matured into a powerful *genre* that captures the wide range of human experience, it lends itself to close reading, discussion, integration with classical literature (Probst, 2004), and the development of **intertextuality** through connections to films, television, and other text forms (Hobbs, 2007). For example, the widely circulated young adult novel *Holes* (Sachar, 1998) has an equally popular film version. Carl Hiaasen's Florida-based novel *Hoot* (Hiaasen, 2002), features middle school characters and an ecological mystery. Like *Holes*, *Hoot* also has a film version of the novel. The *Harry Potter* books have legions of fans who read both the books and flock to the film versions. It is possible to weave creatively together films and classical literature. For example, as a high school English teacher in California, Ernest Morrell (2008) combined old episodes of *The Godfather* with classical literature like the *Odyssey*. In addition, reading young adult literature, followed by opportunities to write about it reflectively, engage in dramatic responses, create, design, and present multimedia and art can result in the kind of close reading necessary for a host of other, future readings (Sumara, 2002). In a careful consideration of *Why Reading Literature in School Still Matters*, Dennis Sumara (2000) notes,

> I have come to think of the experience of developing a deep relationship with a literary text as a focal practice—an interpretive event that occurs when one becomes committed to the making of something that provokes attention to detail, requires the development of interpretation and production skills, and sustains attention, energy and interest. (p. 150)

Although this sort of reading is integral to the classroom use of literature in general and of young adult literature introduced in our book, it is important to note that there is nothing wrong with curling up with any good book and reading it for the sheer pleasure of escape, vicarious journeying with characters, and a respite from our fast-paced lives. Picture books also have a place in the middle and secondary English and other content area classrooms

(Carr , Buchanan, Wentz, Weiss, & Brant 2001). For example, in social stud-ies, Dorinda Makanaonalani Nicholson's (1998) eyewitness picture book account of the bombing of Pearl Harbor titled *Pearl Harbor Child* can be paired with the young adult novel *Eyes of the Emperor* (Salisbury, 2005) and related text material and films to illuminate the onset of World War II. Using multiple texts in this fashion is particularly helpful for **struggling/striving readers** and **English language learners (ELLs).**

Efforts to engage adolescents in sustained silent reading and the resulting flow states that accompany immersion in a captivating story are one way to accomplish this connection with literature. Throughout the book, you will find evaluation criteria aimed at selecting high-quality young adult literature across various genres (e.g., fiction, nonfic-tion, historical fiction, biography, science fiction, and other genres). Given the vast array of young adult literature currently available, it is helpful to develop a critical eye toward this burgeoning collection.

It is helpful to develop a critical eye toward the wide variety of young adult literature.

All of the topics mentioned in this chapter and others will be considered in greater detail. In the three major sections and chapters of the text that follow, we introduce you to the following topics.

In Part I: *Foundations for the Teaching of Young Adult Literature,* the current chapter, Chapter 1: *An Introduction to Adolescent Life, Texts, and Teaching* introduces the major topics in the book along with selected young adult novels and recom-mended readings. Chapter 2: *The Nature and History of Young Adult Literature* traces the movement toward realism, and more recently, the postmodern turn in young adult literature. Chapter 3: *The Teaching of Young Adult Literature* introduces various literary response approaches including cul-tural heritage, reader response or personal response, and cultural criticism, along with guidelines for teaching young adult literature including unit planning. Chapter 4: *Young Adult Literature and Exceptional Learners* considers young adult literature that includes English language learners, gifted and talented students, striving and struggling readers, and students with disabilities.

Part II: *Established and Emerging Genres of Young Adult Literature* covers established, contemporary, postmodern, global, and multicultural forms of young adult literature. Chapter 5: *Realistic Fiction, Romance, and Mystery* offers an overview, evaluation criteria, and recommended literature across these popular and well-established categories. Chapter 6: *Science Fiction, Fantasy, and Horror* considers these popular categories with criteria for selection and evaluation. Chapter 7: *Historical Fiction* looks at key titles that illuminate historical events (e.g., Pearl Harbor). Chapter 8: *Short Stories, Poetry, and Humor* considers high-quality collections in this genre that appeal to adolescents. Chapter 9: *Nonfiction, Biographies, Information, and Self-help* reviews this array of popular books in young adult literature. Chapter 10: *Comics, Manga, Graphic Novels, Zines, and Street (Urban) Literature* introduces more avant-garde genres that have wide appeal for adolescents. Chapter 11: *Postmodern Forms of Young Adult Literature* considers emerging forms of young adult literature characterized by postmodern features (e.g., font shifts, point-of-view shifts, time bending, mixed genres, and others), as well as graphic novels and media works. Chapter 12: *Global and Multicultural Literature for Young Adults* introduces the rich array of books set in multiethnic and international contexts. This chapter highlights notions of self and other, local, national, and global identity. Each chapter in Part II includes ideas for using young adult literature in the classroom.

Part III: *Critical Issues in Young Adult Literature* takes up additional topics and resources relevant in the 21st-century classroom. Chapter 13: *Boys Books/ Girls Books? Gender and Sexuality in Young Adult Literature* introduces gender theory, young adult romance, and censorship issues. Chapter 14: *Young Adult Literature and Critical Content Area Literacy* shows how to integrate critical literacy practices with young adult literature from genres including realism and global and multicultural literature in relation to democratic life.

Chapter 15: *Censorship* offers a variety of ways to defuse censorship issues and ensure diverse young adult literature choices. Chapter 16: *Technology and the Future of Young Adult Literature* discusses electronic books (e-books), the Internet, text messaging, and other multimodal ways of reading and responding to young adult literature.

SPECIAL FEATURES OF THIS TEXT

Several teaching and literature response strategies are modeled throughout the text including Discussion Questions, Reader Response, and Critical Literacy. In addition, artistic and multimedia response modes including drawing, role playing, art, video and podcast production, wiki-writing, book reviews for Internet audiences (e.g., Amazon.com), blogging, and other approaches are considered. In the genre chapters, we consider how the Common Core Standards are supported by teaching various young adult genres. In addition, we provide examples of multimedia text sets that illustrate contemporary teaching practices with young adult literature. We also include vignettes of teens and classroom practices like the one at the beginning of this chapter to give you a concrete sense of how young adult literature can be an integral part of your classroom. The importance of including cultural histories of the

Myers, W. D. (2010). *Lockdown*. New York, NY: HarperCollins/Amistad.

Main character Reese wants to get out of juvenile hall incarceration early by working in a senior citizens home. Conflict arises with one of the residents and Reese must work hard to redeem himself and leave the criminal world behind. Hope looms large in Walter Dean Myers's novels, and this one takes teen readers into Reese's thoughts and actions.

Sachar, L. (1998). *Holes*. New York, NY: Dell Laurel-Leaf.

This now well-known account of Stanley Yelnat's exile to Camp Green Lake where he and the other boys must dig an endless collection of holes in the desert, for no apparent reason. The detention center warden has another agenda, and *Holes* offers readers an engaging mystery. The film that is now available enhances inclusion of this novel in the classroom.

Salisbury, G. (2005). *Eyes of the emperor*. New York, NY: Wendy Lamb Books.

Eddy Okubo, the main character in this novel, enlists to serve his country in the U.S. Army. The book chronicles Eddie's experiences on Cat Island in the South where he and his fellow Hawai'ian soldiers are sent to serve as dog bait for a canine corps planning to chase Japanese soldiers. The book deals with racism and social injustice.

Vizzini, N. (2000). *Teen angst? Naaah . . . : A quasi-autobiography*. Minneapolis, MN: Free Spirit Publishing.

Young writer Ned Vizzini chronicles his high school experiences with tongue-in-cheek humor. His topics range from high-stakes testing at Stuyvesant High School in New York, to video games, girls, and the huge array of concepts hitting him from all sides in his high school classes.

Yep, L. (1993). *Dragon's gate*. New York, NY: HarperCollins.

This novel chronicles the Chinese workers' experiences while building the transcontinental railroad in rough physical and psychological conditions in the Colorado mountains.

RECOMMENDED FILMS

A huge number of teen films can be found at the following Wikipedia site: http://en.wikipedia.org/wiki/Category:Teen_Films

Each film (e.g., *Dangerous Minds*) listing includes a synopsis, cast, soundtrack, and other useful information if you are planning lessons where teen film might be read in concert with a young adult novel (e.g., *Holes*). In addition, these films portray teen life from a variety of stances including narrow, stereotypical views of teens as bundles of raging hormones to more finely nuanced portrayals.

RECOMMENDED WEBSITES

Quinn, K. B. (2009). *A high-interest novel helps struggling readers confront bullying in schools*. ReadWriteThink Lesson Plan. Retrieved from http://www.readwritethink.org/lessons/lesson_view.asp?id=390

REFERENCES

ACT. (2006). *Reading between the lines: What the ACT reveals about college readiness in reading*. Iowa City, IA: ACT.

Adolescent literacy: A position statement of the International Reading Association. (2012). Retrieved from http://www.reading.org/Libraries/Resources/ps1079_adolescentliteracy_rev2012.pdf

Batalova, J., Fix, M., & Murray, J. (2007). *Measures of change: The demography and literacy of adolescent English learners*. New York, NY: Carnegie Corporation.

Bean, T. W. (2010). *Multimodal learning for the 21st Century adolescent*. Huntington Beach, CA: Shell Education.

Bean, T. W., & Harper, H. (2011). The context of English language arts learning: The high school years. In D. Lapp & D. Fisher (Eds.), *Handbook of research on teaching the English language arts* (3rd ed., pp. 60–68). New York, NY: Routledge.

Bean, T. W., Readence, J. E., & Baldwin, R. S. (2012). *Content area literacy: An integrated approach* (10th ed.). Dubuque, IA: Kendall/Hunt.

Biancarosa, G., & Snow, C. (2004). *Reading next: A vision for action and research in middle and high school literacy: A report to the Carnegie Corporation of New York*. Washington, DC: Alliance for Excellent Education.

Campano, G., & Ghiso, M. P. (2011). Immigrant students as cosmopolitan intellectuals. In S. A. Wolf, K. Coats, P. Enciso, & C. A. Jenkins (Eds.), *Handbook of research on children's and young adult literature* (pp. 164–176). New York, NY: Routledge.

Carr, K. S., Buchanan, D. L., Wentz, J. B., Weiss, M. L., & Brant, K. J. (2001). Not just for the primary grades: A bibliography of picture books for secondary content teachers. *Journal of Adolescent & Adult Literacy, 45*, 146–153.

Hall, S. G. (1904). *Adolescence: Its psychology and its relations to physiology, anthropology, sociology, sex, crime, religion, and education* (Vols. I & II). New York, NY: D. Appleton.

Hobbs, R. (2007). *Reading the media: Media literacy in high school English*. New York, NY: Teachers College Press.

Kist, W. (2010). *The socially networked classroom: Teaching in the new media age*. Thousand Oaks, CA: Corwin.

Knobel, M., & Lankshear, C. (2008). Remix: The art and craft of endless hybridization. *Journal of Adolescent & Adult Literacy, 52* (1), 22–33.

Latrobe, K. H., & Drury, J. (2009). *Critical approaches to young adult literature*. New York, NY: Neal-Schuman.

Lesko, N. (2001). *Act your age? A cultural construction of adolescence*. New York, NY: Routledge.

Moore, D. W., Bean, T. W., Birdyshaw, D., & Rycik, J. A. (1999). Adolescent literacy: A position statement. *Journal of Adolescent & Adult Literacy, 43*, 97–112. Also available from http://explorers.tsuniv.edu/ira-alc

Morrell, E. (2008). *Critical literacy and urban youth: Toward a theory of praxis*. Mahwah, NJ: Lawrence Erlbaum.

National Assessment for Educational Progress (NAEP) (2012). Available from the National Center for Education Statistics: http://nces.ed.gov/nationsreportcard/

National Governors Association Center for Best Practices (2012). Core standards. Available from http://www.corestandards.org

Nicholson, D. M. (1998). *Pearl Harbor child*. Honolulu, HI: Arizona Memorial Museum Association.

Nilsen, A. P., & Donelson, K. L. (2008). *Literature for today's young adults* (8th ed.). Boston, MA: Allyn & Bacon.

Probst, R. E. (2004). *Response & analysis: Teaching literature in secondary school* (2nd ed.). Portsmouth, NH: Heinemann.

Quinn, K. B. (2009). *A high-interest novel helps struggling readers confront bullying in schools*. ReadWriteThink Lesson Plan. Retrieved from http://www.readwritethink.org/lessons/lesson_view.asp?id=390

Smagorinsky, P., & O'Donnell-Allen, C. (1998). Reading as mediated and mediating action: Composing meaning for literature through multimedia interpretive texts. *Reading Research Quarterly, 33*, 198–226.

Sturtevant, E. G., Boyd, F. B., Brozo, W. G., Hinchman, K. A., Moore, D. W., & Alvermann, D. E. (2006). *Principled practices for adolescent literacy: A framework for instruction and policy*. Mahwah, NJ: Lawrence Erlbaum.

Sumara, D. J. (2002). *Why reading literature in school still matters: Imagination, interpretation, insight*. Mahwah, NJ: Lawrence Erlbaum.

genre away from middle-class characters to working-class Ponyboy and his rough-and-tumble Greasers gang. Sequels to this novel and subsequent film adaptations including the surreal black-and-white images in *Rumblefish* furthered interest in Hinton's harsh portrayal of working-class, tough-guy teens. Nevertheless, these were White male characters. Multicultural young adult literature was still not a force in the genre or in the classrooms.

MULTICULTURAL YOUNG ADULT LITERATURE

During the period from 1885 through the 1950s, Mexican and African American characters in novels for young adult readers were usually represented in stereotypical fashion or given only minor roles as characters (Bucher & Manning, 2006). Most of the authors were White. Although the number of minority authors and the number of stories about minority teens and their lives has increased, it remains a problem even now. However, the genre is expanding in this area and includes some very powerful literature with complex characters, for example, Laurence Yep's (1993) *Dragon's Gate*, a chronicle of the plight of Chinese indentured workers on the transcontinental railroad, and Gary Soto's (1999) *Buried Onions*, an inside look at Mexican American barrio life in agricultural Fresno, California. In 1976, a landmark young adult novel by Mildred Taylor, *Roll of Thunder, Hear My Cry,* became a classic within the young adult genre. Taylor's now widely read novel challenged stereotypes of Black families in the South (Bucher & Manning, 2006). This novel is now part of the **literary canon** alongside classics from Hawthorne and other American authors.

What is important about all the novels mentioned thus far is that each of these authors offers the reader an insider's window on human experience, particularly that of minority adolescents. And, each of these novels can be used to illuminate particular historical contexts in a fashion not possible in typical textbook accounts. For example, award-winning Native American author Joseph Bruchac's (2006) *Geronimo* takes the reader on board a prison train in the mid-1800s when Apache leader Geronimo and his men were being transported from their mountain home to a Florida prison.

Written from the point of view of Geronimo's adopted grandson, this young adult novel offers a strong counterpoint to simplistic, "savage warrior" accounts that were popular during the dime novel era. Thus, novels like *Geronimo* can be paired and contrasted with historical accounts in textbooks that may skate across the surface of a topic. For example, in a history class undertaking a unit on Pearl Harbor, Graham Salisbury's (2005) *Eyes of the Emperor* offers an account of Eddy Okubo, a young, very patriotic Japanese American soldier who enlists in Hawai'i and ends up serving as dog bait at a canine corps training operation on an isolated island in the South. Eddy and his mates are seen as surrogates for Japanese soldiers rather than as patriotic Americans (Bean, Readence, & Baldwin, 2008).

The theory that placed Eddy and his fellow soldiers in this canine training operation was based on the fallacious notion that Japanese Americans smelled differently from Caucasian Americans and the dogs could then be trained to detect and root out enemy soldiers. Thus, this novel and a host of others can shed a different light on elements of history that would otherwise go unnoticed and unchallenged. Graham Salisbury's painstaking research, involving interviewing some of the 25 soldiers who were sent to this canine training assignment, offers an alternative reading of diverse adolescents' experiences during Pearl Harbor. We will have more to say about incorporating young adult literature in history and other content areas in Chapter 11. For now, it is important to note that multicultural young adult literature has come into its own after many years of struggle. During the 1980s, independent presses like Piñata Press and Arte Publico Press supported Mexican American authors at a time when the audience and adoption process for multicultural literature was just taking hold.

Arte Publico Press continues to flourish with numerous titles in its catalog that would appeal to contemporary adolescents. For example, *The Throwaway Piece* (Hernandez, 2006) follows main character Jewel moving from one foster home to another. And author Gloria Velasquez's young adult novel *Tyrone's Betrayal* (2006) deals with the main character's absentee father in an African American community. Both novels treat contemporary family issues confronting teens without the sentimentality that was a cornerstone in early young adult literature.

Similarly, Bamboo Ridge Press in Hawai'i has long supported local young adult authors like Graham Salisbury and Lois-Ann Yamanaka since the 1970s (Bean et al., 2008). This tradition has continued with ongoing collections of Hawai'i-based poetry and prose that includes adolescent authors. For example, *Growing Up Local: An Anthology of Poetry and Prose from Hawai'i* (Chock, Harstad, Lum, & Teter, 1998) features multiple voices and genres that, without the support of this homegrown outlet, might not be heard.

A key source in tracing the history of young adult literature and key authors got its start in 1973 as a newsletter sponsored by the National Council of Teachers of English. Now known as *The ALAN Review*, this journal offers teachers a powerful vehicle for author study with interviews and commentaries on young adult literature (Kelly & Small, 1999). Case 3.1 illustrates the use of this resource in Jason Spring's young adult literature class.

CASE 3.1: Using *The ALAN Review*

Mr. Spring has his students in the university young adult literature course mentioned in the earlier chapter vignette bring in and share an article from *The ALAN Review* that they found useful. At this point in the class, they have left the history section of the course and are now considering specific teaching practices they might incorporate in their own instruction.

Marilyn (Student):	I found a really good article by Anete Vasquez (2009, Fall) called "Breathing Underwater: At-Risk Ninth Graders Dive into Literary Analysis." It showed how to guide students into a close reading of a work. The article also included all the vocabulary typical of literary analysis with a glossary explaining each term on page 26. Words like "metaphor," "juxtaposition," and so on were listed with specific examples from Alex Finn's (2001) *Breathing Underwater*.

Students share the articles they found in small groups and the teaching strategies that accompany *The ALAN Review* selections. Mr. Spring tells them that in the next class, they will need to demonstrate the teaching strategy in their small group with a different young adult selection.

Contemporary Multicultural Literature

By the 1990s, a number of multicultural young adult novels had a strong following, in part because of the early support of small, independent presses. For example, the young adult novel *Heartbeat, Drumbeat* (Hernandez, 1992) dealt with cultural conflict through the eyes of Morgana Cruz. Morgana's mother was Navajo and her father, Mexican. Throughout the novel, she struggles with her identity, on one hand feeling close to her Navajo mentor while trying to fit into the Mexican traditions advanced by her father.

When students read and discussed this novel in a 9th-grade English class, they critiqued its cultural authenticity (Bean, Valerio, Money Senior, & White, 1999). They consulted Internet sites, listened to a guest speaker from the local school district multicultural center, and wrote about their findings. As a result

Only a relatively small percentage of young adult literature focuses on diverse populations.

of this critical reading, these 9th graders were able to detect inaccuracies in some of the Navajo ceremonies portrayed in the novel. Indeed, in some cases, the dramatic intent of the novel took precedent over cultural accuracy. Thus, multicultural young adult literature can be a site for critique around issues of cultural history and accuracy, as well as a window on diversity.

It is important to note that, despite the steady infusion of multicultural literature for young adults in bookstores and school libraries, the actual number of books about African Americans, Asian Americans, American Indians, and Latinos, among others, numbers less than 10% of all the young adult books that were published in 2002 (Bucher & Manning, 2006). In Chapter 5, we take up a more extensive look at multicultural and international young adult literature. For now, it is worth noting that when searching for literature in these categories, local bookstores are a reasonable starting place, but online searches and reviewing the catalogs of smaller presses like Arte Publico and Bamboo Ridge, among others, may yield additional titles that are not stocked in mainstream bookstores. Young adult books for gay, lesbian, and transgendered teens have traveled a similar trajectory to multicultural literature in their development and history.

LITERATURE FOR GAY, LESBIAN, AND TRANSGENDERED AND TRANSSEXUAL YOUTH

Although it has taken some 40 years for multicultural young adult literature to come of age, literature for gay, lesbian, transgender, transsexual, and bisexual youth traveled a similarly laborious road categorized by an initial period of problem-based novels about the plight of being gay (Cart & Jenkins, 2006). More recently, with the popularity of television shows featuring gays in sitcoms where one's sexual preference is simply one facet of life, young adult novels in this genre present more realistic portraits of gay youth dealing with coming-of-age issues common in other books for teens. Nevertheless, the small number of young adult novels representing gay, lesbian, transgender, transsexual, and bisexual youth is less than that available in the multicultural arena. For example, in 2002, multicultural literature occupied a bit less than 10% of the novels published in young adult literature, whereas fewer than 2% of the books published addressed gay themes and experiences. And, according to an analysis of gay young adult literature, "books with *GLBTQ* content remain among the most challenged titles in America's public and school libraries" (Cart & Jenkins, 2006, p. xvii).

The evolution of GLBTQ young adult literature progressed from an initial coming out stance, to a stage of gay assimilation, and finally to a more advanced stage represented in contemporary novels of queer consciousness and community (Cart & Jenkins, 2006). Beginning with John Donovan's 1969 novel *I'll Get There. It Better Be Worth the Trip*, GLBTQ literature featured characters that, like their heterosexual counterparts in mainstream novels for teens, were male, White, and upper middle class. But unlike the explosion of books for teens in this mainstream literature in the 1970s, comparatively few books with GLBTQ were published. Just seven other novels were published over the next 10 years with GLBTQ characters, and even they were flawed by stereotypical characters and predictable plots (Cart & Jenkins, 2006). Being gay was typically equated with negative events in one's life. It was not until the 1990s that this literature came into its own with mature, realistic portrayals of gay families, communities, and the 1999 creation of the Michael L. Printz Award by the American Library Association for literary merit (Cart & Jenkins, 2006). Indeed, this category included books that overlap multicultural literature. For example, Lois-Ann Yamanaka's (1999) *Name Me Nobody* is centered on teen life on the Big Island of Hawai'i and deals with the main character 14-year old Emi Lou Kaya whose best friend Yvonne is in a lesbian relationship with a baseball player on their Hilo, Hawai'i, team (Bean et al., 2008). During the four years from 2000 to 2004, 66 young adult titles appeared with GLBTQ content (Cart & Jenkins, 2006). By 2004, a novel by Julie Anne Peters's titled *Luna* was published, the first to address transsexual and transgender issues (Cart & Jenkins, 2006). People uncomfortable with their birth gender are termed "transgender," and those undergoing a physical operation to alter their birth gender, "transsexual." Because of its literary quality, *Luna* was nominated for a National Book Award.

Despite the growth in young adult novels with GLBTQ characters and more real-life dilemmas that parallel other teens' lives depicted in this genre, there is a need for more characters of color. This is important if this subset of young adult literature is to be truly inclusive so that "all young readers might see their faces reflected in it" (Cart & Jenkins, 2006, p. 165). And, the standards of evaluation for any young adult novel apply to this corpus of literature and individual novels. Namely, does a novel provide complex, multidimensional characters and realistic family and life problems? We suspect that, like the multicultural literature that has blossomed over the past decade, GLBTQ young adult literature will continue to evolve and achieve greater recognition and use in classrooms.

In addition to the growing body of multicultural young adult literature and GLBTQ books, a growing array of young adult novels set in international contexts and international war zones offer yet another window on adolescents' experiences and voices (Harper & Bean, 2006).

Young Adult Novels in International Contexts

Young adult literature located in international contexts, particularly those novels relating to war; have been around for quite some time now. For example, books dealing with adolescents' experiences during the Holocaust include the widely read *Diary of A Young Girl* (Anne Frank, 1952/1995). A number of books deal with young soldiers' experiences in Vietnam, most notably, Walter Dean Myers's portrayal of two African American adolescent soldiers, *Fallen Angels* (1988). Other novels dealing with Japanese internment camps during World War II such as *Farewell to Manzanar* (Houston & Houston, 1993), *Hiroshima: A Novella* (Yep, 1995), and Graham Salisbury's (1994) *Under the Blood-Red Sun* are but a few of many novels written about this period in history.

More recently, novels set in the Middle East chronicle the harsh realities of war in Afghanistan, Iraq, and other hot spots, including Nigeria (Harper & Bean, 2006). Some of the most widely read and best-known novels include Canadian author Debra Ellis's trilogy about Parvana, a young Afghanistan girl trying to survive and ultimately flee Kabul (Ellis, 2000, 2002, 2003). Starting with *The Breadwinner* (Ellis, 2000), and following Parvana on her journey toward Pakistan, Ellis treats the harsh landscape of war without sentimentality. In one scene, Parvana and a friend eke out a living by sorting human bones for sale (Ellis, 2000).

Other powerful books set in the Middle East include *Thura's Diary: A Young Girl's Life in War-Torn Baghdad* (Al-Windawi, 2004), offering an insider's view of the 2003 bombing of Baghdad and the onset of war. Similarly, Beverly Naidoo's (2000) novel *The Other Side of Truth* offers an account of a Nigerian family fleeing to England at the onset of a military coup in Lagos, Nigeria. Naidoo captures the psychosomatic trauma of families split apart by war. These young adult novels shed light on the underbelly of war as it impacts youth in far-flung global contexts that lose their human elements when reduced to sound bites and fast-moving television news clips.

Although the above examples speak to the horrors of war from a fictionalized viewpoint, nonfiction works offer another perspective on the experiences of adolescents living in areas of conflict. In two compelling accounts, Palestinian and Israeli teenagers speak out and offer their proposals for peace in the Middle East. *We Just Want to Live Here* (Rifa'i & Ainbinder, 2003) consists of ongoing correspondence between a Palestinian teen and her exchange student friend, an Israeli teen. They met while attending a Switzerland-based student exchange program and maintained their friendship and correspondence upon their return home. In *Three Wishes: Palestinian and Israeli Children Speak* (Ellis, 2004), brief proposals for peace are set forth by youth in this war-torn region. Although neither of these books is a novel, they fit within the larger category of young adult works set in international war zones.

Young Adult Novels Relating to Mental and Physical Disabilities

As early as 1929, psychiatrist Dr. G. O. Ireland used the term *bibliotherapy* to categorize his use of books as a treatment for his psychiatric patients (Donelson & Nilsen, 2005). Although remaining controversial through the 1950s, and loosely supported by notions of emotional catharsis through reading about others going through similar experiences, this early work foreshadowed an array of books encompassing characters with various physical and mental challenges.

Numerous titles are now available in this genre, including *Cut* (McCormick, 2000), dealing with Callie, a teen housed in a mental health facility for teens. True to the title, Callie secretly cuts herself. Along with other novels like *You Remind Me of You* (Corrigan, 2002), revolving around bulimia and anorexia, these accounts stay close to the experiences of adolescents struggling with depression and issues of control.

Cerebral palsy in young adults is at the center of *Stoner and Spaz* (Koertge, 2002). Similarly, *Stuck in Neutral* (Block, 2000) has 14-year-old Shawn McDaniel, a boy born with cerebral palsy, wrestling with the growing realization that his father plans to kill him. Cynthia Lord's (2006) award-winning novel *Rules* chronicles 12-year-old Catherine and life with her autistic brother, David. Lord deals with social difference in a fashion that questions what is normal.

Activity 2.2 asks you to delve into this genre in more depth.

ACTIVITY 2.2: Professional Reflection and Discussion

1. Conduct a search for additional titles in this category (via Amazon, American Library Association, or other lists).

2. Discuss titles and summaries you found with colleagues in your class.

3. In your small group, discuss how you would use this genre in your teaching.

Young adult literature continues to evolve and reflect social difference and social practices. Thus, any list of characteristics of young adult literature is always tentative and dynamic. Nevertheless, we believe that a few of these are worth mentioning as teachers seek out engaging literature for the classroom.

Characteristics of Young Adult Literature

As you seek out young adult literature to use in your classroom, here are just a few of the characteristics noted for this genre:

- Fast-paced

Given the compressed nature of young adult novels, spanning 100 to 200 pages of print, they must move quickly into the source of conflict or problems for the main character and engage the reader in the first few pages (Peck, 1999).

- Diverse

By this we mean that young adult literature should be inclusive and reflect the insiders' experiences of multiple groups of teens. Thus, various ethnic groups, genders, international scenes, disabilities, and other life challenges should be represented in young adult literature.

- Complex

Young adult literature needs to address social justice issues like racism and social class stratification in a fashion that moves beyond replicating narrow stereotypes (Probst, 2004). Characters must be complex and debunk common myths that permeate easy but limited categorization (e.g., "People in that neighborhood are all like that").

- Powerful

One of the reasons we read and watch films, television, and sports is because these activities offer powerful vicarious experiences where we can live through another person's challenges in a dramatic fashion. This is also one of the reasons why teens need ample opportunities to discuss events in a novel, offer their own critique, and consider alternative courses of action for a character or author.

- Insightful

In essence, because young adult novels are dealing with youth, they must "end at a beginning" (Peck, 1999, p. 118). In a truly existential fashion, young adult literature together with appropriate pedagogy must provide its readers greater knowledge and insight.

- Innovative

In the next section, we note a few key features as young adult literature continues to challenge past forms chronicled in this chapter. Starting as moralistic treatises, young adult literature in the 21st century is breaking down borders of what counts as literature. For example, manga (Schwartz &

Rubinstein-Avila, 2006) has become hugely popular and whole sections of mainstream bookstores are devoted to this literature. **Manga** consists of comics in graphic-novel formats. These expanded text forms are part and parcel of new literacies that tap into intersecting elements of print and visual features found in contemporary young adult novels.

This turn in young adult literature toward a blend of print and images is becoming more common. For example, a popular young adult novel *ttfn* (Myracle, 2007) consists entirely of text that mirrors instant messaging (IM) conversations. In the next section, we discuss some of these newer text forms and features, but it is important to note that this is a fast-moving area directly linked to new literacies and the Internet so any effort to freeze-frame and pin down newer text forms is doomed to failure. Rather, visiting bookstores and delving into these diverse text forms will help keep you abreast of this exciting blend of print and images.

The Postmodern Turn in Young Adult Literature

Postmodernism refers to a movement that began in architecture, disrupting modernist building designs that dehumanized their occupants, placing them in identical, formalized structures. Postmodern architecture plays with forms, disrupts the taken-for-granted, and challenges simplistic notions of design (Lyotard, 1984). Similarly, postmodern features in texts expand young adult novels to include graphics, visuals, font shifts, time and space bending, and a host of other features that contemporary readers find attractive. Indeed, the influences of postmodernism cut across various fields including art, music, linguistics, and conceptions of literacy (Cherland & Harper, 2007).

Examples of postmodern features in young adult novels include using font shifts from manuscript to cursive writing to signal private spaces where characters can talk about their problems, to the stark black-and-white graphics in Walter Dean Myers's (1999) *Monster*. Indeed, in this novel, the main character Steve's plight in jail is represented by radical font shifts from his diary entries in cursive form, to court transcriptions in manuscript style, and a screenplay with its unique form. Similarly, in *Shooter* (Myers, 2004), based on the Columbine High School massacre, counselor records, police records, and a diary in nearly unreadable syntax and handwriting provide forward movement and a glimpse at the mind-states of various characters. If we think about readers in the 1960s accustomed to structure of a young adult novel where the main character wrestled with problems that were eventually resolved at the close of the novel, these postmodern works seem pretty radical. But for contemporary teens used to multiple media forms bombarding their space simultaneously, postmodern features in novels simply replicate their worlds.

Expanded Forms of Texts in New Times

Based on adolescents' experiences with communication technology including cell phones, instant messaging, MP3 players, Internet material including audio and visual ipodcasts, multiple-player video global video games, multiple author e-zines and **fanfiction,** to mention a few, our notions of what counts as text needs to be expanded. And, amid many high-technology text forms, **zines** represent a kind of counterpoint genre where the authors create handmade publications that represent their particular interests (Gustavson, 2007). For example, an author may cut, glue, and paste a zine together on the floor and copy it to share with a small audience of readers, generally other youth. Zines are often satirical, lambasting popular television programs and aspects of popular culture (e.g., the summer 2007 B-movie *Snakes on a Plane*). In essence, zines are a form of social commentary, offering a site of resistance to mainstream media.

Fanfiction or **fanzines** follow the careers of bands, stars, sports celebrities, and others, while travel zines offer a kind of diary of the author's travels. Zines operate outside the normalizing forces of mainstream culture and open a space where youth have power and voice (Gustavson, 2007).

Oddly enough, amid these expanded forms of text, older systems of providing books and magazines to readers still flourish. For example, the Book-of-the-Month Club, founded in 1926 to serve rural readers, continues to flourish in new times (Karnitschnig, 2007). Despite Amazon.com, iTunes, and other Internet-based sites offer reading material, more than 20 million people still subscribe to book and record clubs. Similarly, Scholastic Book Clubs and reader choice catalogs still act as an important and simple means of offering adolescents self-selected young adult literature. These older systems coexist with newer online text forms perhaps because of their low cost and relative simplicity.

Activity 2.3 helps reveal many of the newer text forms we take for granted and communication devices that our students routinely use in their daily lives.

ACTIVITY 2.3: Professional Reflection and Discussion

Directions: Together with another student, (a) list all the communication devices you interact with each week in the space below. Then, (b) place a checkmark next to any of these devices that you think represent expanded forms of text. Finally, (c) can you think of any young adult novels you have read that included any of these devices in the story line or used to disrupt the text in a way that plays with conventional print?

   a. Communication Devices Used This Week:
   b. Expanded Forms of Text:
   c. Young Adult Novels Where These Devices Are Used:

Given the dynamic nature of young adult literature, and its relatively long history, we need to consider some implications for teaching.

IMPLICATIONS FOR TEACHING WITH YOUNG ADULT LITERATURE

While we embrace with enthusiasm the expanded forms of text offered by post-modern novels in new times, it is worth noting that older novels still hold students' interest. For example, *The Outsiders* (Hinton, 1967) remains popular amid a plethora of newer novels because students still resonate with Ponyboy's plight as a poor White kid struggling to survive on his own. Thus, from an instructional perspective, many older young adult novels such as *The Outsiders* can be read alongside contemporary titles and compared and contrasted in student discussions and writing around themes such as poverty, loss, and redemption. Strategies that visually display similarities and differences can be very effective as discussion starters. For example, a familiar graphic organizer like the Venn diagram with its intersecting concentric circles might be used to compare Ponyboy with Ruben Wolfe in Marcus Zusak's (2000) *Fighting Ruben Wolfe* where Ruben is also from a poor White Australian family, raising money by fighting in illegal boxing matches.

Classic young adult novels may include perspectives that require a critical stance given overtones of racism or discrimination.

   In addition, because older young adult novels depict the nature of social practices in their particular context and time, they offer a window on the past (Rice, 2006). Linda Rice's (2006) book *What Was it Like: Teaching History and Culture Through Young Adult Literature* offers a listing of key novels depicting historical events and sample units teachers can use to consider Japanese Internment, the Vietnam War, and other topics.

In Chapter 14, we discuss the use of young adult literature to illuminate events in history and other content areas including science and mathematics. Many of the novels mentioned in the present chapter are great resources in content area teaching. You may want to begin thinking about how novels like Graham Salisbury's (2005) *Eyes of the Emperor* might be used in teaching history.

SUMMARY

This chapter explored a brief history of young adult literature including (a) the 1800s; (b) the rise of realism in the 1960s; (c) the development of multicultural literature; (d) literature for gay, lesbian, and transgender and transsexual youth; (e) young adult novels in international contexts; (f) young adult novels relating to mental and physical disabilities; (g) characteristics of young adult literature; (h) the postmodern turn in young adult literature; (i) expanded forms of text in new times; and (j) implications for teaching with young adult literature.

DISCUSSION QUESTIONS

1. Why is the role of realism important in the historical development of young adult literature?

2. What is the importance of multicultural young adult literature?

3. Why is the evolution of young adult literature for gay, lesbian, transgender, and transsexual youth important?

4. What is the importance of young adult literature in international contexts?

5. What are the features of young adult novels relating to mental and physical disabilities, postmodernism, and expanded forms of texts?

6. What are the characteristics of high-quality young adult literature?

KEY TERMS

Bibliotherapy   33

E-zines   36

Fanfiction   36

Fanzines   36

GLBTQ   31

Literary Canon   27

Manga   35

Postmodernism   23

SMALL-GROUP ACTIVITY: OLD AND NEW TEXT FORMS

The value of using multiple forms of text is that it helps students begin to see how they can make connections across these multiple forms (intertextuality). With other members of your group, discuss how you would go about combining young adult literature and newer text forms (e.g., blogs, zines, e-zines, fanfiction, IMs, and other multimedia) in your teaching. Have a recorder take notes and discuss this as a whole class. This could be a prelude to a class project later in the course.

RECOMMENDED READINGS

Bean, T. W. (2008). The localization of young adult fiction in contemporary Hawai'i. *The ALAN Review, 35(2), 27–35.*

Cart, M., & Jenkins, C. A. (2006). *The heart has its reasons: Young adult literature with gay/lesbian/ queer content, 1969-2004.* Lanham, MD: The Scarecrow Press.

   The authors offer a very comprehensive history of this genre along with a chronological bibliography of novels dating from 1969 through 2004.

Donelson, K. L., & Nilsen, A. P. (2005). *Literature for today's young adults* (7th ed.). New York, NY: Pearson.

   Chapter 2 in this book includes a very comprehensive treatment of the history of adolescent literature along with a listing of books from 1864 to 1965.

Gustavson, L. (2007). *Youth learning on their own terms: Creative practices and classroom teaching.* New York, NY: Routledge.

   This book, centered on new literacy studies, offers an in-depth look at adolescents' multiple literacies outside the classroom, including zine writing and music design.

Rice, L. J. (2006). *What was it like? Teaching history and culture through young adult literature.* New York, NY: Teachers College Press.

This resource book includes sample units based on key historical events including the Great Depression, migrant farm workers, Japanese internment camps, and other topics. The author includes featured young adult novels along with various discussion and writing strategies.

The ALAN Review. Urbana, IL: National Council of Teachers of English.

The acronym in this journal's title stands for the Assembly on Literature for Adolescents, and for nearly 30 years, this publication has featured articles by leading young adult authors and useful commentaries by scholars working in this vibrant field. As a teacher resource, *The ALAN Review* offers author studies and cultural histories to support the inclusion of young adult novels and poetry in the classroom.

RECOMMENDED YOUNG ADULT LITERATURE FEATURED IN THIS CHAPTER

Alcott, L. M. (1868). *Little women: Meg, Jo, Beth, and Amy.* Boston, MA: Robert Brothers.

Set amid the turmoil of the Civil War, *Little Women* was one of the first novels of its day to feature primarily female protagonists.

Al-Windawi, T. (2004). *Thura's diary: A young girl's life in war-torn Baghdad.* London, England: Penguin.

Told from the perspective of an Iraqi teenage girl at the onset of the war against Iraq in 2003, Thura recounts her family ultimately fleeing Baghdad. This highly readable, 144-page account includes detailed maps and black-and-white photos of Thura and her family prior to and after the falling of Saddam Hussein's regime.

Block, F. L. (2000). *Stuck in neutral.* New York, NY: HarperCollins.

This is a gut-wrenching novel that features 14-year-old Shawn McDaniel, coping with cerebral palsy and a father who wants to kill him.

Bruchac, J. (2006). Geronimo: A novel. New York, NY: Scholastic.

Award-winning Native American author Joseph Bruchac takes the reader on a journey across the United States with Apache leader Geronimo who is bound on a prison train for Florida. Told from the point of view of his adopted grandson in the 1800s, this historical fiction offers an insider's view of Apache values and courage.

Corrigan, E. (2002). *You remind me of you.* New York, NY: Scholastic.

This novel deals with bulimia and anorexia in a realistic fashion that stays close to the experiences of adolescents struggling with depression and power issues.

Donovan, J. (1969). *I'll get there. It better be worth the trip: A novel*. New York, NY: Harper & Row.

Considered the first young adult book to deal with the theme of homosexuality. It contains several homoerotic scenes between the 13-year-old narrator, Davy Ross, and his friend, Altschuler.

Ellis, D. (2000). *The breadwinner*. Toronto, Ontario, Canada: Groundwood.

The first in the trilogy about Parvana, an Afghani teenage girl surviving in Kabul amid Taliban rule and ongoing war, this novel begins a long journey out of Afghanistan for Parvana and her family. The other novels in the trilogy include *Parvana's Journey* and *Mud City*.

Ellis, D. (2002). *Parvana's journey*. Toronto, Ontario, Canada: Groundwood.

Ellis, D. (2003). *Mud city*. Toronto, Ontario, Canada: Groundwood.

Ellis, D. (2004). *Three wishes: Palestinian and Israeli children speak*. Toronto, Ontario, Canada: Groundwood.

This is a very compelling collection of the voices of Palestinian and Israeli youth with their proposals for peace in the region. The 110-page book includes historical information, photos of the region, and biographical sketches of each of the young writers.

Frank, A. (1995). *Diary of a young girl: The definitive edition*. New York, NY: Doubleday.

This crucial account is now part of any unit on the Holocaust, and it is clearly part of the literary canon. Newer accounts of youth in war zones like Deborah Ellis's trilogy also offer an insider's view of struggle and survival in war-torn nations.

Hernandez, I. B. (1992). *Heartbeat, drumbeat*. Houston, TX: Arte Publico Press.

Main character Morgana Cruz is torn between the cultural pressures of her Navajo mother and Mexican father. The novel is a romance that nicely captures its rural New Mexico setting and Morgana's life as an accomplished artist.

Hernandez, J. A. Y. (2006). *The throwaway piece*. Houston, TX: Arte Publico Press.

This novel follows main character Jewel from one foster home to another and centers on emotions not uncommon for adolescents simultaneously functioning as adults and youth.

Hinton, S. E. (1967). *The outsiders*. New York, NY: Penguin.

Now a classic in the young adult genre, this well-known story, told from the point of view of 14-year-old Ponyboy and his brothers offered a realistic look at gang conflict that still captivates adolescent readers.

Houston, J. W., & Houston, J. D. (1993). *Farewell to Manzanar*. New York, NY: Houghton Mifflin.

Wrenched from their home in Long Beach, California, the family in this account of Japanese internment camps at the onset of World War II goes to the heart of racism and the resilience of Japanese American citizens.

Koertge, R. (2002). *Stoner and spaz*. Cambridge, MA: Candlewick Press.
This novel centers on cerebral palsy and teen life.

Lord, C. (2006). *Rules*. New York, NY: Scholastic.
This award-winning novel looks at disability from the point of view of 12-year-old Catherine whose brother David is autistic and raises questions about what is normal behavior.

McCormick, P. (2000). *Cut*. New York, NY: Front Street.
Housed in a mental health facility for teens, Callie secretly cuts herself.

Myracle, L. (2007). *ttfn*. New York, NY: Amulet Books.
This is the second in an ongoing series of books written as text messages. The pages replicate screens with send and cancel buttons, and adolescents find this format familiar and engaging. Each novel is written in IM form including iconic symbols and abbreviations familiar to adolescent readers.

Myers, W. D. (1988). *Fallen angels*. New York, NY: Scholastic.
A now well-established account of two African American teenage soldiers in the Vietnam conflict. The parallels with the ongoing war in Iraq and Afghanistan make this a powerful novel.

Myers, W. D. (1999) *Monster*. New York, NY: HarperCollins.
Steve, the 16-year-old character in this novel, is implicated in a convenience store robbery and murder. Told through a variety of text forms (screenplay, diary, and court transcripts), Steve takes the reader into the gritty world of a county lock-up where sleepless nights are the norm. Grainy black-and-white photos add to the dark, brooding mood of Steve's life in jail.

Myers, W. D. (2004). *Shooter*. New York, NY: HarperCollins.
Based on the Columbine killings, much like *Monster,* this novel uses diaries, school counselor records, and court documents to tell the story of Cameron, Carla, and Leonard. Seventeen-year-old Leonard is shunned by his peers and seeks revenge at Madison High School.

Naidoo, B. (2000). *The other side of truth*. New York, NY: HarperCollins.
This novel is located initially in Lagos, Nigeria, where Sade's father is a well-known journalist protesting the military coup. He is the target of an assassin who inadvertently kills Sade's mother and the family must flee illegally to London, England, where Sade and her brother are victims of racism and bullying. Sade is resourceful and a survivor, using the media to help her cause.

Peters, J. A. (2004). *Luna*. Boston, MA: Little, Brown.

Nominated for a National Book Award, this young adult novel was the first to take up transsexual and transgender issues.

Rifa'i, A., & Ainbinder, O. (2003). *We just want to live here*. New York, NY: St. Martin's Griffin.

This unique book features the ongoing letters between a Palestinian teenage girl and her Israeli counterpart. Following their meeting at a student-exchange program in Switzerland, they continued writing about their fears and anger at the strife between their respective homes. Their ideas for peace in the Middle East envision a future that is different from their experiences as adolescents.

Salinger, J. D. (1951). *The catcher in the rye*. Boston, MA: Little, Brown.

A classic American novel depicting adolescent alienation and loss of innocence in the protagonist Holden Caulfield.

Salisbury, G. (1994). *Under the blood-red sun*. New York, NY: Delacorte.

Both this novel and *Eyes of the Emperor* approach the onset of World War II and Pearl Harbor from the unique perspective of Japanese Americans residing in Hawai'i.

Salisbury, G. (2005). *Eyes of the emperor*. New York, NY: Wendy Lamb Books.

Eddy Okubo, the main character in this novel, enlists to serve his country in the U.S. Army. The book chronicles Eddie's experiences on Cat Island in the South, where he and his fellow Hawai'ian soldiers are sent to serve as dog bait for a canine corps planning to chase Japanese soldiers. The book deals with racism and social injustice.

Soto, G. (1999). *Buried onions*. New York, NY: HarperCollins.

An inside look at Mexican American barrio life in agricultural Fresno, California.

Taylor, M. (1976). *Roll of thunder, hear my cry*. New York, NY: Dial.

Now a classic in the literary canon, this groundbreaking novel debunked stereotypes of Black families in the South.

Velasquez, G. (2006). *Tyrone's betrayal*. Houston, TX: Arte Publico Press.

This novel takes up the issue of the main character's absentee father in an African American community.

Yamanaka, L. A. (1999). *Name me nobody*. New York, NY: Hyperion.

Emi-Lou Kaya is overweight and struggling with the potential loss of her best friend to a lesbian baseball player in rural Hilo, Hawai'i. Yamanaka captures the local dialect and underbelly of rural Hawai'i where everything that happens in this small island community is magnified in importance.

Yep, L. (1993). *Dragon's gate*. New York, NY: HarperCollins.

This novel chronicles the Chinese workers' experiences while building the transcontinental railroad in rough physical and psychological conditions in the Colorado mountains.

Yep, L. (1995). *Hiroshima: A novella*. New York, NY: Scholastic.

This story focuses on Hiroshima residents and the bomb that shattered their lives.

Zusak, M. (2000). *Fighting Ruben Wolfe*. New York, NY: Scholastic.

Now an established young adult author, Markus Zusak's first novel goes into the gritty world of illegal boxing matches in urban Australia that pits two brothers, Cameron and Ruben, against each other. The dialogue is strong, and this is an action-packed novel that treats masculinity in complex ways.

RECOMMENDED WEBSITES

As you search for information about specific genres, authors, or reviews of films, the following websites should be useful: Amazon.com features an array of book reviews and author information, including reviews of electronic books available for the Kindle reader. The American Library Association website is a rich source of young adult literature by topic, genre, and other categories.

Film reviews can be found at Wikipedia, the online encyclopedia, as well as other sites available by Google search, Bing.com, or other search engines.

REFERENCES

Bean, T. W., Readence, J. E., & Baldwin, R. S. (2008). *Content area literacy: An integrated approach* (9th ed.). Dubuque, IA: Kendall/Hunt.

Bean, T. W., Valerio, P. C., Money Senior, H., & White, F. (1999). Secondary English students' engagement in reading and writing about a multicultural novel. *The Journal of Educational Research*, 93(1), 32–37.

Bucher, K., & Manning, M. L. (2006). *Young adult literature: Exploration, evaluation, and appreciation*. Upper Saddle River, NJ: Pearson.

Cart, M., & Jenkins, C. A. (2006). *The heart has its reasons: Young adult literature with gay/lesbian/queer content, 1969-2004*. Lanham, MD: The Scarecrow Press.

Cherland, M. R., & Harper, H. (2007). *Advocacy research in literacy education: Seeking higher ground*. Mahwah, NJ: Lawrence Erlbaum.

Chock, E., Harstad, J. R., Lum, D. H. Y., & Teter, B. (1998). *Growing up local: An anthology of poetry and prose from Hawai'i*. Honolulu, HI: Bamboo Ridge Press.

Donelson, K. L., & Nilsen, A. P. (2005). *Literature for today's young adults* (7th ed.). New York, NY: Pearson.

Graham, J. (2007, June 29). Nancy Drew and the fountain of youth. *The Wall Street Journal*, p. W11.

Gustavson, L. (2007). *Youth learning on their own terms: Creative practices and classroom teaching*. New York, NY: Routledge.

Harper, H. J., & Bean, T. W. (2006). Fallen angels: Finding adolescents and adolescent literacy in a renewed project of democratic citizenship. In D. E. Alvermann, K. A. Hinchman, D. W. Moore, S. F. Phelps, & D. R. Waff (Eds.), *Reconceptualizing the literacies in adolescents' lives* (2nd ed., pp. 147–162). Mahwah, NJ: Lawrence Erlbaum.

Karnitschnig, M. (2007, April 10). Book-of-the-Month Club to turn a new page. *The Wall Street Journal*, pp. B1–B2.

Kelly, P. P., & Small, R. C., Jr. (1999). *Two decades of The ALAN Review*. Urbana, IL: National Council of Teachers of English.

Lyotard, J. F. (1984). *The postmodern condition: A report on knowledge*. Minneapolis: University of Minnesota Press.

Peck, R. (1999). Some thoughts on adolescent literature. In P. P. Kelly & R. C. Small, Jr. (Eds.), *Two Decades of The ALAN Review* (pp. 115–119). Urbana, IL: National Council of Teachers of English.

Probst, R. E. (2004). *Response and analysis: Teaching literature in secondary school* (2nd ed.). Portsmouth, NH: Heinemann.

Rice, L. J. (2006). *What was it like? Teaching history and culture through young adult literature*. New York, NY: Teachers College Press.

Schwartz, A., & Rubinstein-Avila, E. (2006). Understanding the manga hype: Uncovering the multimodality of comic book literature. *Journal of Adolescent & Adult Literacy*, *50*(1), 40–49.

Stevenson, R. L. (2011). *The novels of R. L. Stevenson*. Di Lernia Publications (Amazon Digital Service).

U.S. Department of Commerce (2003). U.S. Census Bureau population estimates. Retrieved from http://www.census.gov/popest/data/historical/2000,vintage_2003/index.html

Vasquez, A. (2009, Fall). Breathing underwater: At-risk ninth graders dive into literary analysis. *The ALAN Review*, *37*(1), 18–28.

Chapter 3

The Teaching of Young Adult Literature

In this chapter, we consider the *teaching* of young adult literature. Specifically, this chapter addresses what it means to teach young adult literature in relation to three major literary and pedagogical orientations: Cultural Heritage, Reader Response, and Cultural Criticism. The following vignette illustrates a high school teacher's approach to teaching young adult literature through a Reader Response orientation.

Learning Objectives

- Understand the **Cultural Heritage orientation** to the teaching of young adult literature.
- Understand the **Reader Response orientation** to the teaching of young adult literature.
- Understand the **Cultural Criticism orientation** to the teaching of young adult literature.
- Be able to discuss the advantages and disadvantages of each orientation.
- Be able to use professional organization position statements and standards to support your curriculum decisions.

Vignette: High School English

Cheryl Fiero is in her first year of teaching high school English in the Pacific Northwest, and one of her classes consists of a significant number of struggling readers in her urban high school. She has the support of her principal to use a variety of contemporary young adult literature to engage reluctant readers in her classroom. As we look in on Cheryl's classroom, she is introducing her students to an activity based on their reading of the young adult novel *Runner* (Deuker, 2005). The main character, high school senior Chance Taylor, worries constantly about money to pay the bills he and his unemployed father confront. They live together on a small, aging sailboat in Seattle, and Chance never reveals this secret to his classmates. Although not homeless, Chance is embarrassed by the struggles in his life that revolve around his dad, a Vietnam veteran who gets drunk daily in Seattle bars. As a way to cope, Chance runs every day near the harbor, and as the novel progresses, he becomes a drug runner, picking up mysterious packages that are dropped off by boat near his jogging route. It pays the bills for shore power electricity on the old boat and the mooring fee but involves significant personal risk to Chance and the potential to damage his future after graduation. Cheryl believes this captivating, action-packed novel will be one her students will actually read from front to back.

Cheryl's teaching approach combines old-school novel discussion based on a personal reader response orientation she learned about at the university with a critical stance toward social justice and conditions of poverty. She routinely integrates communication technology into her lessons, and her school offers laptops and wireless connectivity. She developed the following lesson based on a ReadWriteThink lesson plan that combines blogging (or weblogs) with pictures using Photovoice (available from www.readwritethink.org/lessons/lesson_view.asp?id=1064).

Cheryl: Okay, as we are reading and talking about Chance Taylor in *Runner*, I want you to consider the following questions:

What is courage in the face of social conditions of poverty?

What does courage look like from Chance Taylor's view?

How is social difference in home life depicted in the novel?

How does Chance cope with his dad and life on a small, aging boat?

How would you handle Chance's life choices?

I'm going to ask you to take or select photos that show examples of courage when homelessness or "home" is different from an apartment or house in a neighborhood. Then, we will scan and upload these photos on our classroom blog (see Blogger.com), and we will discuss them around issues of poverty and living courageously.

Students in Cheryl's class carry out this assignment, ultimately leading to an essay writing assignment where they address whether Chance Taylor and his dad's lives demonstrate courage, and how others (including other characters in the novel) might view their lifestyle.

Cheryl's orientation to young adult literature is fairly advanced and philosophically aligned with a Cultural Criticism orientation. It includes elements of Reader Response but avoids some of the pitfalls of engaging students in a strictly personal reaction to events and characters in a novel.

Although this is one approach to teaching young adult literature, we want to explore in more depth various orientations and options that can guide your own teaching. Activity 3.1 foreshadows some of the choices that are available to you as you create units and lessons in your own classroom.

ACTIVITY 3.1: Professional Reflection and Discussion

The following questions provide a focus for the chapter, but please add your own, and consider your responses to these questions as we begin this chapter. Discuss these questions in a small group before you delve into the chapter:

1. What are the various orientations and teaching strategies associated with the teaching of literature in general and the teaching of young adult literature in particular? From the perspective of the English/Language Arts teacher: "What are my pedagogical choices?"

2. What currently constitutes the "best practices" or "principled practices" in the teaching of literature? In other words, what does "good" or effective teaching (and learning) look like and according to whom? From the perspective of the teacher, "Knowing my pedagogical choices in the teaching of literature, what approach should I choose in teaching young adult literature?"

3. What is required in implementing good teaching practices in relation to young adult literature? Again from the perspective of the English/Language teacher: "Having determined what constitutes the best approach to the teaching of young adult literature, how do I apply it in the context of the 'everyday' realities of my students and my classroom?"

Before going farther, we want to consider the importance of a philosophical and theoretical framework in your teaching. We offer two tables that we hope will offer a starting point for professional refection and action.

ORIENTATIONS AND PRACTICES IN THE TEACHING OF LITERATURE

Table 3.1 maps three general orientations to the teaching of literature: Cultural Heritage, Reader Response, and Cultural Criticism. Each is outlined in relation to its position about text (i.e., literature), the teacher, the learner, and the overall goal or objective. Initially developed by Marnie O'Neill (1993) and addressed in relation to poetry by Carl Leggo (1997), we have enhanced and modified the chart for our purposes here (see Table 3.1). Table 3.2 maps the kinds of learning and teaching activities that each orientation or approach generates. We describe each of the orientations and its teaching foci and associated strategies in detail following the presentation of these two tables.

Please note that these maps are two of many available in the educational literature, and certainly they, like any, are not without their limits, but you will find them useful in sorting through the positions taken by various groups and individuals, and in locating your own current position or stance with regard to the teaching of literature.

Table 3.1. Orientations to the Teaching of Literature

	Cultural Heritage	**Reader Response**	**Cultural Criticism**
Text	The Literary Canon: literature considered unique and original works of art that have universal appeal offering moral instruction and insight into the human condition.	Literature reflects life and possible ways of being in the world. Characters are best thought of as real people with thoughts and motivations. Literature provides a powerful "lived-through" experience	Every text depicts and promotes a particular and invested reading of reality. Texts are sites for the stylized construction of multiple, already-existing meanings.
Teacher	The teacher is central to learning and active in instructing and modeling skills and knowledge. He or she must be completely knowledgeable about literature and literary analysis grounded in a close and authorized reading of text.	The teacher facilitates the learning of others and must be first and foremost knowledgeable about the needs, abilities and interests of the learners. Must know a wide range of texts in order to best match students with text	The teacher encourages social inquiry and therefore must be knowledgeable about the various perspectives or readings possible of any given text or discourse.
Learner	The learner must be receptive to the information provided by the teacher as he or she learns to uncover the intended meaning in the literary work studied.	The learner must be active and genuine in responding to text and to the response to others. Each reader brings his or her personal experience and makes his or her own meaning of text.	The learner and teacher must be receptive to the possibility of finding and challenging various perspectives or readings of the world evident in the text.

	Cultural Heritage	**Reader Response**	**Cultural Criticism**
Goal	A reader who appreciates good literature, has well-developed aesthetic sensibilities, and can generate close readings of literature.	An emphatic and responsive reader who can generate deep and profound connections between text and his or her own life.	A critical reader who can read with, but also against, the text; a reader who can determine how a text is related to the larger discourses that name our world

As stated, Table 3.2 connects the three general orientations with various teaching strategies and practices that are most often associated with each orientation. Of course, teaching practices generated in one approach may be used in other orientations, but they would work differently or serve a different purpose from that which was originally intended.

Table 3.2. Teaching Practices Involved in the Three Orientations to the Teaching of Literature

	Cultural Heritage	**Personal/Reader Response**	**Cultural Criticism**
Text and Text Selection	The Classics: Literature from British or national literary canon, or other authorized reading list: selected by teacher, department, school, or school district usually from a state-approved list; generally privileges print text Usually one work read by the entire class at a time	Reading that has the best chance of connecting with students' interests, abilities, and energies; may or may not be considered literature Different texts for different students: choice and self-selection ideal Contemporary texts important; Nonprint texts considered; strong narratives privileged	Text and most importantly readings of text that allow students to reflect on the rendering of the social and political world in the text and in their own world. Readings generated by teacher, students, and others Multiple texts critical, print and nonprint considered; Minority or divergent readings important
Focus	Text and Author: Focus on author's intention/motivation, on the universal theme and	Reader and Reading Community: Focus on the student's personal reading of the	Reading Practices and the Social Life: Focus on the various readings of text and

(Continued)

Table 3.2. (Continued)

	Cultural Heritage	Personal/Reader Response	Cultural Criticism
	subthemes, and on a close reading of literary and narrative elements (plot, setting, etc.) and style evident in the text	text; his or her connection with the story and characters in relation to his or her own lives and the reading community in which the student interacts	across text made available to readers and their effects on the text, reader, and the larger social order
Common Questions	What is the theme of this text? What is the tone? What did the author intend by his or her use of this literary technique?	What do you think this story is about? Why do you think the characters behaved as they did? Is the character realistically depicted?	How would this story/text be different if told from another perspective? How is this text similar to or different from others you've read? What versions of the "good" life are represented in this text?
Activities	Literary analysis with the development of a single reading Focused on close readings of literary text Finding figurative devices; e.g., metaphors, simile, personification Biographical readings of the author's life	Response journals/logs Literature circles Writing-in-character assignments Dramatic enactments	Content analysis with a focus on multiple readings, multi-texts, multimedia presentations Social action projects Rewriting activities
Teaching Mode	Lecture	Individual and group work	Individual and group inquiry; diverse reading
Classroom Assessment and Testing	Individual student essays; Question and answer tests	Student interest inventories; Personal reflections Group projects Rubrics Anecdotal records	Social action projects related to text study Comparative analysis of texts/discourse across time/space Critical deconstruction

As evident in the Table 3.2, the orientation an educator takes to the teaching of literature will affect the kinds of questions, activities, and texts that dominate in their classroom. Certain activities and questions seem particularly suited to one orientation or another. For example, the opening vignette in this chapter exemplified a Reader Response orientation. It could just as easily be framed as a critique of attitudes toward different ways of living (e.g., on an old sailboat or in a car, tent, or other form of "home" that differs from an apartment or house). Indeed, many young adult novels offer alternative lifestyles that can be read against the normative pressures of White middle-class suburbia.

Of course, teachers can be and often are eclectic in their teaching practices, but ultimately they and the educational policy and collective practices of their school, state, or nation will determine which orientation and therefore which teaching practices will occur most often in their classrooms. What approach dominates is important. It is our contention that reading is a learned rather than a natural practice of meaning making. As such, whatever approaches and strategies dominate a classroom will determine or at least affect how our students learn to make meaning from text and what they think literacy is and whether it is of value to them or not. Therefore, it is worth a close look at the orientations or approaches undertaken in our English/Language Arts classrooms.

CULTURAL HERITAGE ORIENTATION

This orientation or approach to the teaching of literature is also known in English studies as New Criticism or as the Great Tradition (Latrobe & Drury, 2009). This orientation with its lecture format, instructor-selected texts, and essay examinations was and often still is dominant in university English departments. Those using this approach maintain a strong distinction between low and high culture, in the case of literature, between contemporary, popular texts and those found on the literary canon (e.g., British, American, etc.). Works on the literacy canon are considered to be the best writing a culture has produced. They are works that have stood the test of time and will have continuing universal appeal. According to Cultural Heritage, such writing offers unique and profound renderings of the human condition worthy of close, intense study. Indeed the close study of literary classics is considered important for everyone but particularly for children and youth as a means to support the development of a moral and ethical person.

Pedagogically, the Cultural Heritage approach takes its cue from classical education, and it is often associated with the transmission model of teaching. Through modeling and explicit instruction a reader can be trained to uncover the meaning

The Cultural Heritage approach is often associated with the transmission model of teaching.

that resides in text, put there by an inspired and talented author. The text is the guarantor of meaning: the site where, with the aid of a teacher, a reader goes to find a single, unified, and consistent message or theme. The teacher must be knowledgeable about literature and highly skilled in literary analysis in order to impart through lecture and modeling his or her knowledge and skill in uncovering textual meaning. Learners must be receptive to the lessons offered, indeed relatively passive compared with the teacher's active intellectual instruction. Because of their knowledge and passion for literature, teachers will inspire students to love literature and the study of literature. The student, regardless of his or her history, background, or experience, will develop a passion for literature, and a similar aesthetic sensibility along the lines of the most accepted scholars in the field. All will develop a similar language to describe and analyze texts and a similar ability to uncover literary meaning. Most importantly, the close study of text will extend and deepen students' moral and philosophical beliefs.

The questions that are critical in this orientation include those that address (a) the intentions of the author (e.g., why did the author write this work, and what in his or her biography accounts for the themes that characterize the writing?), (b) the single unifying message of the literary work (e.g., what is the theme of this work? What is the tone? What is suggested about human condition in this work?), and (c) questions of aesthetics (e.g., how does the author create an experience of the sublime in this chapter?). Answering these questions will require readers to refer back to the text, often in the form of direct quotations and in some instances to reference the author's life and times.

Although it has dominated much of educational history, there has been considerable criticism of this approach. With regard to literature, the most damning criticism has been the elite selection and therefore the narrowness of the works included in the literary canon. The canonical texts used in the Cultural Heritage model often have been limited to White, middle-class, male, and British or Anglo-American authors. For diverse and multicultural local, national, and global contexts, such narrowness seems inappropriate. Yet, attempts to expand the canon to include more diverse authors and to include contemporary works is difficult to entertain because these authors and texts have yet to pass "the test of time" as the best ever written. Simply put, the works are not considered classics. Moreover, even if the British or say the American canon was expanded or alternative literary canons, for example women's literature, Native American literature, or for that matter, a canon of children's or young adult literature established, this does not undue the notion of an elite selection of works chosen by those in authority for all others to read or at least honor as great literature.

Another criticism of the Cultural Heritage approach concerns its teacher-centered pedagogy and the transmission model of learning. The transmission model of learning assumes that an appropriately receptive learner will absorb information as it is provided by the teacher together with the reading experience. It is at odds with contemporary learning theory that reveals learners to be active producers rather than passive consumers or recipients of text and of information more generally. Rather than simply absorbing information, learners are understood to be actively working with the learning materials, constructing their own meanings and purposes in the contemporary circumstances of their own lives. Thus, learners are best served by lessons that allow for active, engaged, personal manipulation of materials and resources. The transmission model of learning does not focus on the learners' construction of knowledge and active inquiry, but on the content of the knowledge provided and the knowledge of the pedagogue.

Related to this, the master–disciple pedagogical relationship of the Cultural Heritage orientation that requires a passive and ultimately compliant learner does not mesh well with the independent, active, and critical citizen required of democratic life. The social, political, and needs of society would seem to demand more of the pedagogy, of literary lessons, and of schools than the Cultural Heritage orientation and its teaching and learning environment can easily provide.

However, the close examination of text, including the aesthetics of text; the established quality of the works chosen; and the efforts to connect the mind of the reader with the mind of an august author is something many teachers and parents might well find appealing. The seemingly objective nature of literary analysis as well as the focus on individual rather than on group work may be more comfortable for some learners. For some teachers, the lecture and assignment format provides a reassuring sense of control and standardization over the lesson and makes the best use of their presentation skills. Finally, those who place great value on the past and on assuring our continuity with the past would like this orientation. Certainly Cultural Heritage offers the literary past or, more precisely, a construction of the literary past as a solid, stable foundation for students to align themselves with as they work through the circumstances of life now and in the future. Although this may be appealing, educators cannot forget the nature, needs, and circumstances of our adolescent learners and the needs of our society at large.

Considering all of this, the question is whether this orientation should dominate English/Language Arts secondary classrooms, and in the context of this book, what that might mean to the teaching of young adult literature? Activity 3.2 takes up this issue.

ACTIVITY 3.2: Professional Reflection and Discussion

We invite you to consider individually and then collectively these questions and to imagine a classroom where Cultural Heritage was the primary approach taken to the teaching of literature and, if it could be entertained, the teaching of contemporary young adult literature.

1. What kind of learner/reader/citizen would be produced by this method?

2. What skills, personal history, and dispositions would allow a student to succeed with this orientation?

3. What kind of teacher, what kind of school, and what kind of classroom atmosphere would be necessary for this orientation?

4. What titles that would be found in the bookroom of a school that supported this orientation?

A second orientation, Reader Response, has taken hold in many school sites sometimes combined with a Cultural Heritage orientation. Although popular and illustrated in the opening vignette in this chapter, like the Cultural Heritage orientation, Reader Response has its limitations.

READER RESPONSE OR PERSONAL RESPONSE

As the name suggests, this approach is focused on the reader. It is an orientation developed by Louise Rosenblatt (1938, 1978) and forwarded by many others. Variants include Stanley Fish's (1982) notions of interpretative communities. It is an approach that reflects the Progressive Education approach of John Dewey (1938) and his beliefs in a student-centered pedagogy that builds on the contemporary interests, energies, and contexts of the learners. Drawing on the work of John Dewey, Louise Rosenblatt developed a literary approach that privileged the reader in the literary lesson. Specifically, she believed that reading was produced in a transaction between text and reader in which the reader was active in expressing his or her own individual interpretation. She wrote, "The reading of a text is an event occurring at a particular time in a particular environment at a particular moment in the life history of the reader. The transaction will involve not only the past experience but also the present state and present interests or preoccupations of the reader" (Rosenblatt, 1978, p. 20).

From this perspective, there can be multiple readings of any text by an individual reader and certainly by groups of readers. The differences in their readings will be a result of their personal histories and contemporary experiences. What will validate and shape a particular reading is, according to Stanley Fish (1982), the interpretative community, which will provide the context for the individual response. In a school setting, the community is the class and/or small group of learners from the class including the teacher, with whom the reader shares and develops his/her response.

Reader response creates space for multiple readings of young adult literature.

The literature read in the personal or reader response approach could include any form of literary work that exists within the interest and abilities of the readers. Contemporary works are often used as the primary text. Usually they are self-selected with the help of the teacher by the individual reader or small group of readers. Literature in this orientation is viewed as a reflection of life with characters read as real people. The themes and the lived-through experience provided by the text is the key to motivating readers and ensuring their deep reflection on self and the world.

Pedagogically a reader response lesson begins with individual reactions to a text, or a section of text. This response can take many forms (written, dramatic, artistic etc.), although personal writing is the most common form. This response is then shared with a group of readers. Discussion with the group and the class, supported and facilitated by the teacher, follows with a selected section of rereading and a second or later a third response in whatever appropriate form finishes the lesson or series of lessons. This discussion could be in the form of an online classroom blog or with **literature circles** in class. With literature circles, each member of the group is assigned a task to do as a form of response or activity with text (e.g., illustrator) that is then shared with the group. In either case, the activity and focus of a reader response orientation is the reader's interpretation of text, shared, and then modified in the context of other readers. The kinds of questions a teacher might bring to discussion with individuals and groups would be framed in relation to the reader; for example, "What do *you* think will happen?" "In this situation, how would *you* have behaved?" "Why do *you* think the character acted like this?" and "Does this seem realistic to *you*? Explain."

To intensify empathetic reading, a teacher might suggest that an individual or group write in character; to write a letter to a character; or to speculate on what happens to the characters after the resolution of the plot. In this orientation, a powerful transaction between the text and the reader(s) is critical to motivating and inspiring learners. The teacher must be very knowledgeable about his or her students, their prior knowledge and experience, and about the range of text available, appropriate, and of interest to them. The teacher must be able to match text with students and, most importantly, to intensify the transaction between text and reader, so that readers will increase their understanding of the material, and in the process extend and deepen their intellectual and affective knowledge and understanding of text, self, and other.

Observational forms of assessment that address the quality of participation and growth would be integral to this approach. Final response papers or performances would be evaluated more formally on the quality of the response, and the depth of connections made among text, self, and life. Authentic, genuine responses would be assumed.

As one might expect, there has been some criticism of Reader Response. This orientation certainly allows for greater student choice in text selection and for greater freedom in responding to text; however, the subjective nature of the literacy lessons raises concerns, particularly in the area of evaluation, in the rigor of the instruction, and in quality of literary works studied. In addition, some have argued that when meaning is presumed to lie with the reader, it is often the unique, individual, and personal reader who is privileged. Thus, the psychology of the individual rather than the sociology of the reader and his or her context is the focus of lessons. It is argued that the study of literary focused on the individual reader can become a form of individual therapy or bibliotherapy.

Even if this is not the case, locating meaning in individual subjectivity can reduce meaning making and interpretation to a matter, if not of individual psychology, then of personal opinion, particularly in matters of interpretation where the text is not or cannot be explicit. There is often a kind of entitlement and ownership as well as a finality to the reader's statement "Well, that's my opinion!" or "So that's my response and that's just the way I see it" that may be implicitly encouraged in this orientation. Such ownership may make it difficult for a reader to later modify or easily abandon his or her reading in light of the readings and responses of others.

A related concern is that this approach may hold the reader or the community of readers responsible for their response. In the case of controversial readings, for example, a racist response, the reader is set adrift from the social conditions that have resulted in the development of that response. The individual reader is responsible for his or her response. Although taking personal responsibility is an important lesson, the broader social conditions, we would argue, also need to be considered, not simply one's unique and individual psychology, or one's individual history. In general, although it may not preclude it, a reader response approach can limit the possibility of broader political/social criticism of text and context.

This is not easily resolved without invoking the opposite problem: the abandonment or modification of an important or interesting divergent response: a gendered reading, for example. In classrooms where students are encouraged to modify, clarify, or reject their initial responses to text in reaction to the responses of other readers, important and interesting divergent or minority responses can be lost inadvertently. The other readers (including the teacher) can serve to legitimate a particular interpretation or set of responses, allowing a consensus to develop about a text and its meaning. This implicit or explicit consensus building can silence or marginalize, if not immediately certainly over time, minority responses. It takes a strong personality to hold onto an opinion or a response against a group of readers with their own responses and opinions.

Sensitive and critical facilitation of the class discussion helps, but the problem for the teacher is that there may be no way to judge from a Reader Response orientation, what is and is not an important minority or divergent response. Depending on whether a teacher privileges the individual reader or the community of readers, either all responses are valued or group dynamics will decide. Class discussion may become confined to a relatively narrow and comfortable range of responses or readings.

With that said, there is much to commend this approach. It is much more democratic in privileging the text selected by readers rather than elite literary authorities. It allows for individuals to take from text what they will rather than what the teacher demands. It is also democratic in that it demands active participation of the individual and the group: The classroom is a place of many voices. Those who like the active involvement of students, who prefer a noisier classroom with group work, and who are comfortable with giving up some control over the direction and focus of literature lessons will appreciate this approach. The question is whether reader response can go far enough in developing readers who are responsive readers who are also critical readers of text and of their social world. Activity 3.3 asks you to reflect on this issue.

ACTIVITY 3.3: Professional Reflection and Discussion

Again we would like to consider whether a reader response orientation should dominate the secondary English/Language Arts classrooms in general and what this orientation would mean for the teaching of young adult literature in your context. Discuss the following questions with your small group:

1. What would the classroom look like?

2. What kind of texts would be made available?

3. What would students like and dislike about this approach?

4. What kind of learner and teacher would do well in this orientation; that is, what skills, talents, history and dispositions would do well with reader response?

5. What kind of learner, reader, and citizen would be developed in this approach?

6. Moving beyond the limitation of reader response requires a careful consideration of the third curricular orientation, Cultural Criticism.

CULTURAL CRITICISM ORIENTATION

Although reader response approaches have been promoted for the last few decades and Cultural Heritage for even longer and although both may have been a part of your own literary education, Cultural Criticism is relatively new and less likely to have been articulated in secondary classrooms at this point. Cultural Criticism is an amalgamation of various forms of literary criticism: feminism, deconstruction, post-structuralism, Marxism, post colonialism, among others. It begins from the premise that no texts, literary or otherwise, are politically neutral. All texts offer particular and interested readings of the world. All texts are products of the context in which they were written and in which they are ultimately read. They are creative and stylized but not unique constructions. For example, the characterization of women characters, of African American characters, or of adolescent life reflects the author's efforts to work with and against the cultural norms that exist at the time of writing. For example, what might constitute a "happy ending" for women characters (usually marriage) or for adolescent characters (greater maturity) is predetermined by what is understood at the time about women or adolescents. The author writes in relation to the norms for endings in constructing the conclusion of his or her work.

Not only are all texts a product of their context, so are all readings. To make meaning of a text, readers draw the cultural resources or background information they have, along with the reading skills they have developed. These resources include the knowledge they have of common genres, their storylines, themes, and representations of characters, and so on. If one is not familiar with the dominant ways of reading/creating meaning, the work and its characters, storyline, and themes may be unintelligible.

In large part, Cultural Criticism asks the learner to examine the text from a "writerly" rather than a "readerly" perspective, to use Roland Barthes (1975) terms. That is, it asks readers to deconstruct the text by looking at how the text works, more precisely, what it draws on in terms of common and dominant storylines, characterizations, and themes.

Cultural Criticism asks readers to deconstruct the text by looking at common and dominant storylines, characterizations, and themes.

Second, and most important, it asks learners to examine what the cultural or discursive resources used in creating and reading texts mean in terms of how we understand and name the self, others, and our world. That is, this orientation demands that we ask what the text and/or a particular reading of the text promotes socially and politically in our world. In short, it demands we read critically.

Teachers using this approach must be self-critical as well as self-reflective and acknowledge their own position and therefore their own partiality in reading texts, as well as their own power to legitimate readings and texts. Teachers must be familiar with a wide range of "readings," in particular with contemporary literary theory, and with contemporary and classical texts, including media texts. Together with the students, the teacher would choose a genre or a thematic unit or specific text that connects to the world of the students. In addition to more usual prereading activities, developing background information, vocabulary, and so on, students would individually or collectively brainstorm the usual features of the plotline, character, and themes that underpin the genre (e.g., fairytales, comic books, and manga), or larger themes (e.g., teenage romance, violence, and family life) and/or, in the case of a single well-known text, what they already have heard about the work—its previous readings. Although the teacher should begin with genres, themes, or a text that the students have some familiarity with, as with any literature lesson, it may be necessary to supplement the students' background knowledge. Students would work their way through the text recording and discussing how text aligns with common expectations and norms as well as their own expectations. The teacher will extend the discussion by highlighting student-generated readings or offering alternative readings or possible readings of the text. For example,

- What would happen if this were told from the perspective of the wicked witch or the ugly stepsisters?
- What would happen if superman were a female, a Native American, or an African American?

In the case of well-known works or a very familiar theme, there may already exist multiple readings that students may or may not know about. Finding and investigating multiple readings can ideally take the form of student inquiry. For example, students can watch and discuss a single scene or series of scenes from various film versions of Shakespeare's *Romeo and Juliet*. There are films dating back to 1938 as well as other media and print versions. Showing renderings of the same scene through a number of historical and contemporary films allows students to focus on and account for the various interpretations or the "readings" of text. It also allows them to consider their own interpretations or rewriting of the text.

Such learning and teaching are not simply about multiplying the number of readings and texts in the classroom but also about adding and studying readings that make a difference in how we understand ourselves, others, and our social and democratic life. The "critique" aspect of the Cultural Critique orientation means that certain kinds of questions will dominate class discussion. These include questions that go beyond the text and beyond the individual reader, such as

- "What version of the 'good life' is represented in this work or this reading, and in what other texts have you seen a similar representation?"
- "What values are important in this texts/reading?"
- "What does such a representation do in our world?"
- "Who would like this text or this reading?"
- "Who is reading, writing, and publishing this kind of work?"
- "How do we account for popularity or lack of popularity of this text?"

Whatever shape or directions such questions take, the critique is informed by a belief in developing critical and compassionate readers of text and of the world.

Students in this orientation would be assessed on their ability to critique and re-create texts and possibly take on related social projects in their own worlds.

Whether they do such projects or not, the intention is to create the conditions for learners to think deeply about the relationship between world in the text and the texts in the world, in their world.

Despite the important democratic overlay to this work, some educators may not be comfortable with the critical and political approach. Certainly the aesthetic value of texts may seem to get short shrift in this approach. Some teachers may simply want their students to fall in love with reading and with books, and they may fear that a critical edge may take that seemingly innocent love away. Some refuse to acknowledge a critical side to any great work of literature; albeit popular media and literature remain suspect. However, preparing students for a world in which they will be bombarded with texts from various sources, a world in which they will be facing critical social, economic, poltical, and environmental issues on a local and global level, it would seem important for deep, critical, self-reflective thinking and feeling to occur in English/Language Arts class as in every class. Under such circumstances, this orientation becomes difficult to ignore. Activity 3.4 asks you to envision how this orientation might play out in the classroom.

ACTIVITY 3.4: Professional Reflection and Discussion

Imagine what a Cultural Criticism orientation would look like in an English/Language Arts classroom committed to the study of young adult literature. Discuss these questions with your small group.

1. What students would do well in this orientation?

2. What kind of texts and media would be involved?

3. What would the lessons be like?

4. What kind of student/learner/citizen would be produced?

TEACHING WITH YOUNG ADULT LITERATURE

In the teaching case that follows, Case 3.1 asks you to identify the teaching orientation in play and to critique it in terms of its positive and negative aspects. Activity 3.5 that follows expands on Case 3.1.

CASE 3.1: Phil Lebow's Middle School Language Arts Class

Phil Lebow's middle school language arts classroom is located in a rural farm community hours from a major urban center. Phil has been teaching English language arts for 20 years and last took a literature class during his master's degree program years back. He has class sets of one of his favorite young adult novels, Gary Paulsen's (1994) *The Car*.

As we look in on Phil's class, they have read the first part of the novel where 14-year-old Terry Anders realizes his parents have deserted him in their suburban home and his only way out is to finish building a custom-kit car, a Blakely Bearcat sports car, his dad was constructing. Terry completes the project, gathers up his life savings, and heads out West on the highway in the first part of the novel, picking up a hitchhiking, burned-flashbacking out flashbacking, acid Vietnam vet named Waylon Jackson. The road trip adventure begins.

Phil: I want you to consider the questions up on the board in your Literature Circles groups. Write your answers on the Post-it Notes at your table, and we'll have a group discussion in 15 minutes. The questions Phil has on the board are

1. Would you do what Terry did going off on the road on your own?
2. Would you pick up a hitchhiker like Waylon?
3. How would you survive on the road?
4. Do you see any problem with Terry at 14 ditching school?
5. Does the author make you want to read the next part?
6. What do you like or dislike about the novel?

Students report out in a large group discussion, and Phil tells them they will be reading a page he has copied for next time about the author, Gary Paulsen, and his adventures that inform his novels.

ACTIVITY 3.5: Professional Reflection and Discussion

Now that you have read Case 3.1, consider in your small group the following questions:

1. What orientation is Phil Lebow, the teacher, illustrating?
2. What are its advantages?
3. What are its disadvantages?
4. How would you go about teaching this particular novel in terms of orientation?

To provide a clear sense of how you might go about creating a young adult literature unit, we include Case 3.2, which is centered on a short 3-week example created by Erin, a 10th-grade high school English teacher. Erin's case illustrates a thematic unit centered on "youth in times of war and conflict." Thematic units offer students an opportunity to explore a topic through multiple texts (Burke, 2008; Smagorinsky, 2008). Many of her students have family members in the military, displaced to fight in the Middle East.

CASE 3.2: The Unit: Youth in Times of War and Conflict

Erin decides to center this unit on contemporary young adult novels that concern the experiences of youth during war. She also identifies audiotapes of some of the novels for her English language learner (ELL) and struggling reader students. She brainstorms a list of possible novels (listed in the recommended young adult literature for this chapter). In addition, Erin identifies a media interview with Ishmael Beah, a young man who wrote the novel *A Long Way Gone: Memoirs of a Boy Soldier* (2007).

Along the way, Erin anticipates potential censorship issues with some of the novels and she consults the Intellectual Freedom section of the American Library Association's website at www.ala.org/ala/oif. She also anticipates developing rubric assessments that tap into students' thinking about war issues via creating iMovies and other media displays that relate to the novels they are reading. Erin consults RubiStar where teachers can create customized rubrics to evaluate students' work. The website for RubiStar and related templates is as follows: http://rubistar.4teachers.org/

As a way of further exploring some of the issues related to unit development, consider the questions in Activity 3.6.

ACTIVITY 3.6: Professional Reflection and Discussion

Discuss in your small group any obstacles and opportunities that exist in your school or teaching site that you have to consider while planning a unit like Erin's.

1. What are some of the obstacles?
2. How would you overcome these obstacles?
3. What are some of the anticipated outcomes?
4. How would you assess students in your unit?

As you undertake planning and implementing creative units of instruction that encompass young adult literature, the following resources should be helpful.

POSITION STATEMENTS TO SUPPORT YOUR CURRICULUM DECISIONS

To lend support to your efforts to determine and defend your choices in the teaching of young adult literature, let us add position statements about adolescent literacy made by the International Reading Association (IRA), the National Reading Conference (NRC), and the National Council for Teachers of English (NCTE). These are well-established organizations collectively representing thousands of educators and researchers. The positions statements all suggest the following:

1.   The need to recognize the out-of-school lives and literacies and interests of the students, individually and collectively, in their classrooms and to use the resources that students bring to the classroom: NCTE (2004) states that It is important for teachers to recognize and value the multiple literacy resources students bring to the acquisition of school literacy. "NCTE acknowledges that adolescents have literacy lives outside of school and therefore the teachers of adolescents need "continued support and professional development that assist them to bridge between adolescents' rich literate backgrounds and school literacy" (http://www.ncte.org). The IRA Adolescent Literacy Commission speaks of individual differences, stating adolescents deserve "teachers who understand the complexities of individual adolescent readers, respect their differences, and respond to their characteristics" (1999, p. 8). It notes as well that "Factors such as family heritage, language, and social and economic position contribute to the variation that students regularly display during reading and writing activities" (p. 8). Donna Alvermann in her 2001 paper, commissioned by the NRC, on effective literacy instruction for adolescents suggests that, "Many adolescent of the Net Generation find their own reasons for becoming literate—reasons that go beyond reading to acquire school knowledge of academic academics texts" (p. 2). She iterates the need to "address the implications of youth's multiple literacies for classroom instruction" (p. 2).

2.   The need for a wide variety of materials and for student choice: The IRA Adolescent Literacy Commission (2012) insists that adolescents deserve "access to a wide variety of reading materials that they can and want to read" (2012, p. 4). The Commission (Moore, et al., 1999) suggests that adolescents want the independence of selecting "age-appropriate materials they can manage and topics and genres they prefer," which means including "reading materials tied to popular

television and movie productions; magazines about specific interests such as sports, music or cultural backgrounds and books by favorite authors" (p. 5). Similarly, the NCTE states that adolescents need "sustained experience with diverse texts in a variety of genres and offering multiple perspectives on real life experiences. Although many of these texts will be required by the curriculum, others would be self-selected and of high interest to the reader" (2006; www.ncte.org/2004). Both NCTE and IRA insist "[t]exts should be broadly viewed to include print, electronic, and visual media" (www.ncte.org). Pushing further, IRA suggests combining reading material (textbooks, paperbacks, magazines, websites, etc.) with the goal that teen readers, by improving and extending their reading might "expand and strengthen their grasp of the world . . . and nourish their emotions and psyches as well as their intellects" (1999, p. 5).

3. The need for critical deep analysis of texts: NCTE states that adolescents need "conversations/discussions regarding texts that are authentic, student initiated, and teacher facilitated. Such discussion should lead to diverse interpretations of a text that deepen the conversation" (www.ncte.org). NCTE's position statement also suggests that the critical examination of text allows adolescents to "question and investigate various social, political and historical content and purposes within texts" and to "make connections between texts, and between texts and personal experiences to act on and react to the world" (www.ncte.org). Furthermore, they suggest the need to create and engage students in critical examinations of texts as "they dissect, deconstruct, and re-construct in an effort to engage in meaning making and comprehension processes" (NCTE, 2006, p. 6).

So, at this point we invite you to consider what your approach will be in the teaching of literature in general and in the teaching of young adult literature in particular. What will be the primary focus in your teaching of literature; what kinds of texts and what kinds of activities and questions will dominate your classroom, ideally? We invite you to consider and reconsider the nature and articulation of your approach as you work your way through the chapters that follow.

SUMMARY

In this chapter, we considered the three most prominent orientations to teaching young adult literature: Cultural Heritage, Reader Response, and Cultural Criticism. Each of these has advantages and disadvantages, and we offered illustrative examples that provide a window on how these orientations play out in the classroom.

DISCUSSION QUESTIONS

1. What is the Cultural Heritage orientation to the teaching of young adult literature?
2. What is the Reader Response orientation to the teaching of young adult literature?
3. What is the Cultural Criticism orientation to the teaching of young adult literature?
4. What, in your view, are the advantages and disadvantages of each orientation?
5. How can you use professional organization position statements and standards to support your curriculum decisions?

KEY TERMS

Cultural Criticism Orientation   47

Cultural Heritage Orientation   47

Literature Circles   57

Memoir   70

Reader Response Orientation   47

SMALL-GROUP ACTIVITY: USING POSITION STATEMENTS

In your small group, have each member visit the position statements alluded to earlier (e.g., NCTE) that are online and use this information and the three orientations outlined in the chapter to construct a brief, one-page teaching philosophy that supports your approach to teaching young adult literature. Discuss this with other group members, and keep this information as part of our teaching portfolio.

RECOMMENDED READINGS

Boyd, F., & Bailey, N. (2009). Censorship in three metaphors. *Journal of Adolescent & Adult Literacy*, 52(8), 653–661.

This article can be accessed at the International Reading Association website: www
.reading.org. The article features useful information for thinking about and responding to censorship issues. Other helpful readings can be found at the National Council of Teachers of English website and the American Library Association website.

Burke, J. (2008). *The English teacher's companion: A complete guide to classroom, curriculum, and the profession* (3rd ed.). Portsmouth, NH: Heinemann.

This text offers useful information to guide teachers' unit planning efforts along with other teaching resources for the field of English.

O'Neill, M. (1993). Teaching literature as cultural criticism. *English Quarterly, 25*(1), 19–25.

The author offers a detailed look at charting major approaches to teaching literature including Cultural Heritage, Reader Response, and Cultural Criticism.

Smagorinsky, P. (2008). *Teaching English by design: How to create and carry out instructional units.* Portsmouth, NH: Heinemann.

This book provides guidance in creating units that captivate students' interests.

RECOMMENDED YOUNG ADULT LITERATURE FEATURED IN THIS CHAPTER

Beah, I. (2007). *A long way gone: Memoirs of a boy soldier.* New York, NY: Farrar, Straus and Giroux.

This memoir provides an account of the author's experience as a boy solider during the civil war in Sierra Leone.

Deuker, C. (2005). *Runner.* Boston, MA: Houghton Mifflin.

Likely to appeal to disengaged readers, this fast-paced novel chronicles main character Chance Taylor's secret life. As a high school senior, he blends into school but leads a clandestine life living on an old sailboat with his down-and-out veteran dad, a drunk who is unable to hold a job. Chance takes daily jogs to stay healthy and warm. He gets an offer to pick up and deliver packages near the harbor where he runs, giving the title *Runner* a more sinister meaning.

Paulsen, G. (1994). *The car.* New York, NY: Harcourt Brace.

Gary Paulsen's well-known young adult novels are action packed and fast-moving, mirroring many of his own outdoor adventures. In this novel, 14-year-old Terry Anders is abandoned by his parents and sets off across the country in a homemade kit sports car his dad was building. He picks up Vietnam vet, Waylon Jackson, and they head west, getting into various scuffles along the way. This is a captivating book for teens interested in working on cars and solving problems.

RECOMMENDED YOUNG ADULT LITERATURE FOR THE UNIT ON YOUTH IN TIMES OF WAR

Al-Windawi, T. (2004). *Thura's diary: A young girl's life in war-torn Baghdad.* London, England: Penguin.

Written from the point of view of an Iraqi teenager at the onset of war, the author provides an insider's look at the impact of the bombing in Baghdad on people's lives.

Black-and-white photos take the reader into Thura's life from childhood through her teenage years, ultimately fleeing to the United States for college.

Barakat, I. (2007). *Tasting the sky: A Palestinian childhood*. New York, NY: Melanie Kroupa Books.
    Written as a memoir of a Palestinian refugee from the Six-Day War that concluded in 1967, resulting in the Israeli occupation of the West Bank and the Gaza Strip, this firsthand account takes the reader into the heart of the Middle East conflict.

Ellis, D. (2000). *The breadwinner*. Toronto, Ontario, Canada: Groundwood.
    The first of three books chronicling the war in Afghanistan, this novel follows a young teenaged girl, Parvana, as she and her family prepare to flee war-torn Kabul. Two other novels trace her journey out of her home country (*Parvana's Journey*, 2002, and *Mud City*, 2003).

Ellis, D. (2002). *Parvana's journey*. Toronto, Ontario, Canada: Groundwood.

Ellis, D. (2003). *Mud city*. Toronto, Ontario, Canada: Groundwood.

Myers, W. D. (2008). *Sunrise over Fallujah*. New York, NY: Scholastic.
    The war in Iraq is seen from the perspective of a young African American soldier from Harlem working with the local people as part of a Civilian Affairs unit. The contradictions and doublespeak that cover the real purpose of this unit's operation weighs heavily on Robin Perry, the main character.

Rifa'i, A., & Ainbinder, O. (2003). *We just want to live here*. New York, NY: St. Martin's Griffin.
    Following a summer peace camp, two teenage girls carry on a conversation about their respective lives in Palestine and Israel. They correspond through letter writing and create alternatives to feeling trapped in their respective countries.

Salisbury, G. (2005). *Eyes of the emperor*. New York, NY: Wendy Lamb Books.
    Set in Honolulu, Hawai'i, at the start of World War II and the bombing of Pearl Harbor, main character Eddy Okubo enlists in the U.S. Army to show his patriotism. Shipped off to a remote training island in Mississippi, Eddy and the other Japanese American Hawai'i-based soldiers are used as enemy bait to train attack German Shepherd dogs. The way in which Eddy and his compatriots handle this racist situation is based on the author's interviews with eight of the survivors.

Satrapi, M. (2003). *Persepolis: The story of a childhood*. New York, NY: Pantheon.
    This graphic novel traces the life of the author growing up in Iran during the Islamic revolution and the impact of war on Tehran and its people. Through the use of haunting black-and-white comic strip frames, the author shows the human impact of war and oppression. A major motion picture based on the novel is available.

RECOMMENDED WEBSITES

Blogger.com: www.blogger.com
This site offers a freeware site to organize a classroom blog that accommodates uploading photos for Photovoice discussions.

ReadWriteThink: *Blogging with Photovoice: Sharing pictures in an integrated classroom*: www.readwritethink.org/lessons/lesson_view.asp?id=1064

Censorship Issues:
See the Intellectual Freedom section of the American Library Association's website at www.ala.org/ala/oif

Rubric Assessments:
Customized rubrics to evaluate students' work can be found at the RubiStar site listed by content areas. Templates can be modified to fit your teaching needs: http://rubistar.4teachers.org/

REFERENCES

Alvermann, D. (2001, Sept.). Effective literacy instruction for adolescents: Executive summary and paper commissioned by the National Reading Conference. Available from: http://nrconline.org

Barthes, R. (1975). *The pleasure of the text*. New York, NY: Hill and Wang.

Burke, J. (2008). *The English teacher's companion: A complete guide to classroom, curriculum, and the profession* (3rd ed.). Portsmouth, NH: Heinemann.

Dewey, J. (1938). *Education and experience*. New York, NY: Collier.

Fish, S. (1982). *Is there a text in this class? The authority of interpretive communities*. Cambridge, MA: Harvard University Press.

International Reading Association (IRA) Adolescent Literacy Commission. (2012). *Adolescent literacy: A position statement of the International Reading Association*. Retrieved from http://www.reading.org/Libraries/resources/ps1079adolescentliteracyrev2012.pdf

Latrobe, K. H., & Drury, J. (2009). *Critical approaches to young adult literature*. New York, NY: Neal-Schuman.

Leggo, C. (1997). *Teaching to wonder: Responding to poetry in the secondary classroom*. Vancouver, British Columbia, Canada: Pacific Educational Press at the University of British Columbia.

Moore, D. W., Bean, T. W., Birdyshaw, D., & Rycik, J. A. (1999). *Adolescent literacy: A position statement for the Commission on Adolescent Literacy of the International Reading Association*. Newark, DE International Reading Association.

National Council of Teachers of English (NCTE). (2006). *Adolescent literacy: A policy research brief produced by The National Council of Teachers of English*. Retrieved from http://www.ncte.org/libraryjNCTEFiles/Resources/Positions/Chron0907Research Brief.pdf

O'Neill, M. (1993). Teaching literature as cultural criticism. *English Quarterly, 25* (1), 19–25.

Rosenblatt, L. (1938). *Literature as exploration*. Chicago, IL: Modern Language Association.

Rosenblatt, L. (1978). *The reader, the text, the poem: The transactional theory of the literary work*. Carbondale IL: Southern Illinois University Press.

Smagorinsky, P. (2008). *Teaching English by design: How to create and carry out instructional units*. Portsmouth, NH: Heinemann.

Chapter 4

Young Adult Literature and Exceptional Learners

In this chapter, we consider young adult literature aimed at learners with special needs including English-as-Second-Language (ESL) students, gifted students, striving/struggling readers, and nonreaders, as well as students with disabilities. The key idea to take away from this chapter is the degree to which adolescents are unique individuals with diverse interests (M. Smith & Wilhelm, 2006). As an English teacher infusing young adult literature in your classroom, knowing your students' in- and out-of-school talents and interests will go a long way toward helping them select fiction and nonfiction that is responsive to their reading interests and levels. The teacher examples featured in this chapter demonstrate the practical value of getting to know your students.

Learning Objectives

- Understand the impact of English Language Learners (ELLs) on young adult literature teaching and learning.
- Know the stages of language development and related instructional strategies.
- Become familiar with young adult literature relevant to ELLs.
- Know some teaching approaches designed to assist struggling readers through young adult literature.
- Be able to address gifted learners' needs through young adult literature.
- Develop an initial understanding of young adult literature resources addressing students with disabilities.

Vignette: Mr. Antonio Papa's 9th-Grade Class

English teacher Mr. Antonio Papa takes special care to get to know all his students as individuals with unique talents in and out of school, as well as diverse interests. Teaching in urban San Francisco, California, Mr. Papa's literature classes include students from all over the globe. As we look in on his period 3 class, we see a rich classroom library with books including popular young adult novels. In addition, we also see racks of high-interest, low-vocabulary fiction and nonfiction selections designed to accommodate the wide-ranging reading levels and interests represented by Mr. Papa's students. In the scene that follows, 9th-grader Rafael Jimenez is browsing through the racks of high-interest, low-vocabulary nonfiction. Mr. Papa knows that Rafael moved to California from Mexico City and that Rafael loves his science classes. As a resident of Mexico City, Rafael experienced strong earthquakes, and now in San Francisco, he knows he is at the epicenter of earthquake history. However, reading extended literary material in English in Mr. Papa's classroom is, at this stage of Rafael's grasp of English, untenable. It is Monday, and for the opening part of class, Mr. Papa has his students do sustained silent reading (SSR) in books they self-select from the classroom library. They also keep a log of how many pages they read and a statement praising or critiquing the section of the book they have been reading.

Mr. Papa: How's it going, Rafael? Are you finding a book that interests you?

Rafael: Nah, I would like to read San Francisco—the earthquakes. In earth science class, we saw a video—how measure earthquakes. I want to do that.

Mr. Papa: Take a look at this one: *Earthquakes* by Anne Schraff (2004). It tells about huge earthquakes that hit various parts of the United States, including San Francisco.

Rafael: Thanks, Mr. Papa.

THE ENGLISH LANGUAGE LEARNER

Changing Student Population

As discussed in other chapters, one of the most powerful and certainly most visible changes in the American schools is the nature of the student population. Over the last 30 years, the student population has become more racially, culturally, linguistically, and ethnically diverse. As noted by the U.S. Department of Education's National Center for Education Statistics (NESC; 2009), between 1972 and 2007, the percentage of White students decreased from 78% to 56%, while the minority population increased from 22% to 44%. In the western states, increasing racial and ethnic diversity is particularly evident: As of 2004, minority enrollment exceeded White enrollment in Alaska, Arizona, California, Colorado, Hawai'i, Idaho, Montana, Nevada, New Mexico, Oregon, Utah, Washington, and Wyoming (http://nces .ed.gov/programs/coe). The increase in minority enrollment mirrors changes in population in general. As of 2005, Hispanics, African Americans, Asians, Pacific Islanders, and Native Americans made up 33% of the U.S. population with Hispanics the largest minority group at 14% (NESC, 2007; Pilonieta & Medina, 2007). The U.S. Bureau of Statistics predicts that by 2042, no one racial or ethnic group will constitute a clear majority.

The increasing diversity of the population is in part a result of accelerated immigration rates brought about by globalization and the intensification of global capitalism. As noted by Margaret Gibson and Anne Rios Rojas (2006), globalization and the rapid social and economic changes it has engendered "are as much about deterritorialization and the displacement of a large and growing number of peoples, as it is about the free movement of capital, information and services" (p. 69). In the United States, current estimates place the total number of foreign born at around 12% of the total population. School enrollment figures suggest that 20% (1 in 5) of all children in the United States are either foreign born or have at least one immigrant parent (Hernandez, Denton, & Macartney, 2009; NESC, 2009; Suarez-Orozoc, Saurez-Orozco, & Todorova, 2008). This number is expected

The increasing diversity of the population is in part a result of the effects of globalization.

to double within the next 20 years (Jimenez & Teague, 2009; NESC, 2005). This is not the first time that there has been a large influx of immigrants to the United States, but families immigrating in these times originate not from Europe but predominately from Latin America (62%) and Asia (22%) and to a lesser extent from Africa (2%). This shift together with existing minority groups has dramatically increased the racial, ethnic, religious, cultural, and linguistic diversity of the country as a whole and, thus, the population of students in our schools.

One effect of increasing and changing immigration patterns is that large numbers of students speak a language other than English at home. According to the NESC (2008), the number of these students doubled from 3.8 to 10.8 million between 1979 and 2006. Most of these students require English language instruction. Lee Gunderson (2008), drawing on statistics from the National Clearinghouse for English Language Acquisition and Language Instruction, reports that the percentage of ELLs in America has risen by 57% since 1995 and now comprises more than 10% of the total student population. In some states, the increase in the number of ELLs has been nothing short of dramatic. North Carolina reports a 500% increase in the number of ELLs; Colorado, Nevada, Oregon, Nebraska, Georgia, and Indiana, more than 200% (Batalova, Fix, & Murray, 2002; Pilonieta & Medina, 2007). Of particular interest to high school English teachers is the fact that the highest increase in the number of ELLs is occurring in grades 7 through 12 (Gunderson, 2008, p. 185). This increase reflects only those students who are classified as ELL, but not the whole range of students of second-language learners who may still require English language support during the to years it takes to become proficient in academic English (Cummins, 2009).

Changing immigrant patterns and increasing diversity suggests that more than ever, a wider range of linguistic and cultural backgrounds and a wider range of English language proficiencies exist in the high school English/Language Arts (ELA) classroom. Although this has always been true in urban schools, in some border communities, and in Native American/Alaskan/Hawai'ian communities, it is now the rule rather than the exception. English language learning and teaching is becoming part and parcel of "everyday" life in high school ELA classes across the nation. More generally, growing awareness of the cultural, social, and linguistic diversity that exists not only across but also within groups, along with the acknowledgment of individual differences, makes it increasingly evident that heterogeneity rather than homogeneity characterizes the contemporary ELA classroom. This is especially true in relation to English language proficiency and the ELLs that increasing compose the student population. Activity 4.1 asks you to reflect on some of these changes in your school and classroom.

ACTIVITY 4.1: Professional Reflection and Discussion

Directions: In small groups, discuss the current demographics with regard to ELL and foreign-born students in your classroom and school district. Is your student population as diverse as suggested by the previous discussion? If so, is this diversity mirrored in the teaching population?

ENGLISH LANGUAGE LEARNERS (ELLS, ESL, LEP)

For the sake of clarity, *English Language Learners* (ELLs) refers to students whose first language (L1) is not English. A multitude of other terms are also used: ESL refers to English-as-Second-Language learners; however, for some multilingual students, English may be a third or fourth language; LEP stands for Limited English Proficiency learners. Other terms include bilingual learners, dual language learners, nonnative speakers of English, and language minority students.

Whatever the term, these students whose first language is not English are over-represented among struggling readers, and they face great challenges in attaining academic success. For example, only 4% of 8th-grade ELLs and 20% of students labeled as "former ELLs" scored at the proficient or advanced levels on the reading portion of the 2005 National Assessment of Educational Progress (Perie, Grigg, & Donahue, 2005).

As with the general population, many factors can affect student achievement, such as intellectual ability, motivation, and teacher–parent expectations, and, of course, quality of instruction. Although there is considerable variation across the ELL population, unique factors affect the reading and academic success of ELLs as a group. These may include previous education and experience, including students' first language literacy, socioeconomic status, and legal immigration status (Pilonieta & Medina, 2007).

In terms of previous life and school experience, there can be considerable variation among ELLs. Some may have had considerable schooling, either in their home country or in the United States, which may or may not have included English language study, whereas other ELLs may have had no or limited schooling, and they may have had no study in English. Indeed may possess only limited literacy in their first language. Students with strong literacy skills in their first language often require less time to learn a second language. Also students' first language may or may not share some degree of similarity to English; for example, it may use the same or similar alphabet as with French or German, or not at all, as in the case of Chinese, which will affect how quickly a student will pick up English. These educational and linguistic factors also will affect how and where a teacher begins with any particular ELL. In addition, as noted by Janice Pilgreen (2007), a 22-year ESL teacher, now a researcher, teachers need to be aware that ELLs often have developed a reservoir of knowledge and experience that is unlike what children in the United States have usually developed linguistically and culturally. In addition, "Some, as young as they are, have experienced the trauma of war, violence, hunger, family crisis, and displacement" (Pilgreen, 2007, p. 239).

Furthermore, ELL students and their families are more likely to be struggling financially, which means that students may have to work after school or help out at home (e.g., babysit) in order to help their families to support themselves. As well, families may have to move frequently to find work, resulting in intermittent schooling for their children. These added responsibilities and circumstances could negatively affect students' academic progress and English language proficiency. Finally, legal immigration status, particularly in light of changing state policy, can affect students psychologically and can affect whether they get access to college, financial aid, and employment. Only 8.9% of immigrants who arrived between 1990 and 1999 have obtained legal citizenship (National Institute of Literacy, 2007). Obtaining citizenship, even if one has superior English Language skills, is, as one of the authors of this text can fully attest, an expensive, time-consuming process that requires easy access to documents in one's home country. Immigration status can be another challenge to the efforts of ELLs. Being aware of these factors can help educators to understand and better meet the needs of their ELLs in their classroom. However, there are still other things teachers should know in order to best serve their ELLs.

STAGES OF LANGUAGE DEVELOPMENT

According to Paola Pilonieta and Adriana Medina (2007), there are four acknowledged stages of language development: (a) preproduction in which students listen and watch (hey may go silent during this stage and not communicate at all for some time); (b) early production, a stage in which learners may understand and speak some English but are still assimilating language and vocabulary; (c) speech emergence, a stage where students begin communicating with some fluency; and (d) intermediate fluency where students function quite well in English. Also helpful for teachers are Jim Cummins's (2003) three levels of language proficiency. These are not discrete levels but develop concurrently: (a) basic interpersonal conversation (**BIC**). This level usually requires 1 to 2 years of exposure to L2. At this level, students use simple, high-frequency words and simple syntax supported by gestures and facial expressions to communicate. (b) The second level occurs when students acquire through formal and informal instruction-specific literacy, phonological and grammatical knowledge. This level includes student's knowledge and use of discrete language skills, for example spelling, punctuation, and capitalization conventions as well as grammatical rules. (c) The third level involves cognitive academic language proficiency (**CALP**). This stage comprises the knowledge and use of less frequently used vocabulary and the ability to produce and understand complex written and oral material. This is the more abstract and complex academic language often required in content area disciplines.

Pilonieta and Medina (2007) maintain that "Only when students have CALP is their academic achievement comparable to their monolingual English counterparts" (p. 131).

Teachers need to be aware that students may be orally quite proficient (L1) and indeed may become very talkative in English, but they still may not do well academically because they have not had sufficient explicit instruction to allow them to work at L2 or attain L3 (CALP).

INSTRUCTIONAL STRATEGIES

Although the research in the area of effective instructional practices for ELLs is limited, there is support for the following instructional elements: vocabulary instruction, developing and activating background knowledge, the use of peer tutoring strategies, and cooperative learning groups, culturally responsive instruction. Vocabulary instruction involves teaching not only the unfamiliar words students will encounter in their reading materials, but also, particularly for those without previous schooling, the language of schooling associated with instructional activities, including discuss, explain, list, describe, outline, and reflect. As with other students, ELLs will benefit from visuals, gestures, graphic organizers, semantic maps, charts, and concept and story maps and with abstract words, explicit instruction. Activating background knowledge means providing experiences (film, visual displays, artifacts, presentations, field trips, and engaging popular culture) or discussion of personal experiences/stories that relate to the topic or theme to be studied, and linking those experiences to the text to be read. The use of peer tutoring and cooperative learning groups helps improve the comprehension and fluency of both tutor and tutee; often more language is used, and there is more immediate feedback as well as greater development of conversational and interactional skills than if an ELL struggles by themselves on a task. Teachers should note that ELLs working with a peer who speaks the same language might resort to their native language, which may not necessarily be a bad thing.

Use of Native Language

Among the general public and the academic community, the use of native language or first language during the school day for instructional purposes is a controversial topic. However, according to many researchers, the use of L1 can be beneficial to ELLs. L1 use can work as a cognitive tool to help scaffold content knowledge and support higher level thinking than restricting students to the sole use of L2 (Garcia & Godina, 2004; Gersten & Baker, 2000). As a result, we suggest teachers consider the *strategic* use of L1 rather than constant translation or exclusive use of L2 as an additional strategy to help students acquire English language proficiency and improved academic success.

Culturally Responsive Instruction: This instruction incorporates or bridges home school and community similarities and differences and often increases students' level of participation and learning (Goldenberg, Rueda, & August, 2006). It works with youth and respectfully recruits their cultural experiences and out of school interests in efforts to develop school and disciplinary skills and knowledge that are meaningful and relevant (Moje & Hinchman, 2004). It stands to reason that better understanding of ELLs, their cultural experiences, and their individual interests can lead to the design of learning environments and pedagogical activities and materials that can result in better educational outcomes.

ELLS AND YOUNG ADULT LITERATURE

Considering this text, it is perhaps not surprising that we believe that young adult literature can be used to help ELLs. We believe that reading this popular, engaging form of fiction can help ELLs in vocabulary and linguistic development, acquiring background knowledge, and when carefully selected, help bridge self, community, and school knowledge, allowing for a more culturally responsive, and personally relevant instruction, enriching individual and collective learning. As with other students, careful matching of text to students is paramount. With ELLs, depending on their level of proficiency, supporting textual material is critical, along with supporting instruction. Fortunately there exists in this genre a wide array of books, including picture books, audio books, and simplified books that will work as texts or supplementary reading for ELLs; we suggest teachers explore the following texts and resources for their ELLs.

If you are working with students whose native language is Spanish, consider the now well-established authors at Arte Publico Press (www.latinoteca.com/arte-publico-press). For example, Genaro Gonzalez's (2009) *A So-Called Vacation* follows two brothers in a Texas high school whose father has them spend a summer in California doing immigrant field work so they come to understand the harsh conditions and racist treatment experienced by undocumented farm workers.

Award winning author Rene Saldana Jr.'s young adult novels reflect his desire to hook reluctant readers on reading. "I had been a reluctant reader (I attributed much of my aversion to the fact that I'd never seen nor heard myself in books), so the question became: 'How many more brown would-be readers are not reading due this glaring omission?'" (Saldana & Moore, 2010, p. 690). As a result of his frustration with the absence of engaging young adult literature, he undertook an ongoing project to create a wiki-style *Annotated Bibliography for Culturally Relevant Literature* (2009) that students and teachers contribute to and use. A copy of this resource can be obtained by e-mailing rene.saldana@ttu.edu.

Rene Saldana's young adult novels are fast-paced and realistic. In *A Good Long Way* (2010), we follow high school senior Roelito as he decides to drop out of school in his Texas–Mexico border town. Despite liking school and handling his classes successfully, Roel is pigeonholed as a mirror image of his rowdy, hard-drinking brother. The story follows Roel and his teen friends as they wrestle with family issues and school perceptions that stereotype and misjudge their potential.

STRUGGLING READERS

Although "struggling readers" is a blanket term that masks the wide-ranging diversity in this category, teachers know that they are instructing many students for whom the assigned texts and readings in their content areas are too difficult. Estimates are that 6 out of 10 adolescents struggle with required texts they are assigned to read and that as many as 65% of high school students may be struggling readers (Lenski, 2008).

Confounding any simple category label, *struggling readers* (sometimes called "striving readers" or "reluctant readers"), may be ELL students, students assigned to read material well outside their comfort zone with little guidance, students whose interests go unmet in the school setting, and a host of other diverse causes. For example, a 9th grader assigned to read science fiction in his English class called the assignment "stupid," yet he played video games like Halo at home (Jolley, 2008). The vocabulary load in science fiction print proved to be daunting for this student. However, if the Halo video game connection had been made by this teacher, along with adequate vocabulary assistance (e.g., in the form of a teacher-made laminated bookmark glossary), he might have warmed up to reading in this genre.

Students' literacy identities are socially constructed in and out of school.

Because students' literacy identities are socially constructed in and out of school, they may react differently to reading in these very different settings. The same student who sits silently in class, hiding out and avoiding displays of reading difficulty, may well function just fine writing lyrics for a rock band on the weekends (Lesley, in press).

In addition, struggling readers may cling to an array of misconceptions about reading ability including the following (Lesley, in press):

- Reading ability is a static, fixed trait that some people just have.
- Making mistakes in school is fraught with serious consequences.
- It is better to remain silent and avoid displaying problems.

Case 4.1 offers an alternative to adopting a position of learned helplessness as a struggling adolescent reader.

CASE 4.1: Brian Hidalgo's High School English Class

Brian Hidalgo is a new English teacher in his first position at an inner-city urban high school. Brian's school is in a partnership grant with the downtown university campus to fund and offer after-school tutoring for struggling adolescent readers. English teachers are paid well for their time in this important activity and are provided professional development sessions aimed at sensitizing them to students' out-of-school literacy interests that can be tapped as a bridge to in-school reading tasks. Brian is excited to be part of this effort, and as a new teacher, he finds the extra professional development and payment helps. In the session that follows, Brian is getting to know his tutee, Nathan Sanchez.

Brian: Tell me about your hobbies outside of school?

Nathan: I play guitar and listen to Los Lonely Boys a lot. I'm trying to learn some of their songs.

Brian: There's a really good documentary about the brothers in that Texas band. Also some books about them. Maybe we can start with the film, doing some dictation writing about it, and then move to a short story by Gary Soto (1990) called "No Guitar Blues." What do you think?

Nathan: Yeah, I'd like that. I need help with reading so I don't embarrass myself in English class. We're reading *The Crucible* by Arthur Miller, and the words are too hard.

Brian: Okay, well there's also films that relate to that classic tale that we can check out. Sometimes it helps to have some background about the history and people you are going to read about first. So, we can work on both your reading fluency in material you like and also do some work on the assignments you have to do for English.

Nathan: Thanks, Mr. Hidalgo. I'm looking forward to these meetings, and I think they will help me stay in school.

Helping struggling readers like Nathan is absolutely crucial but certainly not easy. Beliefs about the negative climate in school settings for the struggling reader are compounded by schools that offer only a limited selection of young adult literature and few opportunities for self-selected reading. Fortunately, there are some solutions to these dismal conditions, and young adult literature offers support for engaged, enthusiastic reading for students who might otherwise disengage. For example, something as simple as a Read Aloud that you do to introduce struggling readers to the subtle nuances of a novel in terms of text structure, vocabulary, and the way language can flow helps scaffold further independent reading (Crawford-McKinney & Hogan, 2008).

Another great way to engage students in self-selected reading that is appropriate for their reading development involves the use of **high-interest, low-vocabulary books** (Crawford-McKinney & Hogan, 2008). High–Low books feature vocabulary in the 3rd- to 4th-grade range and interests likely to be appealing to adolescent readers including sports, horror, science fiction, romance, nonfiction, and other popular genres. The popularity of high-interest, low-vocabulary books is understandable, given that they look similar to young adult trade books in size and layout. This feature makes them appealing to students who may be stigmatized and marginalized by a history of "remedial reading" treatment.

Although there are many sources for high-interest, low vocabulary books at educational conferences and on the Internet, we profile a few that we know are in wide use in classrooms. Most come with teacher's guides and websites designed to stimulate student engagement, discussion, and comprehension. For example, High Interest Publishing (HIP) includes an array of hard-to-put-down novels (www.hip-books.com). These span sports, romance, problem-based novels, and horror and other genres. Books are leveled from 2nd-grade reading difficulty on but feature interests that fit adolescent students. For example, *Running for Dave* by Lori Jamison deals with a track star who gets cancer. The novel is at a 3rd-grade reading level but designed to appeal to a reader audience from grades 6 to 10. A novel like this one could be paired with a teacher read aloud of young adult author, Jordan Sonnenblick's (2010) *After Ever After* chronicling a teen's perspective on cancer survival that takes to task many of the myths and clichés that surround adolescence.

Other popular high-interest, low-vocabulary collections include nonfiction and fiction titles offered by Artesian Press (www.artesianpress.com). This publisher also features electronic books that can be downloaded and read-along MP3s for reluctant readers. In the nonfiction area, Anne Schraff's (2006) *Fashion* takes the reader through a very approachable history of fashion in 60 double-spaced pages. Written at a mid-4th-grade reading level, this selection and others are designed to appeal to reluctant and struggling readers from grades 6 through 12. Other titles in this series discuss tattoos and natural disasters (e.g., wildfires, earthquakes, and volcanoes). Fiction selections span horror and mystery genres, as well as sports, and multicultural titles.

Other major publishers of young adult materials also feature nonfiction and fiction books. One of the best ways to preview these curriculum resources for your classroom is to attend a state, regional, national, or international conference like those of the National Council Teachers of English (NCTE), American Library Association (ALA), or International Reading Association (IRA). Numerous publishers exhibit their titles and generally offer free materials as well.

Another event that may help engage reluctant and struggling adolescent readers with captivating young adult literature is Teen Read Week, an annual literacy initiative of the Young Adult Library Services Association (YALSA) of the ALA. Teen Read Week runs in mid-October each year. Curriculum support materials and program ideas are available, along with the top 10 books based on teens' ratings for each year. The website supports this important event (www.ala .org/teenread).

To fully address struggling readers' needs in your classroom, Gary Ivey (2010) recommends having an enticing and print-rich classroom book collection including books in students' first language (e.g., Spanish), bilingual picture books, easy reading English picture books centered on themes of friends and family, lots of high-quality young adult novels, and providing time and space for sustained silent reading.

THE GIFTED STUDENT

Myths about gifted students abound. Nowhere is this more apparent than in media portrayals of gifted students as nerdish intellectuals, often interested in the arcane aspects of science or history. For example, the popularity of the television show *The Big Bang Theory* rests in part on the social awkwardness of Sheldon, Leonard, and the other characters. Nevertheless, 21st-century problems and issues cry out for gifted and talented citizens who can solve many of the daunting health and environmental problems facing the planet. Narrow conceptions and stereotypical accounts of gifted students need to be challenged by more complex notions of **giftedness**, as well as a good grasp of young adult reading material likely to appeal to students excelling in a variety of endeavors. In this section, we begin by taking to task some of the more common myths surrounding giftedness and offer some guidelines as you work with students who need to go beyond the prescribed mainstream curriculum. Indeed, differentiating curriculum and young adult literature is a dominant theme in this chapter.

By all accounts, our "one-size-fits-all" curriculum fails to acknowledge the tremendous individual diversity displayed by our students. Moreover, there is a huge need to develop students' creative potential, but this development often happens outside the classroom. Author Richard Florida (2010), in an account of critical historical periods where society charted a new course (he calls these "Resets)", argues that "We need a system of learning and human development that mobilizes and harnesses human creative talent en masse" (p. 183). Within this notion of creative talent, how might we define *giftedness* and counter simplistic notions often attached to this term?

Defining Giftedness

One myth is that giftedness is something possessed by some students and not by others, as if it occurred through some miraculous, yet mysterious, process. In fact, gifted students are often gifted in a particular area of learning that involves mathematics, science, music, the arts, and other domains (Davis, Sumara, & Luce-Kapler, 2000). This is understandable given the tremendous effort it takes to be truly exceptional in a particular domain (e.g., classical piano). *Giftedness* can be defined as "optimal universal cognitive development that leads to actualized or potential mastery of a domain" (or domains) (Cohen, 2003, p. 35).

Indeed, the myth that genius or giftedness is something that simply exists in some people and not in others has been widely challenged. Gifted individuals are curious and creative, but most importantly, they are persistent (Howe, 2004). In the face of challenges and setbacks, gifted students will persist and work for hours undaunted by failure. "By and large, geniuses live their lives, and create their triumphs and their failures, by the same rules that govern everyone else" (Howe, p. 111). The value of hard work is just as critical to the creative production of novel things (e.g., the Apple computer) as it is to any endeavor that requires effort (e.g., golf prodigies). This view of creative genius is generally supported by the "10 year rule" (Weisberg, 2006). In essence, it takes at least 10 years of immersion in a particular field or creative endeavor to produce master works, novel inventions, and so on. Although highly creative individuals may well be loners, this may well be a conscious effort to protect valuable time so that ideas can develop, incubate, and be acted on (Murphy & Pauleen, 2009). This is especially true in a social media world where attention can be fragmented by constant interruptions from smartphones and other media. Solitude and free time to let the mind putter often lead to creative ideas. For example, George de Mestral, the inventor of Velcro, thought of this hugely useful product while hiking in the Swiss Alps where thistles would attach themselves to his clothing (Beghetto & Kaufman, 2007). Increasingly, novel and creative things are the end result of collaboration (e.g., the Apple iPad), rather than solitary puttering. What does all this mean for the literature classroom?

In addition to domain-specific talents, gifted students are likely to share the following characteristics (Weber & Hedrick, 2010). They may do the following:

- Read early and at an advanced level
- Use advanced, metacognitive processes when they read (e.g., comprehension monitoring, self-questioning, and critiquing an author's ideas)
- Have advanced language (i.e., general and academic vocabulary)
- Devote more time to reading than other students in their peer group
- Continue reading broadly as adults, tapping into a wide-ranging and eclectic variety of literature

Having a rich classroom library, access to e-books, and at the very least, a strong working relationship with your library/media specialist will go a long way toward accommodating the diverse interests of this group of students. "Gifted students have greater need for large numbers of books with increased depth, scope, and variety than might be found in most traditional school or classroom libraries" (Weber & Hedrick, 2010, p. 57). Reading interest inventories like the one we introduced earlier can help identify potential literature for gifted students. In addition, online interest inventories are available (e.g., www.ala.org/ala/yalsa/teenreading/tipsenc/reading_interest_survey.pdf).

Keeping in mind our role as literature teachers, indications are that gifted students benefit from careful teacher mentoring and guidance to read widely, even outside the comfort zone of their particular talent area (G. Smith, 2004). Wide reading offers gifted students a wealth of material to draw on in problem solving and creative production. Researchers studying giftedness and creativity have found that classrooms embodying a learner-centered inquiry approach are likely to foster student creativity (Beghetto & Plucker, 2006). Thus, as a literature teacher, you can support students' interests and guide them toward wide reading in areas where they express interest. (See Activity 4.2.) Biographies of creative people like the Velcro inventor and others are an obvious choice. Nonfiction books that tap into a student's unique interests, as well as fictional young adult literature that is age-appropriate, can add to the usual emphasis on the classics for gifted students.

ACTIVITY 4.2: Professional Reflection and Discussion

Directions: Visit the Duke University Duke Gifted Letter site describing various teaching program delivery models for gifted students (www.dukegiftedletter.com/articles/vol5no1_ef.html).

Consider the various models described and their advantages and disadvantages (e.g., pull-out, push-in, cluster grouping, full-time grouping, and special classes). In your small group, rank order the five teaching models and be ready to defend your position.

In addition to grouping practices, literature response strategies that have been shown to be effective with gifted students include the following (Weber & Hedrick, 2010):

- Book talks
- Read alouds
- Independent reading
- Self-selection of reading material
- Reading conferences
- Books on tape (and media players)
- Paired reading

The Great Books Foundation reading lists spanning grades 6 through 8 and 9 through 12 offers notable fiction along with interpretive activities (www.greatbooks.org/programs-for-all-ages/junior /jgbseries/grades-6-8.html).

Books in the 9–12 list include classics like H. G. Wells's, *The Time Machine*, contemporary poetry by young adult author Gary Soto, and philosophical works by Plato. In addition to these books, searching Amazon.com by topics that interest gifted students will unearth a host of other books that may be outside the classical literary canon but of interest to particular students.

Students with disabilities bring yet another array of challenges to the classroom. Similar to working with gifted learners, taking some time to learn about your students' unique interests will help guide literature recommendations.

STUDENTS WITH DISABILITIES

This is a complex topic, and we touch on a few young adult novels and resources you may find helpful. The topic of disabilities spans physical and mental categories, and extensive lists of young adult novels for middle and secondary students can be found at the American Library Association website (www.ala/awardstrecords/

Young adult novels aim to expand teens' awareness and acceptance of difference in others.

schneideraward/bibliogrpahy.cfm). In addition, Amazon.com includes an extensive listing of contemporary, realistic young adult fiction on disabilities.

Novels in this realm aim to expand teens' understanding, awareness, and acceptance of difference in others who may have disabilities (Adomat, 2009). Ideal media body images contrast sharply with characters who have lost a limb as a result of an accident and now see themselves as different and abnormal. In addition, novels in this area explore how family members of physically and mentally disabled adolescents cope. For example, the award-winning young adult novel *Rules* (Lord, 2006) features 12-year-old Catherine whose autistic brother David breaks rules at home and gets away with it. She resents her brother's freedom to violate rules she has to adhere to, and she feels David gets all her parents' attention. As the novel progresses, Catherine develops a more sophisticated and nuanced grasp of difference.

Family coping strategies where a family member may be disabled range from denial, keeping hyper-organized in support of the teen with the disability (further accentuating this fact), and preserving appearances as if nothing has changed as a result of a teen's accident and disability (Adomat, 2009). For example, in Melody Carlson's (2009) young adult novel *Just Another Girl*, Aster resents spending all her free time with her younger sister, Lily, who is mentally handicapped. Ultimately, families in many of these novels and disabled teens as protagonists learn to accept difference and disability, seeing strengths that evolve in difficult times.

To have a truly comprehensive classroom young adult book collection, you need to explore this category and locate the growing array of titles that your students will find engaging.

SUMMARY

In this chapter, we considered young adult literature aimed at learners with special needs including English-as-Second-Language students, gifted students, striving/struggling readers, and nonreaders, as well as students with disabilities. Demographic data on the growing second-language (ELL) student population, theories of second language acquisition, instructional strategies, and specific young adult titles were offered. The section on struggling readers provided an overview of this diverse group of students along with specific strategies and young adult titles including high-interest, low-vocabulary selections. Background on gifted students debunked myths in this area and provided specific strategies and young adult titles appropriate for this group. Finally, we considered students with disabilities, a wide-ranging category with a growing list of powerful young adult titles. Throughout the chapter, we have been emphasizing individual differences and identities that need to be acknowledged and supported as adolescents grapple with a host of family and relationship issues.

DISCUSSION QUESTIONS

1. What is the impact of English Language Learners on young adult literature teaching and learning?

2. What are the stages of language development and related instructional strategies?

3. What are some young adult literature titles relevant to English Language Learners?

4. What are some teaching approaches designed to assist struggling readers through young adult literature?

5. How would you address gifted learners' needs through young adult literature?

6. What are some young adult literature resources that address students with disabilities?

KEY TERMS

BIC   78

CALP   78

Creativity   86

English Language Learners   76

Giftedness   84

High-Interest, Low-Vocabulary Books   83

SMALL-GROUP ACTIVITY: CREATE AN ANNOTATED BIBLIOGRAPHY

In your small group, assign each member a topic from this chapter (e.g., struggling readers, gifted readers, ELL students, and students with disabilities) and locate at least two high-quality young adult titles. Using a wiki or Google documents approach, and create an annotated bibliography you can all use to address these crucial topics with young adult titles.

RECOMMENDED READINGS

Adomat, D. (2009). Issues of physical disabilities in Cynthia Voigt's *Izzy, Willy-Nilly* And Chris Crutcher's *That Crazy Horse Electric Game. The ALAN Review, 36*(2), 40–47.

This article looks at difference portrayed in two novels that deal with teen identity troubled by body image changes as a result of an accident, as well as issues of how normalcy is socially constructed.

Ivey, G. (2010). Making up for lost time: Connecting inexperienced teenage readers with books. In K. Dunsmore & D. Fisher (Eds.), *Bringing literacy home* (pp. 245–261). Newark, DE: International Reading Association.

This book chapter offers advice and curriculum resources aimed at engaging reluctant adolescent readers' in self-selected materials that they can feel competent reading. The author has worked extensively with struggling adolescent readers.

Pilgreen, J. (2007). Teaching the language of school to secondary English learners. In J. Lewis & G. Moorman (Eds.), *Adolescent literacy instruction: Policies and promising practices* (pp. 238–262). Newark, DE: International Reading Association.

This book chapter features a rich collection of ideas and approaches aimed at accelerating ELL students' grasp of school-based literacy.

Pilonieta, P., & Medina, A. L. (2007). Meeting the needs of English language learners in middle and secondary classroom. In K. Wood & W. Blanton (Eds.), *Literacy instruction for adolescents: Research-based instruction* (pp. 125–143). New York, NY: Guilford Press.

Another excellent chapter aimed at providing middle and secondary English/Language Arts teachers with resources to effectively address the needs of their ELL students.

VanTassel-Baska, J., & Reis, S. (2004, Fall). Expert's forum: Program delivery models for the gifted. *Duke Gifted Letter, 5*(1), 1–4.

This article reviews the dominant program delivery models for gifted students, finding that the predominant model at middle and secondary levels is the special class, often labeled "honors." Other models like the pull-out are reviewed and critiqued.

Weber, C., & Hedrick, W. (2010). Let's not leave advanced and gifted readers "behind." *Voices from the Middle, 17*(4), 56–58.

This article contains a wealth of useful information about gifted students and offers websites and teaching approaches likely to tap into students' individual interests and talents.

RECOMMENDED YOUNG ADULT LITERATURE FEATURED IN THIS CHAPTER

Carlson, M. (2009). *Just another girl*. New York, NY: Revell.

Aster resents spending all her free time with her younger sister, Lily, who is mentally handicapped. At 17, she wants to be out dating and having a social life.

Gonzalez, G. (2009). *A so-called vacation*. Houston, TX: Arte Publico Press.

This engaging novel follows two brothers in a Texas high school whose father has them spend a summer in California doing immigrant field work so they come to understand the harsh conditions and racist treatment experienced by undocumented farm workers.

Jamison, L. (2009). *Running for Dave*. Buffalo, NY: High Interest Publishing (HIP).

This is one of an array of high-interest, low-vocabulary books available from HIP. Each book has a readability level and Lexile level to guide their use with struggling readers. This novel deals with a track star who gets cancer. The novel is at a 3rd-grade reading level (Lexile 560), and it is designed to appeal to a reader audience from grades 6 to 10.

Lord, C. (2006). *Rules*. New York, NY: Scholastic.

Catherine's autistic brother David breaks rules at home and gets away with it. She resents her brother's freedom to violate rules she has to adhere to, and she feels David gets all her parents' attention. The novel explores how Catherine comes to understand difference and disability.

Saldana, R. (2010). *A good long way*. Houston, TX: Arte Publico Press.

We follow high school senior Roelito as he decides to drop out of school in his Texas–Mexico border town. Despite liking school and handling his classes successfully, Roel is pigeonholed as a mirror image of his rowdy, hard-drinking brother.

Schraff, A. (2004). *Earthquakes*. Buena Park, CA: Artesian Press.

This high-interest, low-vocabulary work of nonfiction offers struggling readers an account of earthquakes and their history from 1812 on. As part of the publisher's Natural Disaster Series, each short chapter offers readers an account of major earthquakes and their impact on the people experiencing these catastrophic events.

Schraff, A. (2006). *Fashion*. Buena Park: CA: Artesian Press.

This book takes the reader through a very approachable history of fashion in 60 double-spaced pages. Written at a mid-4th-grade reading level, this selection and others are designed to appeal to reluctant and struggling readers from grades 6 through 12.

Sonnenblick, J. (2010). *After ever after*. New York, NY: Scholastic.

Chronicles a teen's perspective on cancer survival that takes to task many of the myths and clichés that surround adolescence.

Soto, G. (1990). *Baseball in April and other stories*. New York, NY: Houghton Mifflin Harcourt.

RECOMMENDED WEBSITES

Artesian Press: www.artesianpress.com. Buena Park, CA

This publisher of high-interest, low-vocabulary books for struggling and reluctant adolescent readers includes nonfiction and fiction selections with readability levels down to 3rd grade and interest appeal through 12th grade.

The books are tradebook novel sized and run to 60 pages, double-spaced, making them appealing to students.

www. eslcafe.com

This website has information on teachers' professional development focused on ELLs. In addition, there are activities and lesson plans teachers can use in their classes and links for students as well.

www.everythingesl.net

Created by an ESL teacher and author, this website has resources, teaching tips, lesson plans, and a blog.

High Interest Publishing: www.hip-books.com. Buffalo, NY

This publisher of high-interest, low-vocabulary books for struggling adolescent readers offers a leveled collection of young adult novels designed to engage reluctant readers. The books deal with realistic topics for teens, and they can be paired with teacher read alouds from other young adult novels.

www.readwritethink.org is hosted by the International Reading Association

This site contains lesson plans created by teachers that have been used successfully with English Language Learners.

Rene Saldana, Jr.'s *Annotated Bibliography for Culturally Relevant Literature* (2009).

This resource can be obtained by e-mailing Rene Saldana at rene.saldana@ttu.edu

Teen Read Week: www.ala.org/teenread. American Library Association

Each year in mid-October, the American Library Association's Young Adult Library Services Association (YALSA) sponsors this event. The website includes program planning ideas, book titles, and curriculum materials to support your students.

The Great Books Foundation. Retrieved July 7, 2010 from http://www.greatbooks.org?programs-for-all-ages/junior/jgbseries/grades-6-8.html

REFERENCES

Adomat, D. (2009). Issues of physical disabilities in Cynthia Voigt's *Izzy, Willy-Nilly* And Chris Crutcher's *That Crazy Horse Electric Game. The ALAN Review*, 36(2), 40–47.

Batalova, J., Fix, M., & Murray, J. (2002). *English language learner adolescents: Demographics and literacy achievements* (Report to the Center for Applied Linguistics). Washington, DC: Migration Institute.

Beghetto, R. A., & Kaufman, J. C. (2007). *Creativity in the classroom: Between chaos and conformity.* Paper presented at the annual meeting of the American Educational Research Association, Chicago, IL.

Beghetto, R. A., & Plucker, J. A. (2006). The relationship among schooling, learning, and creativity. In J. C. Kaufman & J. Baer (Eds.), *Creativity and reason in cognitive development* (pp. 316–332). New York, NY: Cambridge University Press.

Cohen, L. M. (2003). A conceptual lens for looking at theories of creativity. In D. Ambrose, L. M. Cohen, & A. J. Tannenbaum (Eds.), *Creative intelligence: Toward theoretic integration* (pp. 33–77). Cresskill, NJ: Hampton Press.

Crawford-McKinney, K., & Hogan, K. (2008). Engaging struggling adolescent readers, In conversations about texts. In S. Lenski & J. Lewis (Eds.), *Reading success for struggling readers* (pp. 116–132). New York, NY: Guilford Press.

Cummins, J. (2003). Reading and the bilingual student: fact and friction. In G. G. Garcia (Ed.), *English learners: Reaching the highest level of English literacy* (pp. 2–33). Newark, DE: International Reading Association.

Cummins, J. (2009). Literacy and English-language learners: A shifting landscape for students, teachers, researchers, and policy makers. *Educational Researcher, 38*, 382–384.

Davis, B., Sumara, D., & Luce-Kapler, R. (2000). *Engaging minds: Learning and teaching in a complex world.* Mahwah, NJ: Lawrence Erlbaum.

Florida, R. (2010). *The great reset.* New York, NY: HarperCollins.

Garcia, G. E., & Godina, H. (2004). Addressing the needs of adolescent English language learners. In T. L. Jetton & J. A. Dole (Eds.), *Adolescent literacy research and practice* (pp. 304–320). New York, NY: Guilford Press.

Gersten, R., & Baker S. (2000). What do we know about effective instructional practice for English-Language learners. *Exceptional Children, 66*(4), 454–470.

Gibson, M. A., & Rojas, A. R. (2006). Globalization, immigration, and the education of "new" immigrants in the 21st century. *Current Issues in Comparative Education, 9*(1), 69–76.

Goldenberg, C., Rueda, R. S., & August D. (2006). Synthesis: Sociocultural contexts and literacy development. In D. August & T. Shanahan (Eds.), *Developing literacy in second-language learners: Report of the National Literacy Panel on Language-Minority Children and Youth* (pp. 249–267). Mahwah, NJ: Lawrence Erlbaum.

Gunderson, L. (2008). The state of art of secondary ESL teaching and learning. *Journal of Adolescent & Adult Literacy, 52* (3), 184–187.

Hernandez, D., Denton, N., & Macartney, S. (2009). School-age children in immigrant families: Challenges and opportunities for America's schools. *Teachers College Record, 11*(3), 616–658.

Howe, M. J. A. (2004). Some insights of geniuses into the causes of exceptional achievement. In L. V. Shavinina & M. Ferrari (Eds.), *Beyond knowledge: Extracognitive aspects of developing high ability* (pp. 105–117). Mahwah, NJ: Lawrence Erlbaum.

Ivey, G. (2010). Making up for lost time: Connecting inexperienced teenage readers with books. In K. Dunsmore & D. Fisher (Eds.), *Bringing literacy home* (pp. 245–261). Newark, DE: International Reading Association.

Jimenez, R., & Teague, B. (2009). Language, literacy, and content: Adolescent English Language Learners. In L. Morrow, R. Reuda, & D. Lapp (Eds.), *The handbook of research on literacy and diversity* (pp. 114–136). New York, NY: Guilford Press.

Jolley, K. (2008). Video games to reading: Reaching out to reluctant readers. *English Journal, 97*(4), 81–92.

Lenski, S. (2008). Struggling adolescent readers: Problems and possibilities. In S. Lenski & J. Lewis (Eds.), *Reading success for struggling readers* (pp. 38–57). New York, NY: Guilford Press.

Lesley, M. (in press). Preservice secondary teachers discourse models of "struggling" readers and school literacy tasks. *Journal of Adolescent & Adult Literacy.*

Moje, E., & Hinchman K. (2004). Culturally responsive practices for youth literacy learning. In T. L. Jetton & J. A. Dole (Eds.), *Adolescent literacy research and practice* (pp. 321–350). New York, NY: Guilford Press.

Murphy, P., & Pauleen, D. (2009). Managing paradox in a world of knowledge. In M. A. Peters, S. Marginson, & P. Murphy

(Eds.), *Creativity and the global knowledge economy* (pp. 257–276). New York, NY: Peter Lang.

National Center for Education Statistics. (2005, 2007, 2008, 2009). Available from http://nesc.ed.gov

National Institute of Literacy. (2007). *What content area teachers should know about adolescent literacy*. Washington, DC: Department of Education, National Institute of Literacy, National Institute of Child Health and Human Development (NICHD).

Perie, M., Grigg, W. S., & Donahue, P. L. (2005). *The nation's report card: Reading 2005*. Washington, DC: U.S. Government Printing Office.

Pilgreen, J. (2007). Teaching the language of school to secondary English learners. In J. Lewis & G. Moorman (Eds.), *Adolescent literacy instruction: Policies and promising practices* (pp. 238–262). Newark, DE: International Reading Association.

Pilonieta, P., & Medina, A. L. (2007). Meeting the needs of English language learners in middle and secondary classroom. In K. Wood & W. Blanton (Eds.), *Literacy instruction for adolescents: Research-based instruction* (pp. 125–143). New York, NY: Guilford Press.

Saldana, R., & Moore, D. W. (2010). Research connections: Writing, teaching, and researching: An interview with Rene Saldana, Jr. *Journal of Adolescent & Adult Literacy, 53*(8), 688–690.

Smith, G. J. W. (2004). The role of unconscious processes in the evolvement of creativity. In L. V. Shavinina & M. Ferrari (Eds.), *Beyond knowledge: Extracognitive aspects of developing high ability* (pp. 27–37). Mahwah, NJ: Lawrence Erlbaum.

Smith, M. W., & Wilhelm, J. D. (2006). *Going with the flow: How to engage boys (and girls) in their literacy learning*. Portsmouth, NH: Heinemann.

Suarez-Orozco, C., Suarez-Orozco, M. M., & Todorova, I. (2008). *Learning a new land: Immigrant students in American society*. Harvard, MA: Belknap Press of Harvard University Press.

Weber, C., & Hedrick, W. (2010). Let's not leave advanced and gifted readers "behind." *Voices from the Middle, 17*(4), 56–58.

Weisberg, R. W. (2006). Expertise and reason in creative thinking. In J. Kaufman & J. Baer (Eds.), *Creativity and reason in cognitive development* (pp. 7–42). New York, NY: Cambridge University Press.

PART II

Established and Emerging Genres of Young Adult Literature

Chapter 5

Realistic Fiction, Romance, and Mystery

The three established genres considered in this chapter offer readers some of the most captivating forms of literature. Indeed, these genre categories continue to evolve, and we focus on the major figures contributing to an increasingly rich array of literature you can draw from in your teaching. Teen issues including family life, sexuality, bullying, drugs, friendships, relationships, poverty, homelessness, and a host of other realistic life experiences underpin these works.

Learning Objectives

- Be able to state how the features of these three genres (**realistic fiction**, **romance**, and **mystery**) contribute to students' understanding of Common Core Standards related to theme and complex characters.

- Be able to state the criteria for selecting high-quality young adult fiction within the three genres considered in this chapter.

- Know some of the key titles within realistic young adult fiction.

- Know some of the key titles within romance young adult fiction.

- Know some of the key titles within mystery young adult fiction.

Vignette: Nat Taylor's High School Literature Class

Mr. Taylor's class consists of high school students who are reluctant, struggling readers. He uses realistic fiction, short stories, and other selections to engage his students in reading and discussion. In this lesson, Nat has his students do a quick write on a writing prompt prior to reading and discussing African American young adult author Sharon Flake's (2005) short story "So I Ain't No Good Girl." The story is one of the selections in *Who Am I Without Him: Short Stories About Girls and the Boys in Their Lives*. Mr. Taylor learned about this strategy in a journal article (Fournier & Graves, 2002).

In this opening story, the narrator juggles her hot boyfriend Raheem's indifference to her anger at his eyeing (and ultimately hanging out with) other girls, often those who are "good girls" on the Dean's list and doing all the right things. Mr. Taylor previews the story and reads a short quote from a section where the narrator sees a redhead get off the city bus to hook up with Raheem.

Mr. Taylor has his students do quick writes to consider issues in the young adult literature they read, putting their responses on a class blog (e.g., blogger.com). He begins by reading an excerpt from the story:

> I lean over and stare out the window and see the redhead standing on the corner with Raheem.
> She must have sneaked out the back of the bus as soon as she got on. Raheem's all up in her face.
> Sunglasses off. Arms wrapped around her neck. His sweet, brown lips pressed tight to hers. (p. 8)

Mr. Taylor: "Okay, assume that you are in love with a person that you see every day. I want you to write in response to two key questions: Would you put up with your boyfriend or girlfriend stepping out on you? If that happened, how would it make you feel, and how could you change that situation?"

Following their reading of the story, students in small groups return to the two writing prompts and create an advice columnist's letter from the narrator about her wandering boyfriend Raheem. Other small groups read the letter and offer an advice column style of response, generally recommending that this girl should dump Raheem.

Common Core Standards

The following standards are addressed in this chapter.

RL.9-10.1, 11-12.1 Cite strong and thorough textual evidence to support analysis of what the text says explicitly as well as inferences drawn from the text.

RL.9-10.2, 11-12.2 Determine a theme or central idea of a text and analyze in detail its development over the course of the text, including how it emerges and is shaped and refined by specific details; provide an objective summary of the text.

> RL.9-10.3, 11-12.3 Analyze how complex characters (e.g., those with multiple or conflicting motivations) develop over the course of a text, interact with other characters, and advance the plot or develop the theme.
>
> RL. 9-10.5, 11-12.5 Analyze how an author's choices concerning how to structure specific parts of a text (e.g., the choice of where to begin or end a story and the choice to provide a comedic or tragic resolution) contribute to its overall structure and meaning as well as to its aesthetic impact.

Like the story in the vignette, *contemporary realistic* fiction takes up real-life problems that teens experience. Themes include family struggles, sexuality, and a host of other issues.

DEFINING GENRES

Genre boundaries continue to blur and evolve, sometimes leading to new categories of young adult literature (Latrobe & Drury, 2009). Nevertheless, there are several enduring genres including those considered in this chapter. For example, contemporary realistic fiction has moved away from a dependence on plot to forms that feature multiple viewpoints, imagery, flashbacks, and time shifts (Latrobe & Drury, 2009). Among the characteristics that define quality realistic fiction, the following are important to consider:

Does the story feature a young adult main character?

Will your young adult students identify with this protagonist?

Is the protagonist complex and multidimensional?

Does the protagonist's experience mirror those issues common to adolescents?

Does the theme support universal experiences and truths as the novel progresses?

Romance novels consider young adults' quest for love and friendship amid sometimes overly simplistic views of gender and socioeconomic status (Beach et al., 2008). Much like the characteristics offered for realistic fiction, high-quality romance novels should realistically portray the intricacies of relationships, particularly in situations where life is not all rosy and bright.

Genre boundaries continue to blur and evolve, sometimes leading to new categories of young adult literature.

In addition, this genre is ideal for engaging young adults in critical discussion of characters and the degree to which they mirror the life experiences of today's students (Glenn, 2008). Paranormal romances combine elements of romance with unusual powers that often trouble the characters' desire for each other.

Young adult mysteries abound and represent an enduring genre. They generally introduce a challenging problem, puzzle, or element of suspense where the protagonist is an adolescent able to unravel the mystery. High-quality young adult mysteries should be fast paced with a suspenseful, credible plot (Latrobe & Drury, 2009). In addition, they are likely to feature plots that illuminate the protagonist's life and personal conflicts.

WORKING WITH ESTABLISHED GENRES OF YOUNG ADULT LITERATURE

As you consider selecting contemporary realistic young adult fiction, romance, and mystery, the following criteria may be helpful. Look for the following:

- Authentic selections that realistically capture teen coming-of-age dilemmas and problems
- Stories and situations teens can identify with as they search for ways to cope with their own life issues
- Selections that provoke questions and offer a forum for discussion of teen issues

Contemporary realistic fiction goes to the heart of adolescent life experiences and continues to mirror the particular social context of the time. Early 1960s ground-breaking novels like S. E. Hinton's *The Outsiders* (1967) and main character Ponyboy gave this genre a jump-start that contemporary authors like Gary Soto, Walter Dean Myers, Sharon Flake, and others have run with. These are stories with teeth and vivid depictions of teens coping with an increasingly fast-moving, diverse, transnational world. Although it has never been easy to make it as an adolescent, the statistics we offered in the introductory chapters suggest that issues of poverty, racism, homelessness, and family challenges including job losses have escalated. Contemporary realistic young adult fiction in these times takes readers into the visceral realities of our world like no textbook can.

Case 5.1 offers an example of how to engage students in comparing and contrasting contemporary paranormal romances with classical romance novels.

Numerous mystery novels invite teen readers to solve cases that elude others.

CASE 5.1: Paranormal Romance Novels and Classical Literature

Students in Ms. Tiffany Field's high school literature class have been reading classical romances and beginning a project where they have to self-select a contemporary paranormal romance novel. They must read it and then compare and contrast it with the classical romance (e.g., *Pride and Prejudice*).

Ms. Field: We are going to be using Edmodo (www.edmodo.com), a secure social learning network application that looks a lot like Facebook but one the district will let us use to post our discussions about the novels you select.

Student 1:   I really like Karly Kirkpatrick's (2010) new novel, *Into the Shadows*. It is a paranormal romance with a main character, Paivi Anderson, who, like us, is a high school freshman with a potential boyfriend. But the problem is that she has special powers and enemies that want to take her down.

Ms. Field: Whew, that sounds good! Let's use the rest of this class to identify the paranormal romance you are going to read and tomorrow we will get logged on to Edmodo and I can model how to post your comments about the two novels.

Student 2:   Hey, Ms. Field, we already know how to post to Facebook at home and on our phones so this should be easy.

Ms. Field: That's great. Let's get started.

Many of our students (inservice teachers) use Edmodo, and it has many of the features of Facebook but in a closed system that allows for secure social learning like novel discussions. We suggest trying it out across various genres and including some of the photo uploads and other features it offers to augment young adult novel discussions.

CONTEMPORARY REALISTIC FICTION

In this genre, we consider the long-standing body of work under the label "Contemporary Realistic Fiction." With its roots in early young adult novels like S. E. Hinton's (1967) *The Outsiders*, realistic fiction generally deals with problems adolescents face in coming of age. The natural tensions between adolescent and adult life loom large in these stories, along with questions of the self, others, and identity in flux. Learning to cope with family crises, friendship issues, and a host of other problems characterizes these works. Adolescent readers can often recognize elements of themselves in these novels, and this vicarious experience may help readers think of problem-solving approaches they can adopt. Thus, well-crafted realistic fiction should offer accurate portrayals of the protagonist's problems and paint a realistic picture of day-to-day life in various urban and rural settings.

Coming-of-age stories generally find adolescent characters confronting the common struggles of growing up amid racial issues, poverty, bullying, class and ethnic struggles, family issues, disability, and other realistic problems. These and other characteristics of the adolescent human condition must ring true and take the reader into the characters' lives in a way that seems credible.

Several well-established, award-winning young adult novelists have ventured into the contemporary realistic fiction territory. For example, Walter Dean Myers's (2003) *The Beast* explores the growing rift between Anthony Witherspoon, a successful African American student bound for the university, and his high school girlfriend, Gabi, saddled with taking care of her family from the Dominican Republic. She copes with not going on to college by writing poetry and sinking further into heroin addiction.

Gary Soto's young adult novels offer a powerful look at Latino life in rural California. In *Accidental Love* (Soto, 2006), Marisa accidentally picks up the wrong cell phone. When she returns it to its owner, Rene, her psychic opposite, she finds herself in love. Polar opposites, Rene is bookish, nerdy, and uninterested in typical macho athletic pursuits. In contrast, Marisa is street tough and uninterested in books.

Matt de la Pena's (2009) *We Were Here* charts main character Miguel's journey from juvenile detention to the beaches of Venice, California, and south to Mexico in search of himself and a new life away from the mean streets of Stockton, California. Written as a series of dated journal entries, the reader is invited into Miguel's thoughts and reflection on a world that is harsh and saved by friendship.

In Native American author Sherman Alexie's (2007) National Book Award–winning young adult novel *The Absolutely True Diary of a Part-Time Indian*, Junior, the main character, leaves his friends in the struggling Spokane, Washington, reservation high school to attend a high-powered town school. This commute off the reservation angers Junior's friends and creates powerful inner conflicts as Junior experiences firsthand the radical differences in material resources in the two settings. Autobiographical and moving, Junior's life parallels many Native Americans and the obstacles that lower self-esteem and derail opportunity (Blasingame, 2008).

In one scene on the reservation school, Junior opens his science text only to see his mother's name written on the inside flap. The book that Junior was studying was more than 20 years old! When he moves to the off-reservation school, Junior's opportunities for upward mobility increase, but not without tragedy and lots of self-examination on his part.

Undoubtedly, one of the best-known authors in this genre is Laurie Halse Anderson. The 2009 winner of the American Library Association's Margaret A. Edwards Award for a significant and lasting body of work, novels like *Speak* (1999), *Catalyst* (2002), and *Twisted* (2007), Anderson's characters confront the cliques and social boundaries common to high school.

In *Twisted*, main character Tyler Miller is required to do summer physical labor tarring his high school roof after getting in trouble. The physical labor transforms him from a skinny geek into a muscular hunk, attractive to popular Bethany Milbury. Tyler must deal with the plusses and minuses of his new attractiveness to the opposite sex and confront the dark side of high school game playing.

In an interview with Laurie Halse Anderson about writing books that interleave comedy and tragedy, she said, "I come from a fairly messed-up family with a dark and twisted sense of humor . . . laughter fights off the darkness and keeps you warm until dawn" (Kaywell & Kaywell, 2008). Indeed, most realistic young adult fiction has many of the same elements. Trying to cope with what, from an adolescent's point of view, seems to be a badly flawed adult world is a common theme.

For example, in *The Last Exit to Normal* (Harmon, 2008), 14-year-old urban skateboarder Ben Campbell is spirited away to tiny rural Butte, Montana, by his dad and his dad's new boyfriend. Ben clashes with his father and the boyfriend's mother, a tyrannical but kindhearted old lady. Next door, more trouble brews with a single-parent family where the dad is abusive to his 11-year-old son and nasty to cats, Ben, and the neighbors in general. Petty violence peppers the novel in this rural, traditional male landscape, balanced by Ben's falling in love with a cowgirl and working on her uncle's farm. Ben matures as the novel progresses, transforming into a more responsible and understanding person but still at odds with the deck of cards life dealt him.

Numerous titles abound in this category with authors like Canadian writer Martha Brooks (*True Confessions of a Heartless Girl*, 2002); Christopher Paul Curtis (*Bucking the Sarge*, 2004); the latest novel by Louanne Johnson, the author of *Dangerous Minds*, *Muchacho* (2009); Jacqueline Woodson (*Behind You*, 2004); Jerry Spinelli (*Stargirl*, 2000); Walter Dean Myers (*Lockdown*, 2010; *Sunrise over Fallujah*, 2008); Nancy Osa (*Cuba 15*, 2003); and many others writing in this genre.

Activity 5.1 provides an opportunity to explore young adult titles dealing with adolescent problems.

ACTIVITY 5.1: Professional Reflection and Discussion

Directions: In your small group, share any issues you confronted as a teen and realistic young adult fiction titles that helped you see other adolescents struggling with similar issues. Do an Internet search of other contemporary young adult titles that deal with problems (e.g., teen pregnancy, relationships, crime, gangs, poverty, racism, bullying, and so on). Share these titles in a subsequent class with your small group.

ROMANCE NOVELS

Long a staple of young adult novels with historically popular series such as Sweet Valley High and others enjoying a wide following through library and retail outlets, romance novels are alive and well. The quest for love and friendship endures in these novels. Teen readers of romance novels are a complex, highly diverse group with varying views of their life trajectories in relation to romance and relationships (Beach et al., 2008). Stereotypical views of teens, especially girls, suggest they are preoccupied with love, sex, and romance. Indeed, these traditional and fairly static views persist in write-ups about teen romance novels (e.g., Debraski, 2007). However, an intensive classroom study of 14 working-class high school seniors and juniors in the Midwest paints a very different picture. These researchers devoted considerable attention to mapping students' responses to multicultural literature in a course that featured a significant amount of reading and discussion across genres (Beach et al., 2008).

In general, the six males in this study defined themselves in relation to masculine notions of hard work and individual accomplishments. Nevertheless, their English teacher was able to engage both the boys and the girls in his class in discussions that challenged dominant cultural models around gender issues. For example, girls in the study "defied any simplistic notions of how the culture of romance operates" (Beach et al., 2008, p. 54). They were often ambivalent about long-term relationships with a boy that would lead to marriage and family, realizing that in unstable economic times, very little about their future would be predictable. In essence, while reading young adult literature including romance novels, these students entertained multiple and conflicting life trajectories and identities. In some cases, female students were already significant caretakers of younger siblings, resulting in very realistic views of childcare and its demands.

Thus, although we are not saying that adolescents cannot enjoy young adult romance novels as a captivating escape into alternative life pathways, we believe these novels offer an ideal forum for critiquing narrow portrayals of young adults. This idea is especially important given the popularity of a subset of the romance novel genre that valorizes wealthy teens as conspicuous consumers, devoid of any sense of social justice (Glenn, 2008). High-end, brand-name products including Versace and Chanel parade across the pages, along with the importance of "in" clothes. In one reported study examining the prevalence of brand names in the Gossip Girl, Clique, and A-List titles, communications professor Naomi Johnson found that brand names referring to brand-name alcohol, cigarettes, or prescription drugs occurred on average more than once per page (Conant, 2008). These novels include titles that suggest an alluring jet-set lifestyle often well out of reach of most young adults. Indeed, popular but reasonably priced brand names like Keds served to label their wearers as losers, as did bikinis purchased at Target. Novels like *Beautiful Stranger: An A-List Novel* (Dean, 2007), *The A-List* (Dean, 2003), *The Insiders* (Minter, 2004), and *The It Girl* (Von, 2005) are just a few examples of this popular but disturbing trend in young adult romantic fiction. In the recommended reading section of this chapter, we highlight Wendy Glenn's (2008) article offering guidelines for helping adolescent readers critique the message of conspicuous consumption in these novels and series.

Some of the novels in this upscale neighborhood vein manage to avoid being shallow wastelands of rich teen angst. For example, Alyson Noel's (2007) *Kiss and Blog* chronicles long time teen friends Winter and Sloane as high school freshmen intent on moving up the social ladder in their sophomore year. Sloane manages to get accepted to this clique by simultaneously dumping Winter, her long time childhood friend. Winter retaliates by writing a blog as revenge on Sloane. This humorous, fast-moving story will captivate reluctant teen readers with its allusions to popular communications technology.

Amid romance novels that read like advertisements for an array of high-end brand-name products, the American Library Association profiles lists of notable titles adolescents and teachers have recognized as worth reading and talking about. For example, in the online newsletter of the Young Adult Library Services Association, a division of the American Library Association, you can find a column on "Romantic Reads" (Debraski, 2007).

Genre categories often blur into hybrid young adult novels that combine elements of horror, the paranormal, fantasy, mystery, and romance. For example, the widely popular House of Night Series includes paranormal romance novels like *Tempted* (Cast & Cast, 2009). These are highly engaging novels with characters endowed with superpowers that appeal to young adult reluctant readers. Themes surrounding friendship, romance, and trust are common and series like this one enjoy a loyal following of readers and high-profile marketing in mainstream bookstores.

MYSTERY

Mystery novels have their roots in the work of Edgar Allan Poe and Sherlock Holmes, among others. They appeal to readers who enjoy considering clues and trying to speculate on possible solutions to a murder, bank robbery, or other crime. They must be carefully plotted with strong main characters that engage the reader. Mystery novels can include *CSI*-like crimes, historical puzzles, private investigators, and teens as detectives. Suspense is a key ingredient in young adult mysteries.

Young adult mystery novels include Carl Hiassen's (2002) bestseller *Hoot* and its sequel *Flush* (2007). *Hoot* chronicles the main character's amateur detective work to figure out who the mysterious figure is that seems to be sabotaging a proposed pancake house development. The site is the home to an endangered species, and Roy, a middle school student recently arrived in Florida from Montana, gets in the middle of an ongoing ecological mystery. *Hoot* also has a film version, making it an ideal watch and read for students. *Flush* continues this ecological theme by focusing on the illegal dumping of raw sewage from a floating casino in Florida. Main characters Noah Underwood and his sister Abbey concoct a plan to expose the environmental disaster perpetuated by the casino owner.

Tantalize (2007) by Cynthia Leitich Smith features a strong female main character in Quincie P. Morris, as she cares for an uncle whose gothic girlfriend thinks constantly about vampires. Quincie's relationships suffer from overarching elements of horror. For example, her potential boyfriend Kieren is a werewolf, the restaurant she remodels with her uncle ends up with its chef murdered just before opening, and this event propels Quincie into a world of vampires and intrigue. In a review of this engaging multigenre novel with its elements of horror and mystery told via menus, advertisements, and other pop culture artifacts, book reviewer Elle Wolterbeek (2007) noted that "*Tantalize* is a thinking reader's horror novel and an entertaining, empowering ride" (p. 75).

Numerous mystery authors and novels take teen readers along for the ride as adolescent amateur sleuths attempt to solve cases that elude others. Award-winning author David Klass's (2007) novel *Dark Angel* finds main character 17-year-old Jeff Hastings leading a fairly idyllic life on the Jersey Shore. However, when a brother he knew nothing about is released from prison after facing a murder charge, Jeff is thrust into a new world that is upside down. Troy, the ex-con brother, is a master manipulator, and the conflict and tension between the two brothers in this novel is palpable.

In *Runner* (Deuker, 2007), Chance Taylor, a high school teenager, lives with his Vietnam Era veteran father who is drunk much of the time. They live a rough-and-tumble life on an old 30-ft sailboat moored in Puget Sound, Seattle, Washington. Chance goes through the motions at school but revels in long afternoon runs at the marina where they live. Struggling for money to pay their mooring fees, Chance agrees to make extra money working for a marina employee who asks Chance to pick up packages at a tree along his running route. He is aware that he may be engaging in criminal activity but is desperate for the money. This haunting, suspenseful novel should appeal to reluctant readers.

In *The Perfect Shot* (2005) by Elaine Marie Alphin, a high school senior basketball player is distraught after the murder of his girlfriend, her sister, and her mother. The girls' father is on trial for the crime, but the main character Brian knows information that could impact the case. Brian is writing a paper based on the 1913 Leo Frank murder case that parallels this contemporary situation. Both a mystery and a commentary on racism in this small Indiana setting, the true killer looms in the shadows as the novel unfolds.

In *The Bloodwater Mysteries: Snatched* (Hautman, 2006), an 11th-grade journalist, Roni Delicata, and a younger science-oriented student, Brian Bain, team up to solve the kidnapping of a snobby new kid in school, Alicia Camden. These two pushy amateur sleuths challenge authority and uncover clues that reveal Alicia's difficulty at home. A sequel to this Pete Hautman novel, *The Bloodwater Mysteries: Skullduggery* (2007), finds Roni and Brian again on the trail of money-hungry developers. An injured archeologist they encounter on a class field trip claims he was attacked by a ghost, which sets the two teen sleuths on a mission to find the truth.

Activity 5.2 asks you to conduct a brief author study of a prominent author from any of the genres we have considered in this section. Increasingly, authors have their own blogs in addition to their publisher's websites. Both places are good spots to start exploring your chosen author's biography and works.

Teen readers of romance novels have varying views of their life trajectories in relation to romance and relationships.

ACTIVITY 5.2: Professional Reflection and Discussion

Directions: In this activity, we ask you to conduct a brief author study of a chosen author from one of the genres considered in this chapter. The author study should be shared with your small group and archived for other students and readers. The following steps should help guide this process:

Look for information on your chosen author using the author's publisher's website, the author's own blog, or information from Amazon.com.

Consider addressing the author's biography and how the author's personal experiences led to becoming a writer.

(Continued)

(Continued)

List some of the author's better-known books. Why were they successful?

How had this author moved his or her particular genre forward?

How do you feel about this author's works?

Once you have developed your author study, you may want to put it in podcast or blog form to share with your small group. This material can then be archived for future students to consult as they develop their own author studies.

MULTIMEDIA TEXT SET

In this multimedia text set, classroom teachers Kristen Cragwall and Megan Kabell have used the realistic fiction novel *A So-Called Vacation* (Gonzalez, 2009) to explore issues of racism, immigration, and tolerance. In making their selections, they wanted to find stories that echoed the experience of difference encountered by immigrants in the United States.

1. Argueta, J. (2001). *A movie in my pillow.* San Francisco, CA: Children's Book Press.

This book is an anthology of poetry from the perspective of a boy from El Salvador who is living in San Francisco. This text was picked because the poetry deals with similar themes of immigration and inclusion in the United States.

2. Argueta, J. (2006). *Talking with mother earth.* Toronto, Ontario, Canada: Groundwood.

This book follows a boy, Tetl, in California who is teased for looking different than other children. He comes to appreciate his Aztec ancestry when he learns about his heritage from his grandmother. This book is about personal acceptance and pride in Latin American culture.

3. Lin, G. (2009). *Where the mountain meets the moon.* New York, NY: Little, Brown.

This book provides students with perspectives on child farm workers in another part of the world. The main character, Minli, works on the rice fields in China out of a strong sense of duty for her family. The text would provide a rich comparison lesson between the differing experiences of both books' characters. It would lead to an interesting discussion on the cultural differences between the Mexican American farm workers and the Chinese farm workers.

4. Immigrant experience through song. Retrieved from http://www.npr.org/templates/story/story.php?storyId=128247391

This link contains songs about the experience of immigrating to America by six artists hailing from different Latin American countries. They highlight both the commonalities and the vast differences experienced by immigrants and offer a more current perspective with which students could connect. These songs also relate more closely to the perspective of the teenage characters in *A So-Called Vacation*, given that they are more current.

5. Nick News video clip: I'm American! They're not! (2010). Retrieved from http://www.nick.com/videos/clip/im-american-theyre-not-full-episode

This Nick News video clip shows children's reactions to possibly losing their parents as a result of deportation. The video focuses mostly on children and how they feel about what would happen if their parents had to leave America and they got to stay (because all of them were born here making them American citizens).

In constructing a rich and varied text set, Megan and Kristen have created an opportunity for their students to explore the many facets and experiences that immigrants face, especially around issues of discrimination. Multimedia text sets such as this one can not only lead to a greater understanding of each component in its relationship to the whole, but they also help students grapple with complex issues in their own communities and lives.

SUMMARY

This chapter introduced three popular genres: realistic fiction, romance, and mysteries, as well as subgenres (e.g., paranormal romance). In addition, we considered key elements and evaluation criteria for the selection of high-quality young adult literature in each of these genres. Suggestions for engaging readers in the critique of some titles where critical approaches would be appropriate were also offered.

DISCUSSION QUESTIONS

1. How do the features of these three genres (realistic fiction, romance, and mystery) contribute to students' understanding of Common Core Standards related to theme and complex characters?

2. What are the criteria for selecting high-quality young adult fiction within the three genres considered in this chapter?

3. What are some of the key titles within realistic young adult fiction?

4. What are some of the key titles within romance young adult fiction?

5. What are some of the key titles within mystery young adult fiction?

KEY TERMS

Realistic Fiction   99

Romance Novels   99

Young Adult Mysteries   100

SMALL-GROUP ACTIVITY: DEVELOPING YOUR DATABASE OF YOUNG ADULT LITERATURE

Locate additional titles in one of the three genres introduced in this chapter and share your list with your small group. Each member of the group should search one of the genres and share these titles, along with a written or electronic summary and bibliographic details.

RECOMMENDED READINGS

Debraski, S. C. (2007, Spring). *Romantic reads. Yattitudes: The official newsletter of the Young Adult Library Services Association*, a division of the American Library Association, 6(3). Retrieved February 12, 2008 from http://www.ala.org/ala/yalsa/yalsamemonly//yattidues/yattiduesarch/spring2007/spring07.cfm

Glenn, W. (2008). Gossiping girls, insider boys, A-list achievement: Examining and exposing YA novels consumed by conspicuous consumption. *Journal of Adolescent & Adult Literacy, 52*(1), 34–42.
   This article features a much-needed critique of shallow romance novels populated by wealthy New York socialites ill-equipped to any sensitivity to others not enjoying a life of privilege and glamour. Nevertheless, these novels offer an excellent forum for critical reading and discussion.

Latrobe, K. H., & Drury, J. (2009). *Critical approaches to young adult literature*. New York, NY: Neal-Schuman.

This valuable book about established genres and teaching does an excellent job of introducing each genre along with key criteria to consider in the selection of high-quality young adult titles.

Rozema, R. (2007). The book report, version 2.0: Podcasting on young adult novels. *English Journal*, 97(1), 31–42.

This article demonstrates how to have students write, revise, and collaborate on book-talk podcasts that feature young adult novels. Examples include podcasts developed by students on young adult science fiction novels and a very useful ReadWriteThink Internet example lesson plan.

RECOMMENDED YOUNG ADULT LITERATURE FEATURED IN THIS CHAPTER

Alexie, S. (2007). *The absolutely true diary of a part-time Indian*. New York, NY: Little, Brown.

Junior, the main character, leaves his friends in the struggling Spokane, Washington, reservation high school to attend a high-powered town school. This commute off the reservation angers Junior's friends and creates powerful inner conflicts as Junior experiences firsthand the radical differences in material resources in the two settings.

Alphin, E. M. (2005). *The perfect shot*. Minneapolis, MN: Carolrhoda Books/Lerner.

A high school senior basketball player is distraught after the murder of his girlfriend, her sister, and her mother. The girls' father is on trial for the crime, but the main character Brian knows information that could impact the case. Brian is writing a paper based on the 1913 Leo Frank murder case that parallels this contemporary situation. Both a mystery and a commentary on racism in this small Indiana setting, the true killer looms in the shadows as the novel unfolds.

Anderson, L. H. (1999). *Speak*. New York, NY: Penguin.

Melinda displays the classic signs of depression after being raped at a high school party. Over the course of the novel, she comes to speak about her trauma and confronts her rapist.

Anderson, L. H. (2002). *Catalyst*. New York, NY: Penguin.

In both *Speak* and *Catalyst*, Anderson's characters confront the cliques and social boundaries common to high school

Anderson, L. H. (2007). *Twisted*. New York, NY: Penguin.

Tyler Miller is required to do summer physical labor tarring his high school roof after getting in trouble. The physical labor transforms him from a skinny geek into a muscular hunk, attractive to popular Bethany Milbury, but he must deal with all the social problems that go with this new notoriety.

Brooks, M. (2007). *True confessions of a heartless girl*. New York, NY: Farrar.

Cast, P. C. (2008). *Immortal: Love stories with bite*. Dallas, TX: BenBella Books.
   This bestselling author of the *House of Night* series offers readers vampires, ghosts, and teenage characters in a captivating collection of short stories.

de la Pena, M. (2009). *We were here*. New York, NY: Delacorte.
   Written as a series of dated journal entries, the reader is invited into Miguel's thoughts and reflection on a world that is harsh and saved by friendship. As Miguel emerges from juvenile detention, he journeys to Venice beach, California and on to Mexico in search of a better life, adding entries to his journal an inviting the reader into his thoughts and dreams of a better life.

Cast, P. C., & Cast, K. (2009). *Tempted*. New York, NY: St. Martin's Griffin.
   As part of the widely popular House of Night Series, this novel includes paranormal romance.

Curtis, C. P. (2004). *Bucking the Sarge*. New York, NY: Wendy Lamb Books.

Dean, Z. (2003). *The A-list*. New York, NY: Little, Brown.

Dean, Z. (2007). *Beautiful stranger: An A-list novel*. New York, NY: Alloy Entertainment.

Dessen, S. (2002). *This lullaby*. New York, NY: Viking.
   This popular and humorous novel features Remy, a girl who, on the heels of her mother's multiple marriages, simply doesn't believe in love. Her cynical view of romance is challenged by a rocker named Dexter who is in love with Remy for the long haul.

Deuker, C. (2007). *Runner*. Boston, MA: Houghton Mifflin.
   Chance Taylor, a high school teenager, lives with his Vietnam Era veteran father who is drunk much of the time. They live a rough-and-tumble life on an old 30-ft sailboat moored in Puget Sound, Seattle, Washington. Chance goes through the motions at school but revels in long afternoon runs at the marina where they live. Struggling for money to pay their mooring fees, Chance agrees to make extra money working for a marina employee who asks Chance to pick up packages at a tree along his running route. He is aware that he may be engaging in criminal activity but desperate for the money.

Flake, S. G. (2005). *Who am I without him? Short stories about girls and the boys in their lives*. New York, NY: Hyperion.
   This short story collection gets at the tensions arising in relationships where the characters' sense of self sometimes gets lost in love. This collection contains realistic accounts of the complex trials of love and longing.

Gonzalez, G. (2009). *A so-called vacation*. Houston, TX: Piñata Books.

In this coming-of-age novel, two high school brothers, Gabriel and Gustavo, leave their Texas home with their father for a summer in California doing field work. Although they are native-born Texans, and less than thrilled about this trip, their dad was an immigrant worker as a kid and he feels this will be an important growth experience for Gabriel and Gustavo.

Harmon, M. (2008). *The last exit to normal*. New York, NY: Knopf.

Urban skateboarder Ben Campbell is spirited away to tiny rural Butte, Montana by his dad and his dad's new boyfriend. Ben clashes with his father and the boyfriend's mother, a tyrannical but kindhearted old lady. Next door, more trouble brews with a single parent family where the dad is abusive to his 11-year-old son and nasty to cats, Ben, and the neighbors in general.

Hautman, P. (2006). *The bloodwater mysteries: Snatched*. New York, NY: Putnam Juvenile.

An 11th-grade journalist, Roni Delicata, and a younger science-oriented student, Brian Bain, team up to solve the kidnapping of a snobby new kid in school, Alicia Camden. These two pushy amateur sleuths challenge authority and uncover clues that reveal Alicia's difficulty at home

Hautman, P. (2007). *The bloodwater mysteries: Skullduggery*. New York, NY: Putnam Juvenile.

Roni and Brian are again on the trail of money-hungry developers. An injured archeologist they encounter on a class field trip claims he was attacked by a ghost, which sets the two teen sleuths on a mission to find the truth.

Hinton, S. E. (1967). *The outsiders*. New York, NY: Penguin.

Now a classic in the young adult genre, this well-known story, told from the point of view of 14-year-old Ponyboy and his brothers offered a realistic look at gang conflict that still captivates adolescent readers.

Hiassen, C. (2002). *Hoot*. New York, NY: Knopf.

Hoot chronicles the main character's amateur detective work to figure out who the mysterious figure is that seems to be sabotaging a proposed pancake house development. The site is the home to an endangered species, and Roy, a middle school student recently arrived in Florida from Montana, gets in the middle of an ongoing ecological mystery.

Hiassen, C. (2007). *Flush*. New York, NY: Knopf.

Flush continues with the ecological theme from *Hoot* by focusing on the illegal dumping of raw sewage from a floating casino in Florida. Main characters Noah Underwood and his sister Abbey concoct a plan to expose the environmental disaster perpetuated by the casino owner.

Johnson, L. (2009). *Muchacho*. New York, NY: Knopf.

Main character Eddie Corazon gravitates toward a life of crime, largely ignores school, and loves reading. He writes poetry and finds inspiration and a way to change his life when he meets Lupe and falls in love. Eddie's life circumstances conspire to hand him setbacks, but his determination to meet these challenges will engage teen readers.

Kirkpatrick, K. (2010). *Into the shadows*. Chicago, IL: DarkSide.

It is a paranormal romance with a main character, Paivi Anderson, who is a high school freshman with a potential boyfriend. But the problem is that she has special powers and enemies that want to take her down.

Klass, D. (2007). *Dark angel*. New York, NY: HarperTeen.

Main character 17-year-old Jeff Hastings is leading a fairly idyllic life on the Jersey shore. However, when a brother he knew nothing about is released from prison after facing a murder charge, Jeff is thrust into a new world that is upside down. Troy, the ex-con brother, is a master manipulator, and the conflict and tension between the two brothers in this novel is palpable.

Minter, J. (2004). *The insiders*. New York, NY: Bloomsbury.

Myers, W. D. (2003). *The beast*. New York, NY: Scholastic.

This powerful novel explores the growing rift between Anthony Witherspoon, a successful African American student bound for the university and his high school girlfriend, Gabi, saddled with taking care of her family from the Dominican Republic. She copes with not going on to college by writing poetry and sinking further into heroin addiction.

Myers, W. D. (2008). *Sunrise over Fallujah*. New York, NY: Scholastic.

The war in Iraq is seen from the perspective of a young African American soldier from Harlem working with the local people as part of a Civilian Affairs unit. The contradictions and doublespeak that cover the real purpose of this unit's operation weighs heavily on Robin Perry, the main character.

Myers, W. D. (2010). *Lockdown*. New York, NY: HarperCollins.

Main character Reese wants to get out of juvenile hall incarceration early by working in a senior citizens home. Conflict arises with one of the residents and Reese must work hard to redeem himself and leave the criminal world behind. Hope looms large in Walter Dean Myers's novels, and this one takes teen readers into Reese's thoughts and actions.

Noel, A. (2007). *Kiss and blog*. New York, NY: St. Martin's Griffin.

Longtime teen friends Winter and Sloane are high school freshmen intent on moving up the social ladder in their sophomore year. Sloane manages to get accepted to this clique by simultaneously dumping Winter, her longtime childhood friend. Winter retaliates by writing a blog as revenge on Sloane. This humorous, fast-moving story will captivate reluctant teen readers with its allusions to popular communications technology.

Osa, N. (2003). *Cuba 15*. New York, NY: Delacorte.

Smith, C. L. (2007). *Tantalize*. New York, NY: Candlewick.
   This novel features a strong female main character in Quincie P. Morris, as she cares for an uncle whose gothic girlfriend thinks constantly about vampires. Quincie's relationships suffer from overarching elements of horror. For example, her potential boyfriend Kieren is a werewolf, the restaurant she remodels with her uncle ends up with its chef murdered just before opening, and this event propels Quincie into a world of vampires and intrigue.

Soto, G. (2006). *Accidental love*. New York, NY: Harcourt.
   Marisa accidentally picks up the wrong cell phone. When she returns it to its owner, Rene, her psychic opposite, she finds herself in love. Polar opposites, Rene is bookish, nerdy, and uninterested in typical macho athletic pursuits.

Spinelli, J. (2000). *Stargirl*. New York, NY: Knopf.
   This book is the story of an unconventional girl, Susan Caraway, who tries but fails to conform to the status quo at her school and is shunned by her peers and ultimately her boyfriend, Leo, who realizes too late what he has lost.

Von, Ziegesar, C. (2005). *The it girl*. New York, NY: Little, Brown.

Woodson, J. (2004). *Behind you*. New York, NY: Putnam.

RECOMMENDED FILMS

A huge number of teen films can be found at the Wikipedia site (http://en.wikipedia.org/wiki/Category:Teen_Films). Each film (e.g., *Dangerous Minds*) listing includes a synopsis, cast, soundtrack, and other useful information if you are planning lessons where teen film might be read in concert with a young adult novel (e.g., *Holes*). In addition, these films portray teen life from a variety of stances including narrow, stereotypical views of teens as bundles of raging hormones to more finely nuanced portrayals.

RECOMMENDED WEBSITES

The American Library Association website lists young adult literature annual awards (http://www.ala.org/yalsa/booklists). In addition, a Top 10 Best Books for Young Adults can be found at this website. If you are working with reluctant young adult readers, additional titles are listed aimed at engaging reluctant readers in appealing literature. Finally, each year a Teens Top Ten list is offered.

You can also consult the website for Kirkus Reviews where evaluations of young adult (and children's) literature are offered. In addition, every issue (eight times per year) of the *Journal of Adolescent & Adult Literacy* features Books for Adolescents including author interviews and annotated book listings. *The ALAN Review* (National Council Teachers of English) features articles profiling major young adult authors and themes.

REFERENCES

Beach, R., Thein, A. H., & Parks, D. (2008). *High school students' competing social worlds: Negotiating identities and allegiances in response to multicultural literature*. Mahwah, NJ: Lawrence Erlbaum/Taylor & Francis Group.

Blasingame, J. (2008, Winter). From Wellpinit to Reardan: Sherman Alexie's journey to The National Book Award. *The ALAN Review*, 69–73.

Conant, E. (2008, March 17). Teens: Branding for beginners. *Newsweek*, p. 14.

Debraski, S. C. (2007, Spring). *Romantic reads. Yattitudes: The official newsletter of the Young Adult Library Services Association, a division of the American Library Association*, 6(3). Retrieved from http://www.ala.org/ala/yalsa/yalsamemonly//yattitudes/yattiduelsarch/spring2007.cfm

Fournier, D. N. E., & Graves, M. F. (2002). Scaffolding adolescents' comprehension of short stories. *Journal of Adolescent & Adult Literacy*, 46(1), 30–39.

Glenn, W. (2008). Gossiping girls, insider boys, A-list achievement: Examining and exposing YA novels consumed by conspicuous consumption. *Journal of Adolescent & Adult Literacy*, 52(1), 34–42.

Kaywell, J. F., & Kaywell, S. (2008). A conversation with Laurie Halse Anderson. *Journal of Adolescent & Adult Literacy*, 52(1), 78–83.

Latrobe, K. H., & Drury, J. (2009). *Critical approaches to young adult literature*. New York, NY: Neal-Schuman.

Wolterbeek, E. (2007). Review of *Tantalize*. In J. Blasingame's Books for Adolescents, *Journal of Adolescent & Adult Literacy*, 51 (1),74–76.

Chapter 6

Science Fiction, Fantasy, and Horror

In this chapter, we touch on three of the most engaging and popular genres in young adult literature: science fiction, fantasy, and romance. We also discuss elements you might consider in selecting books that represent quality literature within these genres.

Learning Objectives

- Be able to state how the features of these three genres (**science fiction, fantasy,** and **horror**) contribute to students' understanding of Common Core Standards related to how an author structures a text, orders events within it, and manipulates time to create mystery, tension, or surprise.

- Be able to state the criteria for selecting high-quality young adult fiction within the three genres considered in this chapter.

- Know some of the titles within realistic young adult fiction and consider how you would incorporate these into your classroom.

- Know some of the titles within the fantasy genre and consider how you would incorporate these into your classroom.

- Know some of the titles within the horror genre and consider how you would incorporate these into your classroom.

Vignette: Margo Sabo's High School American Literature Class

Ms. Sabo has her senior English class read both required canonical literature and self-selected literature from popular genres including science fiction. A technology fan, she uses podcasting (audio delivered over the Internet) to enhance students' author studies (Putman & Kingsley, 2009; Rozema, 2007).

Ms. Sabo learned about podcasting through an *English Journal* article on using podcasts for book reports (Rozema, 2007). Podcasting consists of audio content that can be shared on the Internet through MP3 players and iTunes via iPods and other software.

Margo's students each selected a science fiction author and at least one novel to summarize in a 3- to 5-minute author study podcast. The example that follows features Malcolm Zhang's efforts to create an author study podcast on the well-known science fiction author William Sleator after reading his futuristic novel *Test* (2008). In the novel, high school seniors exist in a polluted, urban city where they never read real books, only short paragraphs that mirror No Child Left Behind–like test questions. Teachers are rewarded or fired based on their students' performance each week. Students sit in class based on their weekly test scores with high performers near the front and low performers in the back of the classroom.

Malcolm Zhang has been captivated by the science fiction genre since middle school, and he is interested in William Sleator's background. He begins researching the author by looking at the author's publisher and website (Penguin.com), as well as by crafting a script for his short audio podcast. He discovers that William Sleator created his first story about a fat cat at age 6. Later, Sleator liked to write macabre stories, and he ultimately attended Harvard University as an English major. As it turns out, he did not care much for Harvard and amused himself with his talents as a pianist. He moved to Europe where he made a living as a pianist and composer, accompanying the Boston Ballet on tour. He wrote his first novel while in England and subsequently shifted into the science fiction genre, using real people from his experiences as models for characters in his books. He now splits his time between homes in Boston and Thailand.

Malcolm used this site and others to develop a 5-minute podcast on William Sleator. Other students in Ms. Sabo's class researched authors from horror and other genres, finding author blogs and publisher sites that profiled their chosen authors. Ms. Sabo archives the students' podcasts for real audiences of other students interested in particular genres.

Common Core Standards

The following standards are addressed in this chapter.

RL.9-10.1, 11-12.1 Cite strong and thorough textual evidence to support analysis of what the text says explicitly as well as inferences drawn from the text.

3. Using a jigsaw strategy where each member of your group shares their expertise with the other group members, provide a discussion of what you learned about your genre along with a bibliography of at least five classic and more contemporary titles, annotated for the group.

4. Determine how would you use these selections in your teaching; for example, *A Wrinkle in Time*, although a fantasy, is informed by real-life science (e.g., the molecular makeup of humans).

Mr. Dela Cruz circulates among the small groups of six students and helps them get started on this project, which will span the next two class meetings.

Science Fiction

Science fiction has been an enduring genre with cult followings of fans of *Star Trek* being just one example among many. Dating back to the 19th century, science fiction novels incorporate fantastical elements and more grounded notions from evolving theories in the sciences. Often overlapping with fantasy, mystery, and horror, as well as informed by the hard sciences, science fiction continues to entrance adolescent and adult readers. Imagining possible worlds, interplanetary conflicts, strange creatures, and space exploration, as well as the possibility of highly intelligent mutant beings, all capture the reader's imagination. Excellent histories of the genre abound (Donelson & Nilsen, 2005), but for our purposes, we want to touch on a few newer examples of the genre (and its relatives in fantasy, horror, and mystery), and we urge the reader to browse bookstores, libraries, and the Internet for additional examples. As is the case with young adult literature more generally, the number of titles coming out annually is extensive.

Mystery is often an element in science fiction novels. In Carey Borgens's (2007) *The Wolf Experiments*, the main character, 15-year-old Alex, has amnesia, and she is confronted by nightmares. She must, with the aid of a wolf, solve a murder and look for victims of a genetic experiment that has gone awry. Radiation sickness plagues the world, but wolves are immune to the radiation. Carey resides in a biosphere that shelters the last remaining species on Earth, and as the story unfolds, she must confront her amnesia and reconstruct her life with the help of a journal in an old destroyed laboratory. Adolescent readers note that the story is captivating and that the author plans sequels.

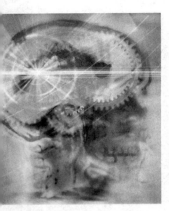

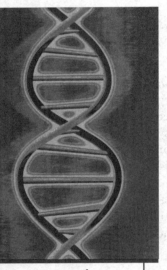

Science fiction is a dynamic genre that defies conventions.

In a first novel that has garnered awards, Mark Wakely's (2005) *An Audience for Einstein* takes up the rapid advances in medical science that could allow a renowned scientist to live beyond the years of normal life expectancy, extending a career and its potential accomplishments into the future. An aging astrophysicist teams up with a neurosurgeon to transplant his memories into the body and mind of a 10-year-old illiterate street urchin. The downside is Miguel, the 10-year-old recipient of Dr. Marlow's brilliance, will have to give up his own identity. The novel nicely weaves together elements of futuristic medicine, mystery, and ethical questions.

Books in a series are generally popular with students once they get hooked on an author. For example, *Uglies* (2005b) by Scott Westerfield is part of a trilogy featuring two additional titles, *Pretties* (2006) and *Specials* (2007). Westerfield creates a future world where social difference is eradicated by a compulsory operation at age 16, designed to transform adolescents into homogenized beauties. That leaves younger teens in an ugly state, rebelling against their older siblings. Futuristic hoverboards (skateboards that swiftly skim through the air) and other inventions permeate Westerfield's mythical world. Themes of rebellion against conformity and valuing social difference coexist with future worlds where wild inventions shrink distances.

Similarly, in James Patterson's widely popular *Maximum Ride: The Angel Experiment* (2005), genetically engineered children who are part human and part bird, escape from the laboratory where they were created. They go after Erasers, a group of wolf-like predators sent to kill the children so their existence will not be discovered.

Matt, the main character in Nancy Farmer's (2002) award-winning novel *The House of the Scorpion,* discovers that, in a future world 100 years from now, he is the clone of El Patron, a very powerful opium lord living on the United States–Mexico border. Matt's existence has little to do with taking over his patron's role as El Patron, and as the novel unfolds, Matt learns his fate.

Dystopian Science Fiction Novels

Dystopian science fiction novels trouble utopian views of the future by offering readers seriously flawed fictional societies. For example, George Orwell's (1949) novel *Nineteen Eighty-Four* created Big Brother and the Thought Police, among other troubling control elements in this well-known dystopian novel.

Young adult literature examples of dystopian novels include Keary Taylor's (2011) *Eden* depicting a world in which human DNA is intermingled with cybernetic matter such that the machine elements overwhelm the human elements.

At 18, Eve navigates a future dystopian world where only 2% of the human population is left. Cyborg elements rule, and Eve and Avian try to save this tiny human population from extinction.

Veronica Roth's (2011) *Divergent* offers another example of this science fiction genre. In a dystopian Chicago in the future, all 16-year-olds must devote their lives to the cultivation of one of five special "virtues." For example, Amity, the peaceful virtue, and Erudite, the intelligent virtue, are two of the five possible choices for main character Beatrice, but she troubles this unity by possessing three of the five virtues, rendering her dangerous to this dystopian society. With a film adaptation of this young adult novel, it joins other popular works enjoying a strong following of enthusiastic readers and viewers.

Sometimes overlapping with science fiction, fantasy offers readers an escape into surreal worlds where anything is possible. Great feats of strength against powerful mythical creatures are possible and heroic acts are not uncommon.

Fantasy

This increasingly popular genre takes the reader on fantastic journeys where magic prevails, creatures of all kinds talk and have magical powers, and anything is possible. Imaginary lands and fairy-tale qualities transport readers out of their ordinary lives to conquer monsters and go on epic journeys. It is no wonder fantasies are hugely popular with young adult audiences and are engaging to teach.

Two types of fantasy compose this genre: high fantasy and low fantasy (Latrobe & Drury, 2009). High fantasy offers readers a journey into alternative worlds where there are no physical and human laws. Low fantasy centers on magical events. High fantasy raises issues about good and evil. The criteria for evaluating fantasy that you should consider include the following (Latrobe & Drury, 2009, p. 103):

- Writing and a plot that is creative, original, and new
- A plot and story line that is believable
- A narrative that elicits a sense of wonder in the reader that helps one suspend belief
- A theme that addresses the struggle between good and evil and a protagonist caught up in this struggle

Nicely overlapping with science fiction and often embedded in these novels, elements of fantasy abound in the following selections. For example, in Roland Smith's (2005) *Cryptid Hunters*, 13-year-old twins Grace and Marty

Fantasy offers readers an escape into surreal world where anything is possible.

are sent to be raised by their Uncle Wolf following the death of their parents in a plane crash. Their Uncle Wolf is a veterinarian who is obsessed with finding cryptids, mythical creatures like the Loch Ness Monster and Sasquatch. This search takes their uncle and the twins to the Congo and secrets about the twins' identities.

In *The Call to Shakabaz* (Wachpress, 2007), two African American brothers and their two sisters are sent to live with their aunt after their mother's death. They learn that they have the power to pass through their own dimension into mystical worlds of talking animals, magical powers, and a crusade against the forces of evil. Combining fantasy, history, and suspense, this novel captivates readers.

Lamplighter: Monster Blood Tattoo, Book Two (Cornish, 2008) finds main character Rossamund Bookchild reevaluating the stereotype that all monsters are evil (Blasingame, 2008). As a result, he can go beyond common monster slayers, taking this heroic role to a new level. Rossamund is assigned as a lamplighter to a post in a desolate and dangerous place called Wormstool. This posting is designed to prevent him from revealing information he has on the corrupt leaders at the lamplighters training facility. Elements of suspense, romance, and engaging writing propel this fantasy forward.

In *Catching Fire* (Collins, 2009), protagonist Katniss Everdeen struggles to recover from her victory during the Hunger Games and the follow-up victory tour. Confronted with rebellion in the districts she must visit, Katniss faces betrayal and dissention. Fast-paced, engaging, and carefully crafted, *Catching Fire* places Katniss in constant conflict.

Also within the fantasy genre, *Eldest* (2005) by young author Christopher Paolini, was an American Library Association young adult top 10 selection. Book two in a trilogy, *Eldest* takes Eragon, the main character, to a land of elves where he is to learn the skills of the Dragon Rider, namely, magic and swordsmanship.

This novel and others show the potential impact of an increasing array of independent publishers on the expansion of young adult literature titles. Christopher Paolini published his first novel through a family publishing operation. By chance, well-known Miami author Carl Hiassen (*Hoot, Flush*, and other books) happened to read the novel and recommended that his New York publisher, Alfred A. Knopf, give Paolini a look. As a result, Paolini's *Eldest* had a print run of 1 million copies. The point is, as you look for novels in the science fiction, fantasy, mystery, and horror genres, among others, cast your net far and wide as many independent publishing houses feature authors and works that appeal to teen readers.

Horror

The horror genre has long been popular with young adult readers, and its impact is enhanced through film. For example, Dracula has been featured in numerous films and was transformed into a more compelling monster in Bram Stoker's version (1897) where Dracula takes on tragic human qualities. Generally, the horror genre appeals to readers because of its shock value, often embedded in well-crafted writing.

The **horror** genre overlaps with gothic literature and its ancient tradition depicting the trials of characters who sell their souls to the devil for material gain (Latrobe & Drury, 2009). Set in dark, foreboding places including old castles and haunted houses, these stories have a long history that includes well-known classics like Bram Stoker's *Dracula* (1897) and Mary Shelley's *Frankenstein* (1818), as well as a host of modern film adaptations and spoofs.

Selecting high-quality literature within the horror genre should include the following elements (Latrobe & Drury, 2009, p. 104):

- Complex psychological figures
- An emotionally charged setting and overall atmosphere
- Creative treatment of familiar archetypes (e.g., the film adaptation of Bram Stoker's *Dracula*)

In the horror genre, vampires continue to reign. Stephanie Meyer's (2005) novel *Twilight* is the first book in a series featuring a companion movie as well. Set in a rural northwestern town, the story centers on main characters Bella and Edward, and on Edward's life as a teenage vampire. The sequels to *Twilight* have enjoyed a huge worldwide fan base with more than 85 million copies sold (Clarke, 2010). As a popular culture success, the *Twilight* novels and film have spawned a body of critical essays in a fashion typically reserved for canonical, classical literature. For example, Pamela H. Demory (2010) argued that Stephanie Meyer's books are attracting female fans because the books provide pleasure for them. Capturing the passion and excitement of falling in love for the first time, a young female reader may identify with Bella and the tensions that surround her love for Edward. Demory (2010, p. 213) noted that *Twilight* "offers a model of the female adolescent struggle to negotiate love and sex, family and career, dependence and independence." And, like the book, the film adaptation of *Twilight* and its sequels been hugely successful at the box office.

In Stephanie Meyer's (2010) vampire novella *The Short Second Life of Bree Tanner*, various vampire characters continue the *Twilight* tradition

The horror genre appeals to readers because of its shock value and well-crafted writing.

(Blasingame, 2011). Also in the vampire vein of the horror genre, Scott Westerfield's (2005a) novel *Peeps* mixes horror and mystery as 19-year-old Cal, who is a carrier of vampire elements but not a predator, uses his powers (super night vision and strength) to save New York City from a growing population of peeps (parasite-positive) vampires with cannibalistic needs.

Gothic elements in young adult horror fiction abound (Crawford, 2008). For example, in *The Haunting of Alaizabel Cray* (Wooding, 2005), main character Thaniel must confront a host of supernatural villains called "wych-kins" in Victorian London, England. The underbelly of the city is overrun with horrible creatures. Beautiful Alaizabel Cray has been possessed by an old "wych," and it is Thaniel's duty to wrest this evil spirit from Alaizabel by slaying an endless array of awful monsters. This novel and the one that follows were both nominated for awards.

In Celia Rees's (2006) *The Wish House*, 15-year-old Richard finds that his favorite abandoned cabin (Wish House) near his family's summer vacation spot in Wales is occupied by an eccentric artist and his family. Richard becomes attached to the artist and his daughter Clio, and the family's dark fantasy world is based on British mythology. As the layers of this family's secrets unfold, Richard learns that his trust in this seemingly free-spirited family has been violated. He goes on a rampage, destroying his bonds with the family until he achieves redemption 6 years later.

Numerous gothic and vampire-laden novels are popular with young adult readers, and they generally feature the following typical characteristics (Crawford, 2008). A villain or monster is at the center of the narrative, along with a creepy, dark setting like an ancient castle with gargoyles and secret passageways, and societal taboos related to elements of life (e.g., mental illness) many would like to sweep under the carpet.

ACTIVITY 6.1: Professional Reflection and Discussion

Directions: In this activity, we ask you to conduct a brief author study of a chosen author from science fiction, fantasy, or horror genres. The author study should be shared with your small group and archived for other students and readers. The following steps should help guide this process:

1. Look for information on your chosen author using the publisher's website, the author's own blog, or information from Amazon.com.

2. Consider addressing the author's biography and how the author's personal experiences led to becoming a writer.

3. List some of the author's better-known books. Why were they successful?

4. How had this author moved their particular genre forward?

5. How do you feel about this author's works?

Once you have developed your author study, you may want to put it in podcast or blog form to share with your small group. This material can then be archived for future students to consult as they develop their own author studies.

MULTIMEDIA TEXT SET

In this multimedia text set, classroom teacher Lindsey Woods uses the sci-fi horror text *Miss Perrigrine's Home for Peculiar Children* (Riggs, 2011) as a cornerstone to explore social justice issues including discrimination and prejudice toward the Other. Her selections cover a variety of perspectives and media that contribute not only to a better understanding of the genre but also to social issues.

1. Telgemeier, R. (2009). *X-men: Misfits 1*. New York, NY: Del Rey.

This graphic novel retells the X-men story from a girl's perspective of being a mutant in a mutant school for extraordinary young people. In many ways, the story offers parallels to *Miss Perregrine*. Written in the format of a graphic novel, it adds the same elements of the picture/text experience explored in the cornerstone text.

2. O'Connor, B. (2010). *The fantastic secret of Owen Jester*. New York, NY: Farrar, Straus and Giroux.

Owen Jester happens on a "secret" that falls off a freight train in Georgia. This secret guides him and his two friends through a summer to remember forever. This book gives readers a vision toward fantasy hitting reality, much like the idea of the peculiar children going from imagination to real life. This story allows readers another link to connect creativity with reality. By gaining a more solid perspective on fantasy, the reader can better analyze how the fantasy elements in the cornerstone text play into the ideas of difference and discrimination experienced by Jacob, his grandfather, and the children in *Miss Perrigrine*.

3. Asimov, I. (1954, February). The fun they had. *The Magazine of Fantasy & Science Fiction*.

In this short story by legendary sci-fi writer Asimov, two young characters discover a key to the ancient past, where students read real books with real teachers. Connections can be made between these characters and Jacob in the cornerstone text, who must also endure some immense, and often unsettling, discoveries. Both stories delve into the introspection of our own times and enable readers, much like the protagonists, to see an "outsider," as someone else that they just do not understand.

4. Blomkamp, N. (Director), & Jackson, P (Producer). (2009). *District 9* [Motion picture]. United States: Sony Pictures and Tristar Pictures.

This feature film takes place in Johannesburg, South Africa, where an alien society lands on Earth. Initially welcomed with curiosity, the aliens come to be recognized as a menace to the city and are treated with a level of disrespect and inequality comparable with South Africa's times of apartheid. One character involved with the aliens becomes exposed to a chemical that turns him into an alien himself, and the viewer sees the disrespect that comes with difference and discrimination through his journey. Although the movie is meant for more mature audiences, clips can be shown to illustrate the same sci-fi effect that revolves around the concepts of difference and discrimination.

5. *Issac Asimov: Three Laws of Robotics* (http://www.youtube.com/watch?v=AWJJnQybZlk)

Isaac Asimov is a known creator of several sci-fi theorems and laws. One is the law of robotics, used in such works as the film *I, Robot*. In this video clip, Asimov outlines his laws and their relevance to science fiction. The class can discuss why the author of a fictional work would integrate rich descriptions of context and nonfiction elements, such as the Welsh culture depicted in *Miss Peregrine* or the descriptions of District 12 (Appalachia) in *Hunger Games*.

When engaging students in complex and challenging genres such as science fiction and horror, teachers can use multimedia text sets such as this one to provide rich and varied experiences for their students that also facilitate discussions of social issues such as alienation that may not be readily connected to the texts individually but that become more visible as the text set is explored.

SUMMARY

This chapter explored three popular genres: science fiction, fantasy, and horror. Descriptions of each genre were offered along with selection criteria. Finally, a few titles were profiled in each genre with the caveat that all of these genres have new titles coming out.

DISCUSSION QUESTIONS

1. How do the features of these three genres (science fiction, fantasy, and horror) contribute to students' understanding of Common Core Standards related to how an author structures a text, orders events within it, and manipulates time to create mystery, tension, or surprise?

2. What are the criteria for selecting high-quality young adult fiction within the three genres considered in this chapter?

3. What are some of the titles within realistic young adult fiction, and how you would incorporate these into your classroom?

4. What are some of the titles within the fantasy genre, and how would you incorporate these into your classroom?

5. What are some of the titles within the horror genre, and how would you incorporate these into your classroom?

KEY TERMS

Dystopian Science Fiction Novels   122

Fantasy   123

Horror   125

Science Fiction   121

SMALL-GROUP ACTIVITY: INTERVIEW A YOUNG ADULT ABOUT HIS OR HER READING PREFERENCES

Interview a young adult about his or her reading preferences related to one of the three genres considered in this chapter, and discuss the results with another class member. In addition, how would you go about locating reading titles for this student? What are some examples of young adult novels and related films you might recommend to the student?

RECOMMENDED READINGS

Clarke, A. M. (2010). Introduction: Approaching *Twilight*. In A. M. Clarke & M. Osborne (Eds.), *The Twilight mystique: Critical essays on the novel and film* (pp. 3–13). London, UK: McFarland.

Crawford, P. C. (2008). A new era of Gothic horror. *School Library Journal Mobile*. Retrieved from http://www.schoollibraryjournal.com/article/CA6600683.html

This article profiles Gothic elements in some of the award-winning horror novels published, and it offers a useful history tracing the genre back to Edgar Allen Poe and others. The author argues that many well-crafted examples of the genre are available, which serve to counter narrow views that this genre only appeals to readers' desire for lurid tales.

Demory, P. H. (2010). The pleasure of adapting: Reading, viewing, logging on. In A. M. Clarke & M. Osborne (Eds.), *The* Twilight *mystique: Critical essays on the novel and film* (pp. 201–216). New York, NY: McFarland.

Donelson, K. L, & Nilsen, A. P. (2005). *Literature for today's young adults* (7th ed.). Boston, MA: Allyn & Bacon.

These authors devote separate chapters to various genres and offer detailed historical references charting the development of science fiction and other genres.

Putman, S. M., & Kingsley, T. (2009). The atoms family: Using podcasts to enhance the development of science vocabulary. *The Reading Teacher*, 63(2), 100–108.

Although this article deals with science content, the information on podcasting is first rate and includes a number of useful websites to guide your use of podcasting in the classroom.

Rozema, R. (2007). The book report, version 2.0: Podcasting on young adult novels. *English Journal*, 97(1), 31–42.

This article demonstrates how to have students write, revise, and collaborate on book-talk podcasts that feature young adult novels. Examples include podcasts students developed on science fiction young adult novels and a very useful ReadWriteThink Internet example lesson plan.

Wolterbeek, E. (2007). Review of *Tantalize*. In J. Blasingame's books for adolescents, *Journal of Adolescent & Adult Literacy, 51*(1), 74–76.

RECOMMENDED YOUNG ADULT LITERATURE FEATURED IN THIS CHAPTER

Borgens, C. (2007). *The wolf experiments*. Parker, CO: Outskirts Press.

The main character in this science fiction novel, Alex, is a 15-year-old girl, orphaned and living in a biosphere with no memory of how she got there. A biosphere protects her from massive radiation in the Earth's atmosphere, and wolves are immune to its effects. Alex must use a series of clues to recover who she is and ameliorate a genetic experiment gone awry.

Collins, S. (2009). *Catching fire*. New York, NY: Scholastic.

In this fantasy/dystopia novel, main character Katniss Everdeen returns from victory at the Hunger Games only to face dissention and conflict at every turn on her victory tour. The towns she visited have citizens that mock her achievements, and the plot is fast-paced and engaging.

Cornish, D. M. (2008). *Lamplighter: Monster blood tattoo, book two*. New York, NY: Putnam.

Main character Rossamund Bookchild reevaluates the stereotype that all monsters are evil. As a result, he can go beyond common monster slayers, taking this heroic role to a new level.

Farmer, N. (2002). *House of the scorpion*. New York, NY: Atheneum.

In a future world 100 years from now, Matt learns he is the clone of El Patron, a very powerful opium lord living on the United States–Mexico border. Matt's existence has little to do with taking over his patron's role as El Patron, and as the novel unfolds, Matt learns his fate.

Hiassen, C. (2002). *Hoot*. New York, NY: Knopf.

This book chronicles the main character's amateur detective work to figure out who the mysterious figure is that seems to be sabotaging a proposed pancake house development. The site is the home to an endangered species, and Roy, a middle school student recently arrived in Florida from Montana, gets in the middle of an ongoing ecological mystery.

Hiassen, C. (2007). *Flush*. New York, NY: Knopf.

This book continues this ecological theme by focusing on the illegal dumping of raw sewage from a floating casino in Florida. Main characters Noah Underwood and his sister Abbey concoct a plan to expose the environmental disaster perpetuated by the casino owner.

L'Engle, M. (1962). *A wrinkle in time*. New York, NY: Random House Children's Books.

This well-established young adult classic won a Newbury Medal. The main characters, Meg, Charles Wallace, and Calvin, visit planets outside our solar system where thinking aliens reside and the struggle between good and evil is palpable. The novel mixes science fiction, fantasy, and science in a fashion that stands the test of time, even 50 years after its publication.

Meyer, S. (2005). *Twilight*. New York, NY: Little, Brown.

Set in a rural northwestern town, the story centers on main characters Bella and Edward and on Edward's life as a teenage vampire. This book is the first in a four-part series. *New Moon, Eclipse,* and *Breaking Dawn* are also available.

Meyer, S. (2010). *The short second life of Bree Tanner*. New York, NY: Little, Brown.

Depicts vampire characters' struggle against the power of super vampires.

Paolini, C. (2005). *Eldest*. New York, NY: Knopf.

Book two in a trilogy, Eldest takes Eragon, the main character, to a land of elves where he is to learn the skills of the Dragon Rider, namely, magic and swordsmanship.

Patterson, J. (2005). *Maximum ride: The angel experiment*. New York, NY: Warner.

Genetically engineered children who are part human and part bird escape from the laboratory where they were created. They go after Erasers, a group of wolf-like predators sent to kill the children so their existence will not be discovered.

Rees, C. (2006). *The wish house*. Somerville, MA: Candlewick Press.

Richard finds that his favorite abandoned cabin (Wish House) near his family's summer vacation spot in Wales is occupied by an eccentric artist and his family. Richard becomes attached to the artist and his daughter Clio and the family's dark fantasy world based on British mythology.

Riggs, R. (2011). *Miss Peregrine's home for peculiar children*. Philadelphia, PA: Quirk Books.

This *New York Times* bestseller combines elements of fantasy and horror to take the reader into a time warp during World War II where peculiar children (featured in haunting black-and-white photos with period dress) are hiding to escape a mythical beast that killed the main character's grandfather.

Roth, V. (2011). *Divergent*. New York, NY: HarperCollins, Katherine Tengen Books.

Dystopian Chicago in the future has main character Beatrice coping with a society based on total devotion to mastering one of five virtues (e.g., peace). Unfortunately, she has three virtues in her possession, rendering her dangerous to the programmed harmony of this time in the future.

Sleator, W. (2008). *Test*. New York, NY: Amulet Books.

This science fiction novel takes No Child Left Behind into a future where high school students are only allowed to read short, paragraph-length material to prepare for their high-stakes exit exam in English. Students are seated each week in rows that represent their test performance, and they live in a completely stratified world of the very rich and the very poor. The main character, Ann, is regularly stalked by a black motorcycle that follows her as she walks home through the polluted urban city where she lives.

Smith, C. L. (2007). *Tantalize*. New York, NY: Candlewick Press.

This multigenre novel features a strong female main character in Quincie P. Morris in the care of an uncle whose gothic girlfriend thinks constantly about vampires. Quincie's relationships suffer from overarching elements of horror. For example, her potential boyfriend Kieren is a werewolf, the restaurant she remodels with her uncle ends up with its chef murdered just before opening, and this event propels Quincie into a world of vampires and intrigue.

Smith, R. (2005). *Cryptid hunters*. New York, NY: Hyperion.

Thirteen-year-old twins Grace and Marty are sent to be raised by their Uncle Wolf, a veterinarian who is obsessed with finding cryptids, mythical creatures like the Loch Ness Monster and Sasquatch. This search takes their uncle and the twins to the Congo and reveals secrets about the twins' identities.

Taylor, K. (2011). *Eden*. New York, NY: CreateSpace (Amazon).

The reader enters a dystopian world where human DNA is intermixed with cybernetic matter, leaving only 2% of the human population left. Main character Eve must negotiate this complex universe where machine elements threaten what is left of Eden.

Wachpress, A. (2007). *The call to Shakabaz*. Talmage, CA: Woza Books.

Two African American brothers and their two sisters are sent to live with their aunt after their mother's death. They learn that they have the power to pass through their own dimension into mystical worlds of talking animals, magical powers, and a crusade against the forces of evil.

Wakely, M. (2005). *An audience for Einstein*. Cincinnati, OH: Mundania Press.

This futuristic novel takes up the rapid advances in medical science that could allow a renowned scientist to live beyond the years of normal life expectancy, extending a career and its potential accomplishments into the future. An aging astrophysicist teams up with a neurosurgeon to transplant his memories into the body and mind of a 10-year-old illiterate street urchin. Issues of ethical consciousness that often collide with medical expediency make this novel a good one for critical discussions.

Westerfield, S. (2005a). *Peeps*. New York, NY: Penguin, Razorbill.

Nineteen-year-old Cal, who is a carrier of vampire elements but is not a predator, uses his powers (super night vision and strength), to save New York City from a growing population of peeps (parasite-positive) vampires with cannibalistic needs.

Westerfield, S. (2005b). *Uglies* (Uglies Trilogy, Book 1). New York, NY: Simon & Schuster, Simon Pulse.

Westerfield creates a future world where social difference is eradicated by a compulsory operation at age 16, designed to transform adolescents into homogenized beauties. That leaves younger teens in an ugly state, rebelling against their older siblings.

Wooding, C. (2005). *The haunting of Alaizabel Cray*. New York, NY: Scholastic Point.

Thaniel must confront a host of supernatural villains called "wych-kins" in Victorian London, England. The underbelly of the city is overrun with horrible creatures. Beautiful Alaizabel Cray has been possessed by an old "wych," and it is Thaniel's duty to wrest this evil spirit from Alaizabel.

REFERENCES

Blasingame, J. (2008). Review of *Lamplighter: Monster blood tattoo, book two*. *Journal of Adolescent & Adult Literacy, 52* (2), 177–178.

Blasingame, J. (2011). Review of *The short second life of Bree Tanner*. *Journal of Adolescent Literacy, 54* (4), 307–308.

Clarke, A. M. (2010). Introduction: Approaching *Twilight*. The *Twilight* mystique. In A. M. Clarke & M. Osborne (Eds.), *Critical essays on the novel and film* (pp. 3–13). London, UK: McFarland.

Crawford, P. C. (2008). A new era of Gothic horror. *School Library Journal Mobile*. Retrieved from http://www.schoollibraryjournal.com/article/CA6600683.html

Demory, P. H. (2010). The pleasure of adapting: Reading, viewing, logging on. In A. M. Clarke

& M. Osborne (Eds.), *Critical essays on the novel and film* (pp. 202–216). London, England: McFarland.

Donelson, K. L., & Nilsen, A. P. (2005). *Literature for today's young adults* (7th ed.). Boston, MA: Pearson.

Latrobe, K. H., & Drury, J. (2009). *Critical approaches to young adult literature.* New York, NY: Neal-Schuman.

Meyer, S. (2010). *The short second life of Bree Tanner.* New York, NY: Little, Brown.

Orwell, G. (1949). *Nineteen eighty-four.* London, England: Secker & Warburg.

Putman, S., & Kingsley, T. (2009). The atoms family: Using podcasts to enhance the development of science vocabulary. *Reading Teacher, 63* (2), 100–108.

Rozema, R. (2007). The book report, version 2.0: Podcasting on young adult novels. *English Journal, 97* (1), 31–42.

Shelley, M. (1818). *Frankenstein.* New York, NY: Penguin.

Stoker, B. (1847). *Dracula.* New York, NY: Penguin.

Von, Ziegesar, C. (2005). *The it girl.* New York, NY: Little, Brown.

Westerfield, S. (2006). *Pretties* (Uglies trilogy, book 2). New York, NY: Simon & Schuster, Simon Pulse.

Westerfield, S. (2007). *Specials* (Uglies trilogy, book 3). New York, NY: Simon & Schuster, Simon Pulse.

Chapter 7

Historical Fiction

Historical fiction takes the reader into an insider's view of events. Young adult novel accounts of Native American historical figures like *Geronimo* (Bruchac, 2006) and *Eyes of the Emperor* (Salisbury, 2005) chronicling Japanese American soldiers after the bombing of Pearl Harbor are captivating accounts. They take readers into the rich and compelling contours of famous events in history from the characters' perspectives.

Learning Objectives

- Be able to state how the features of this genre (**historical fiction**) illuminate Common Core Standards related to political, social, or economic aspects of a particular time period.

- Be able to state the criteria for selecting high-quality historical young adult fiction.

- Know some of the titles within this genre related to significant historical periods and consider how you would incorporate these into your classroom.

- Be able to engage students in a cultural criticism stance to critique historical fiction that may contain racist or sexist elements.

Vignette: Adair Garrett's Middle School Social Studies Class

In Ms. Garrett's 8th-grade social studies class, an exploration into the slave trade has begun. To engage her students in this topic, Ms. Garrett has constructed a *multimodal text set* that centers on Sharon Draper's (2010) novel *Copper Sun*. This excellent example of historical fiction is a character-rich story describing the shocking realities of the slave trade and plantation life while portraying the perseverance, resourcefulness, and triumph of the human spirit.

As an active proponent of global human rights, Ms. Garrett wants her students to explore not only the historical slave trade but also the ongoing human rights violations associated with present-day human trafficking. To that end, she has included in her multimodal text set videos from the organization *Youth for Human Rights* (www.youthforhumanrights.org) and has created a Web Quest around human trafficking that centers on the CNN Freedom Project (http://thecnnfreedomproject.blogs.cnn.com/). This project seeks to end modern-day slavery by creating slavery awareness and outlining methods of tracking and prevention worldwide. Ms. Garrett knows that this source will provide her students with several articles, videos, and other media that revolve around issues of modern-day slavery, and it lists real-world concepts that illustrate the points brought up in *Copper Sun*.

Ms. Garrett provided her students with additional slave narratives including Gary Paulsen's (1993) *Nightjohn* about a slave who risks his life to teach reading to 12-year-old Sarny. In Newberry Award–winning author Mildred D. Taylor's (1976) well-established *Roll of Thunder Hear My Cry,* main character Cassie Logan endures racist threats and taunts, rising above the humiliating comments against her family and the land that is so important to them. The third book in the series, *The Road to Memphis* (Taylor, 1990), chronicles Cassie at 17 and her friend Moe's clash with his White tormentors. Cassie takes it on herself to accompany Moe on his journey to Memphis and safety. With these titles, Ms. Garrett has provided cornerstone texts for her students as they develop their text sets.

As her class has already set up a Ning (www.ning.com) site, a type of social network, as a means of facilitating online discussions and responses around topics in class, Ms. Garrett asks her students to create and post Venn diagrams that compare and contrast the historical slave trade with modern human trafficking by drawing on the titles she has provided along with ones they will find in their own exploration of this topic. She has also assigned them the task of finding poems, songs, or other texts about slavery, past and present, to add to their multimodal text sets. The students will work in small groups to create a film using movie-making software to share what they have learned about historical slavery and modern-day human trafficking.

Common Core Standards

The following standards are addressed in this chapter.

RL.6.9, 7.9 Compare and contrast texts in different forms or genres (e.g., stories and poems as well as historical novels and fantasy stories) in terms of their approaches to similar themes and topics.

RL.9-10.5 Analyze how an author's choices concerning how to structure a text, order events within it (e.g., parallel plots), and manipulate time (e.g., pacing and flashbacks) to create such effects as mystery, tension, or surprise.

RH.9-10.4 Determine the meaning of words and phrases as they are used in a text, including vocabulary describing political, social, or economic aspects of history/social science.

VOICES FROM THE PAST . . . PERSPECTIVES ON THE FUTURE

Historical fiction presents the human condition in a way that exposes readers to conflict and dreams set against the backdrop of a particular place and time. It also allows for reflection on present-day circumstances that may mirror historical events. It is an unfortunate truth that sometimes history does repeat itself when we do not learn from its lessons. Characters' emotions and resistance to prejudice and cruelty give voice to those who were likely silenced in a particular place and time (e.g., Salisbury's soldiers treated like dog bait but resisting by adopting a devotion to their assignment) as well as raise questions and points for discussion around those who may be silenced or treated cruelly today.

Novels like Laurence Yep's (1993) *Dragon's Gate* endure because of their strong social justice elements. *Dragon's Gate* takes up the construction of the transcontinental railroad where Chinese workers were essentially enslaved to do the hard labor of chiseling out the route through bitterly cold mountain passes. Set at the time of the Civil War, this novel remains a powerful account of the human spirit overcoming oppression. In the next section, we review a selection of historical fiction texts that relate to discrimination and prejudice and its sometimes horrific consequences. Perhaps by exploring these topics as a teacher of young adult literature, you can guide your students to a better understanding of historical events and the way they shape our world.

Historical fiction presents the human condition against the backdrop of a particular place and time.

World War II and Japanese American Internment

Historical young adult fiction that explores the prejudice and discrimination faced by Japanese Americans after U.S. engagement following Pearl Harbor provides for rich discussions around the tenets of freedom and democracy and what it means in times of war. Kathleen Tyau's (1999) *Makai* explores such themes. This book is set in Hawai'i just after the bombing of Pearl Harbor and the declaration of martial law.

> All of Honolulu was black. All of Oahu, all of the islands. No lights shining, everything shut down, everything quiet. I pressed my face against the screen and strained to see the dark. The night sky punched with stars. The moon hiding too. A few cars creeping by with blue paint on their headlights or black paper, like big eyelids, with only a little bit of the white eyeballs showing. (p. 107)

Deborah Iida's (1996) *Middle Son* follows Spencer Fujii, a Japanese American raised in the sugar plantation culture, who returns to O'ahu to look after his ailing mother. Spencer recounts being born amid World War II:

> I am of the Sensai generation. We are the dreams of our parents, dreams Scarred with thorns of cane leaves and pineapples. My own children are Yonsei, and with each generation, we lose more tradition. My daughter Teresa does not care for rice, and I find this disturbing. (p. 21)

Unlike the Japanese Americans in California who were interned without rights, Spencer notes 1% of Hawai'i Japanese Americans were interned immediately after the bombing of Pearl Harbor. In California, Japanese Americans experienced a harsh period of internment, chronicled in *Farewell to Manzanar* (Houston & Wakatsuki, 1995). Wrenched from their homes and jobs in communities like Long Beach, California, these patriotic citizens were treated like prisoners, relegated to mass internment camps.

The Holocaust

"Works of historical fiction and creative non-fiction written about the Holocaust have come to occupy an important place in both the literary and history curricula in K to 12 schools" (Krasny, 2012, p. 3). Few other events in history up to that point have witnessed such profound violations of the most basic of human rights. Indeed, the Holocaust and the hopes of nations to prevent future atrocities led the United Nations to create the Universal Declaration of Human Rights on December 10, 1948. In exploring young adult literature that centers on the Holocaust, one must avoid the pitfall of "othering" both the victims and the perpetrators into simple stereotypes locked in a particular time and place. Yet, rather than a simplistic adherence to George Santayana's (1905/1936) admonition, "Those who cannot remember the past are doomed to repeat it" (p. 284), these novels might be used to examine critically the prejudice, intolerance, and apathy that permitted these tragic events to unfold in the past, to raise awareness and advocacy efforts in the present and future.

Such is the dilemma for Hannah, the main character in Jane Yolen's now classic tale of the Holocaust *The Devil's Arithmetic* (1990). In this novel, Hannah is bored and embarrassed about her relatives' stories about the Nazis. Then during a Passover Seder, when she open the front door symbolically to welcome the prophet Elijah, she is transported back to 1940s Poland where she is captured and sent to a death camp. There, Hannah is befriended by a young girl named Rivka. In an act of final self-sacrifice, Hannah exchanges places with Rivka as she is being sent to the gas chamber. As the chamber door swings closed on Hannah, she is transported back to her grandparents' Seder with a new understanding of her relatives' ordeal and the importance of remembrance.

In contrast to the Yolen's fictional account of the Holocaust, Susan Goldman Rubin and Ela Weissberger give us the nonfiction account of Ela Stein in their book *The Cat With the Yellow Star: Coming of Age in Terezin*. In 1942 when she was 11 years old, Ela was sent to the Terezin concentration camp with other Czech Jews. This book chronicles Ela's 3½ years until she was liberated from the camp at the age of 15 in 1945. In those 3½ years of sickness, terror, separation from loved ones, and loss, Ela managed to grow up. In the bleakest of conditions, Ela forged lifelong friendships with other girls from her barracks. A children's opera called Brundibar was even performed, and Ela was chosen to play the pivotal role of the cat. Yet amid all of this, transports to death camps and death itself were a part of daily life. Full of sorrow, yet persistent in its belief of the triumph of hope over evil, this memoir tells the story of an unimaginable coming of age that puts a human face on the Holocaust.

In portraying the human experience of a global event, the novel *Emil and Karl* is a unique work of literature. Originally written in Yiddish in 1938, *Emil and Karl* (Glatshteyn, 1938/2006) focuses on the dilemmas faced by two young boys—one Jewish, the other not—when they suddenly find themselves without families or homes in Vienna on the eve of World War II. As the book was written before World War II, and before the global knowledge of the Third Reich's persecution of Jews and other civilians, it offers a fascinating look at the moral challenges people faced under Nazism.

Each of these novels and many others reflect the struggles of marginalized characters in the harshest aspects of the human condition. High-quality writing in this genre does not shy away from including gritty details and compelling narratives. As you look for high-quality young adult historical fiction, the following characteristics are important to consider.

DEFINING GENRES

"Good historical fiction moves beyond the mere introduction of factual material: It reconstructs the past both materially and emotionally, showing the impact that major social and cultural events had on the lives of people at the time" (Sprague & Keeling, 2007, p. 88). These authors recommend specific criteria for selecting high-quality historical fiction, including the following:

- The work should offer an authentic portrayal of the time, place, and people being featured.
- The characters should be believable.
- The work should immerse the reader in the experiences of people in a way that illuminates the human condition.

Historical fiction reconstructs the past illustrating the impact that major social and cultural events had on the lives of people at the time.

In addition, young adult historical fiction author L. M. Elliott noted that "Good historical fiction fills a reader's mind with the *human drama* that is history" (Rice, 2006, p. 45). L. M. Elliott (Rice, 2006) argued that engaging historical fiction should not shy away from including gritty details. For example, during the 18th century, common colds were treated with a hideous blend of curdled milk, wine, and pickled deer antler slices. These and other gory details catch readers' attention and make the cold, hard facts of history closer to the real human condition.

For example, *Fever: 1793* (Anderson, 2002) takes the reader into the world of Mattie, a young girl living in 18th-century Philadelphia during an outbreak of yellow fever. The awful conditions are punctuated by actual quotes from historical records of the fever's devastation on the city and families during this period.

As a way of getting started in this genre, Activity 7.1 asks you to conduct a brief author study of a prominent author from historical fiction. Increasingly, authors have their own blogs in addition to their publisher's websites. Both places are good spots to start exploring your chosen author's biography and works.

ACTIVITY 7.1: Professional Reflection and Discussion

Directions: In this activity, we ask you to conduct a brief author study of a chosen author from the historical fiction genre. The author study should be shared with your small group and archived for other students and readers. The following steps should help guide this process:

1. Look for information on your chosen author using the author's publisher's website, the author's own blog, or information on Amazon.com.

2. Consider addressing the author's biography and how the author's personal experiences led to becoming a writer.

3. List some of the author's better-known books. Why were they successful?

4. How had this author moved his or her particular genre forward?

5. How do you feel about this author's works?

Once you have developed your author study, you may want to put it in podcast or blog form to share with your small group. This material can then be archived for future students to consult as they develop their own author studies.

WORKING WITH ESTABLISHED GENRES OF YOUNG ADULT LITERATURE

One issue when you are working with historical fiction is the tendency for classical novels from the past to include racist and sexist elements (Latrobe & Drury, 2009). You may want to help your students adopt a cultural criticism stance that engages them in rich discussions of historical contexts that supported prejudice.

For example, during the bombing of Pearl Harbor, Japanese Americans were interned and viewed as sympathetic to the enemy. Hawai'ian young adult author Graham Salisbury's *Eyes of the Emperor* (2005) shows how super-patriotic Japanese American soldiers from Hawai'i were sent to an isolated island in Mississippi where they were used as dog bait to train German shepherds to hunt them down under the belief that they smelled differently from Caucasians. Accounts like this one lend themselves to critique and cultural criticism, an approach we described in Chapter 3. When you are considering young adult historical fiction, the following elements should be considered (Latrobe & Drury, 2009, p. 75):

- A style that hooks the reader into the historical place, time, and plot
- A writing style that avoids long, cumbersome passages
- Characters with whom adolescents can identify
- Settings, time, and places that entice adolescents into the story
- Historically accurate events
- A chain of evidence that the novel is based on research
- A realistic depiction of the period through careful attention to details of dress, family life, and so on
- A powerful, universal theme that spans time and place

Young adult novels in this genre include fiction chronicling the Great Depression (1929–1939), migrant farm worker experiences (1940s–1960s), the Holocaust (1939–1945), Japanese World War II internment (1941–1945), the civil rights movement (1950s–1960s), and various wars (e.g., Vietnam, 1959–1975) (Rice, 2006). The sheer volume of historical young adult fiction is huge and easily searchable by the period you are interested in exploring.

For example, Christopher Paul Curtis's novel *Elijah of Buxton* (2007) deals with the town of Buxton, Ontario, at the end of the underground railway as people fled to Canada to escape slavery. Elijah is the first free-born African American in the town. He learns that a group of slaves have been sold back into slavery after a con man took their money. Elijah sets out to rescue them.

The American Revolution has an endless array of young adult novels that captivate readers. For example, Gary Paulsen's (2010) *Woods Runner* follows 13-year-old Samuel and his family, living in the British colony of Pennsylvania at the onset of American patriots challenging English rule. His parents are ultimately taken prisoner, and Samuel sets out to follow their trail using his tracking skills. But he is faced with the daunting brutality of war and enemy territory. In typical Gary Paulsen style, this story personalizes the profound impact the Revolutionary War had on this country.

The Battle of Bunker Hill was the battle that began the Revolutionary War. In Gregory Edgar's (2009) *Patriots*, three teenage boys, two American and one British, quickly jettison any romantic delusions about the realities of war.

In L. M. Elliott's World War II novels *Under a War Torn Sky* (2001) and its sequel *A Troubled Peace* (2009), American pilot Henry Forester is shot down during a bombing raid in France's Vercors Mountains. He must travel at night to avoid being captured behind enemy lines. Henry depends on the kindness of villagers to survive. In the sequel *A Troubled Peace,* Henry returns home to Virginia but agonizes over a local boy Pierre who helped him in France. As the novel unfolds, Henry returns to France to search for the lost Pierre, encountering more of the aftereffects of World War II.

Navajo author Joseph Bruchac's (2005) *Code Talker* chronicles the main character Ned Begay as a very young Marine enlistee during World War II assigned to use his native language to send coded messages related to assist the war against Japan. His Pacific theater experiences span stints in Hawai'i to work out details of the code these Navajo soldiers used and on to Guadalcanal and Iwo Jima.

Teachers and students can adopt a cultural criticism stance to promote rich discussions of historical contexts.

In Case 7.1 that follows, a very creative English teacher, Maria Bascon, has her students capitalize on iPad2.0 tablets purchased from a grant she wrote aimed at engaging students in historical simulations. She starts this inquiry project by having her students read Gary Paulsen's (2010) *Woods Runner* to learn about tracking skills. She then has her students search for iPad applications that illuminate some aspect of the Revolutionary War, including weaponry, tracking skills, and first aid.

CASE 7.1: Maria Bascon's English Classroom

Ms. Bascon: Once you have located some of the many apps available about the American Revolution, I want you to locate an app that focuses on the particular topic you have (these have been drawn randomly from a hat). For example, if weaponry is the one you have, then a free app like *Musket & Artillery: American Revolutionary War* might be good.

Student: Okay, and we can use the star rating system and comments to see what other people thought about it.

Ms. Bascon: Right, but that's just one part of this assignment. I want you to go beyond the app you locate and, in your small group, critique this app and offer design changes that you feel would make it more exciting and engaging. In particular, try to answer the question: How does this app help us understand what was happening to people on both the British and American sides during this war?

(Continued)

(Continued)

During the next class, the students who selected the website Ms. Bascon recommended provided their evaluation of this application, loaded on the class iPads they each used.

Small Group: This app (*Musket & Artillery: American Revolutionary War*) uses strategies and military tactics to defeat enemies during the American Revolutionary War. We could join forces with the British, France, United States, Germany, or Spain. You can take over territories as the game progresses. It had three and a half stars out of five, and it's pretty good. It's free but, as with all apps, they try to get you to buy the upgraded version for $2.99, and many of the other war apps were even pricier. Our group agreed that we have become more careful buying apps because we work in minimum-wage jobs at the mall and we have to budget carefully. This free one is fine for class though, and the reviews were mostly positive.

Ms. Bascon: Okay, that's great. Do you feel that it helps us visualize and are there any design changes you would recommend?

Small Group: Definitely! When we tried out the app, we found that the computer wins most of the time. We had an American army with 60 soldiers that got defeated by a British army of only 20 soldiers! So, based on our experiences with this iPad app, we would say it needs serious debugging and a design that seems more fair to the players. In fact, we would only give it two stars out of five. The graphics aren't too bad, but we don't recommend this app. We will search from one that is better designed and has more visual depth and definition.

Ms. Bascon: Okay, nice work on this. We'll consider the next group's application evaluation.

MULTIMEDIA TEXT SET

This multimedia text set was constructed by classroom teacher Meagan M. Vieta-Kaball. It uses picture books and websites to expand on and further explore the issues of slavery raised in Sharon Draper's *Copper Sun*. In the following, Megan shares her multimedia text set and her rationale for including the sources for the set.

1. McCully, E. A. (2007). *The escape of Oney Judge: Martha Washington's slave finds freedom.* New York, NY: Farrar, Straus and Giroux.

In this book, Mrs. Washington declares that young Oney is just like one of the Washington's own children, but Oney is not fooled. On the night Mrs. Washington tells Oney she will not grant her freedom on her death, Oney thinks quickly, acts courageously, and flees. Expressive watercolors within this well-researched biography portray the bravery of Onah Maria Judge, an African American woman who claimed, and fought for, the right to have "no mistress but herself." This book was labeled a Winner for Younger Children in 2008.

2. Curtis, C. P. (2007). *Elijah of Buxton.* New York, NY: Scholastic Press.

This book is a sensitively written historical novel infused with the spirit of youth. Eleven-year-old Elijah bursts with pride at being the first child born free in Buxton, a settlement of runaway slaves in Canada just across the border from Detroit. When a scoundrel steals money saved to buy an enslaved family's freedom, Elijah impulsively pursues the thief into Michigan. The journey brings him face-to-face with the terrors of slavery, pushing him to act courageously and compassionately in the name of freedom. This book was named an Honor Book for Older Children in 2008.

3. Tingle, T. (2008). *Crossing Bok Chitto: A Choctaw tale of friendship & freedom.* El Paso, TX: Cinco Puntos Press.

The Choctaw people live on one side of the River Bok Chitto; plantation owners and African American slaves live on the other. A secret friendship between a Choctaw girl and an African American boy is the first link in a chain of humanity that spirits the boy's family across the river to freedom. The folktale is a tribute to the Choctaws and Indians of every nation who aided African Americans running from slavery. Earth-tone paintings and striking use of white express the story's blend of reality and magic perfectly. This book was named an Honor Book for Younger Children in 2007.

Connections and Rationale

These books were selected because they are about slaves trying to find freedom/stay free like Amari. I also thought a story about a slave being born free (*Elijah of Buxton*) would be a good book to bring in to tie to the end of *Copper Sun*. I thought having a book related to a runaway slave settlement would be interesting because Polly and Amari spent time in one in the novel. I also thought *Crossing*

Bok Chitto would be a good addition because of the friendship that brings a slave family freedom, which is very similar to Polly and Amari's friendship in *Copper Sun*.

The Underground Railroad: Escape from Slavery
   http://teacher.scholastic.com/activities/bhistory/underground_railroad/activities.htm
   I chose this website because I thought it would be a fun and informative way for students to learn what life was like being a slave in early America.

BBC News: "Mali's Children in Chocolate Slavery"
   http://news.bbc.co.uk/2/hi/africa/1272522.stm
   I chose this article because it ties modern-day slavery to historical slavery and provides students the opportunity to explore a major global news sources in relation to the topics examined in this text set.

SUMMARY

This chapter centered on historical fiction and selection criteria for high-quality young adult historical fiction. Applicable Common Core State Standards were included along with an example multimedia text set.

DISCUSSION QUESTIONS

1. How do the features of this genre (historical fiction) illuminate Common Core Standards related to political, social, or economic aspects of a particular time period?

2. What are the criteria for selecting high-quality historical young adult fiction?

3. What are some of the titles within this genre related to significant historical periods, and how you would incorporate these into your classroom?

4. How would you engage your students in a cultural criticism stance to critique historical fiction containing racist or sexist elements?

KEY TERMS

Historical Fiction   137

SMALL-GROUP ACTIVITY: TEACHING HISTORICAL FICTION THROUGH A MULTIMEDIA FRAMEWORK

Directions: Read one of the selections within the historical fiction genre treated in this chapter. Think about how you would teach this selection through a multimedia framework. Create a plan for a 2-week unit centered on this genre, and share your unit in your small group, including its relation to the Common Core Standards and assessment approaches.

RECOMMENDED READINGS

Rice, L. J. (2006). *What was it like? Teaching history and culture through young adult literature.* New York, NY: Teachers College Press.

This carefully organized book offers specific young adult titles within each chapter dealing with a particular period in history (e.g., The Great Depression). Additional titles and specific teaching strategies are profiled as well.

Sprague, M. M., & Keeling, K. K. (2007). *Discovering their voices: Engaging adolescent girls with young adult literature.* Newark, DE: International Reading Association.

Chapter 4 in this book offers a good account of historical fiction and advice on criteria for the selection of high-quality young adult literature in this genre.

RECOMMENDED YOUNG ADULT LITERATURE FEATURED IN THIS CHAPTER

Alphin, E. M. (2005). *The perfect shot.* Minneapolis, MN: Carolrhoda Books/ Lerner.

A high school senior basketball player is distraught after the murder of his girlfriend, her sister, and her mother. The girls' father is on trial for the crime, but Brian, the main character, knows information that could impact the case. Brian is writing a paper based on the 1913 Leo Frank murder case that parallels this contemporary situation.

Anderson, L. H. (2002). *Fever: 1793.* New York, NY: Aladdin.

This historical fiction novel takes the reader into the world of Mattie, a young girl living in 18th-century Philadelphia during an outbreak of yellow fever. The awful conditions are punctuated by actual quotes from historical records of the fever's devastation on the city and families during this period.

Bruchac, J. (2006). *Geronimo*. New York, NY: Scholastic.

Within the historical fiction genre, this novel takes the reader on Geronimo's train journey to prison from his mountain home in Colorado to the harsh, humid Florida landscape following his imprisonment in Fort Sill, Oklahoma, in 1908. Narrated by his adopted grandson, we see the charismatic Geronimo endure the wrenching journey from his spiritual mountain homeland.

Brucjac, J. (2005). *Code talker: A novel about the Navajo marines of World War Two*. New York, NY: Dial.

Ned Begay is a young Marine enlistee during World War II assigned to use his Native Navajo language to send coded messages to assist the war against Japan.

Curtis, C. P. (2007). *Elijah of Buxton*. New York, NY: Scholastic.

The Canadian town of Buxton, Ontario, was at the end of the underground railway designed to assist African American slaves in their effort to escape slavery. Elijah sets out to rescue a group of slaves sold back into slavery, even after escaping.

Draper, S. (2010). *Copper sun*. New York, NY: Atheneum Books.

After witnessing the destruction of her family and village, 16-year-old Amari boards a slave ship to the Carolinas. This is a tale of endurance, bravery, and hope.

Edgar, G. T. (2009). *Patriots*. St. Augustine, FL: Bluewater Press.

This novel features the Battle of Bunker Hill, the first major battle of the Revolutionary War. The main characters are three teenage boys, one of whom is British.

Houston, J. D., & Wakatsuki, J. (1995). *Farewell to Manzanar*. New York, NY: Laurel Leaf Books.

This well-established novel chronicles the internment of Japanese Americans in camps during the onset of World War II. Manzanar became home to the main characters, taken from their homes and businesses in Long Beach and elsewhere.

Iida, D. (2000). *Middle son*. Chapel Hill, NC: Algonquin Books.

Main character Spencer Fujii returns to Hawai'i as an adult to care for his aging mother, but numerous conflicts occur across the generations.

Paulsen, G. (1993). *Nightjohn*. New York, NY: Laurel Leaf Books.

Nightjohn risks his life teaching other slaves how to read by tutoring them after dark.

Paulsen, G. (2010). *Woods runner*. New York, NY: Ember.

This novel follows 13-year-old Samuel and his family, who live in the British colony of Pennsylvania at the onset of American patriots challenging English rule. His parents are ultimately taken prisoner, and Samuel sets out to follow their trail using his tracking skills while confronting daily the horrors of war.

Rubin, S. G., & Weissberger, E. (2006). *Cat with the yellow star: Coming of age in Terezin*. New York, NY: Holiday House.

Main character Ela Stein, a Czech Jew, is sent to the Terrazin concentration camp in 1942 where she endures and survives horrible conditions and human rights violations. During the three years she is there, Ela manages to make enduring friendships that overshadow the awful reality of the concentration camp.

Ryan, P. M. (2000). *Esperanza rising*. New York, NY: Scholastic.

Set in a Mexican farm labor camp outside Bakersfield, California, this novel chronicles a young Latina girl's life during the Great Depression. The story is based on the author's maternal grandmother who left a rich life in Mexico to immigrate to the United States and work in a San Joaquin Valley labor camp. As historical fiction, the novel can be paired with nonfiction accounts in history to illuminate the grassroots experiences of Mexican immigrant workers during the Great Depression.

Salisbury, G. (2005). *Eyes of the emperor*. New York, NY: Wendy Lamb Books.

It is 1941 and Eddy Okubo enlists in the Army in Honolulu. With the bombing of Pearl Harbor, Eddy, a Japanese American Hawai'ian resident, is assigned to a unit that is sent to a remote island outpost in Mississippi to serve as dog bait for German shepherd dogs trained to detect Japanese enemy soldiers. The Washington, D.C, office that concocted the theory that Japanese soldiers smell different and can be easily detected by trained dogs drives the novel's plot. The reader gets an inside look at the racist treatment of patriotic Japanese Americans during this period.

Taylor, M. D. (1976). *Roll of thunder hear my cry*. New York, NY: Dial Books.

This award-winning novel relates the account of an African American family, the Logans, as they struggle to stay together amid racist conditions in the 1930s Deep South.

Taylor, M. (1990). *Road to Memphis*. New York, NY: Penguin Books.

This sequel follows the Logan family in 1941 with Cassie now in her last year of high school in Jackson, Mississippi, facing harsh racist conditions.

Tyau, K. (1999). *Makai*. New York, NY: Farrar, Straus and Giroux.

The novel features a Chinese-Hawai'ian woman struggling against racism in Hawai'i.

Yep, L. (1993). *Dragon's gate*. New York, NY: HarperCollins.

This novel chronicles Chinese workers' lives while building the transcontinental railroad in brutal conditions.

Yolen, J. (1990). *The devil's arithmetic*. New York, NY: Puffin.

Main character Hannah resists going to her family's Passover Seder, but as the even begins, she is magically transported to a Polish village in 1942 where she experiences the tragic events of this period.

RECOMMENDED WEBSITES

Historical fiction lends itself to an exploration of websites where strong visual support for events can be found. For example, if students are reading *Esperanza Rising*, set in the 1930s Depression era, a number of sites can be consulted, for example, American Experience: Surviving the Dust Bowl at www.pbs.org/wgbh/amex/dustbowl farm life during the Great Depression at www.livinghistoryfarm.org

REFERENCES

Glatshteyn, Y. (2006). *Emil and Karl* (J. Shandler, Trans.). New York, NY: Square Fish. (Original work published in 1938)

Krasny, K. (2012). Between art and testimony: Transforming oral histories of Holocaust survivors into young adult fiction and creative non-fiction. *Oral History Forum, 32*. Retrieved from http://www.oralhistoryforum.ca/index.php/ohf/issue/view/40/showToc

Latrobe, K. H., & Drury, J. (2009). *Critical approaches to young adult literature.* New York, NY: Neal-Schuman.

Rice, L. J. (2006). *What was it like? Teaching history and culture through young adult literature.* New York, NY: Teachers College Press.

Santayana, G. (1905). *Life of reason, Reason in common sense.* New York: Scribners.

Sprague, M. & Keeling, K. (2007). *Discovering Their Voices: Engaging Adolescent Girls With Young Adult Literature.* Newark, Del.: International Reading Association.

Chapter 8

Short Stories, Poetry, and Humor

The three genres considered in this chapter offer readers and struggling readers some of the most engaging reading material, often in compact but powerful packages. Short stories, poetry, and humor are mainstays in the young adult literature world with a strong focus on diverse students and a host of issues important to teens.

Learning Objectives

- Understand the criteria for selecting texts in each of the genres discussed and how they relate to Common Core Standards.

- Consider and be able to discuss the importance of students' having access to literature such as **short stories** that reflect circumstances they may have encountered in their own lives.

- Develop an understanding of the nature of **poetry** and how it might be integrated with technology, performance, and social justice issues.

- Know how to use a wide variety of genres such as **humor** to engage disenfranchised readers.

- Continue to create a database of young adult literature that includes the genres discussed in this chapter.

Vignette: Macy Garth's 11th-Grade Classroom

Eleventh-grade teacher Macy Garth sat down at her desk with a sigh. The school year had just begun and already the "real lives" of her students were intruding on her carefully written plans for a multigenre unit on Shakespeare aligned with the common core standards. One of her students was now homeless, another was pregnant, and many were dealing with issues of racism and discrimination. As she looked out the window at the dense urban neighborhood below, she remembered a recent workshop that used poetry and contemporary short stories focusing on teen experiences to illuminate the complexity of Shakespearean works. Macy opened her file drawer and combed through the workshop materials for the suggested titles of short stories, poetry, and videos that would make the classics come vividly alive for her students.

Common Core Standards

The following standards are addressed in this chapter.

RL.9-10.2, 11-12.2 Determine a theme or central idea of a text and analyze in detail its development over the course of the text, including how it emerges and is shaped and refined by specific details; provide an objective summary of the text.

RL.9-10.311-12.3 Analyze how complex characters (e.g., those with multiple or conflicting motivations) develop over the course of a text, interact with other characters, and advance the plot or develop the theme.

RL.9-10.4, 11-12.4 Determine the meaning of words and phrases as they are used in the text, including figurative and connotative meanings; analyze the cumulative impact of specific word choices on meaning and tone (e.g., how the language evokes a sense of time and place and how it sets a formal or informal tone).

RL.9-10.5, 11-12.5 Analyze how an author's choices concerning how to structure a text, order events within it (e.g., parallel plots), and manipulate time (e.g., pacing and flashbacks) to create such effects as mystery, tension, or surprise.

WORKING WITH ESTABLISHED GENRES OF YOUNG ADULT LITERATURE

As you consider selecting short stories for young adults, the following criteria may be helpful. Look for the following:

- Authentic selections that realistically capture teen coming-of-age dilemmas and problems, stories, and situations teens can identify with as they search for ways to cope with their own life issues
- Selections that provoke questions and offer a forum for discussion of teen issues

Activity 8.1 provides an opportunity to discover additional short story young adult fiction.

ACTIVITY 8.1: Professional Reflection and Discussion

Directions: In your small group, share any issues you confronted as a teen and short story young adult fiction titles that helped you see other adolescents struggling with similar issues. Do an Internet search of other contemporary young adult short story titles that deal with problems (e.g., teen pregnancy, relationships, crime, gangs, poverty, racism, bullying, and so on). Share these titles in a subsequent class with your small group. How might some of those titles explicate the classic works required by common core standards? What text pairings are possible?

The long-standing short story genre now includes some excellent anthologies for young adults that go to the heart of issues teens confront in and out of school.

SHORT STORIES

In the not too distant past, **short stories** read by teens were primarily written by mainstream authors for adult audiences. For example, stories by the American author O. Henry (William Sydney Porter, 1862–1910) with their surprise endings have endured. Like O. Henry, Burmese author Saki (H. H. Munro, 1870–1916) left a rich legacy of stunning, surprise-ending gems that continue to captivate readers.

However, these collections deal mainly with adult characters and, given the social context of their times, may not engage contemporary teens' issues. Nevertheless, short stories remain popular with students, partly because of their compact format where the reader is rapidly propelled into a character's world. Every word counts in a short story, and conflict happens fast. This is a genre that opens the door for struggling and reluctant readers to participate in literary conversations. As you think about incorporating short stories in your classroom, consider the following selection criteria:

High-quality short stories should be the following:

- Realistic
- Fast moving
- Written as if every word counts
- Centered on teen's conflicts (e.g., family, relationships, identity, and sexuality)
- Easily read in a sitting

The short story genre includes anthologies for young adults that address issues teens confront in and out of school.

The young adult short story genre received its biggest boost from Donald Gallo's (1984) initial anthology, *Sixteen: Short Stories by Outstanding Writers for Young Adults*. Subsequent anthologies, including multicultural works like the collection *First Crossings: Stories About Teen Immigrants* (Gallo, 2007), offer a compelling look at many of our diverse students' experiences in a transnational world. The 10 stories in this collection span Latino, Chinese, Korean, and other ethnic groups' immigration stories.

Older multicultural short story collections continue to offer powerful pictures of families struggling with new social mores as they immigrate to the United States. For example, in Anne Mazer's (1993) short story collection *America Street: A Multicultural Anthology of Stories*, author Lensey Namioka explores the cultural minefield a dinner invitation poses for a Chinese family. In "The All American Slurp," the narrator declares at the outset of the story, "The first time our family was invited out to dinner in America, we disgraced ourselves while eating celery" (p. 55). The narrator goes on to recount how the host family stared at their Chinese guests when they ate raw celery, struggling to remove the shoots that got stuck in their teeth. Raw vegetables would have been cooked in China, but in an effort to be polite these guests did their best to eat the unfamiliar food.

Author Gary Soto's (1990) *Baseball in April and Other Stories* appeals to middle school readers and offers a glimpse into Latino teens in Fresno, California, trying to balance poverty and doing the right thing. For example, in "No Guitar Blues" (p. 54), Fausto wants a guitar more than anything. When he finds a lost and very fancy dog, he calls the number on the dog's collar and sets out to get a reward from the dog's owner by lying about where he found the pet. The grateful family gives him $20 and some pastries, making Fausto feel bad about lying to them. He goes to church and donates the $20 bill, forgoing the money that would have gone toward a guitar. At home, his mom gives him an old guitarra that belonged to his grandfather, an instrument played by Los Lobos, his favorite band. Clearly, these are fairly gentle stories with happy endings. More contemporary collections feature relationships and identity issues that are much rawer.

For example, Sharon Flake's (2005) collection *Who Am I Without Him? Short Stories About Girls and the Boys in Their Lives* features Black vernacular and issues of body image, betrayal, and identity. The 12 stories in this anthology treat teen relationships realistically, and as the vignette demonstrated, they provide problem-based situations for discussion. The collection was acknowledged as a Coretta Scott King honor book.

In a short story collection that capitalizes on many teens' interest in all things vampire related, P. C. Cast's (2008) anthology *Immortal: Love Stories With Bite* features stories by the horror genres major authors.

In addition to these short story collections featuring established authors, Hanging Loose Press produces anthologies drawn from the high school section of *Hanging Loose* literary magazine (http://hangingloose press.com). The fourth in this series of anthologies, *When We Were Countries: Poems and Stories by Outstanding High School Writers* (Pawlak, Lourie, & Hershon, 2010) features teen voices and issues of coming of age, living and caring for aging grandparents, special moments with a mom or dad, and accentuating the taken-for-granted moments in daily life.

Each of the collections profiled offers models for student writing, as well as themes that include coming-of-age issues, multicultural and international dimensions, and other themes that lend themselves to unit planning. In addition, a number of websites support outlets for teen reviews, journaling, and creative writing.

For example, *Teen Libris: Your Link to Teen Lit* (www.teenlibris.com) offers reviews, interviews, book lists, and a forum and blog for book discussion.

Another site, www.authors4teens.com, includes prominent young adult authors being interviewed by Donald Gallo. The site displays authors' biographical information, lists of their works, and other material.

Activity 8.2 explores teaching through guided reading and discussion of short stories.

ACTIVITY 8.2: Professional Reflection and Discussion

Directions: Locate a contemporary young adult short story collection. Identify a story you would like to use with your class. Share this selection with your small group, and brainstorm how you would go about teaching this selection in terms of guided reading and discussion. In particular, think about online support elements and websites that will expand students' interest and understanding of the short story genre. In addition to short story collections, poetry offers another genre that is compact but powerful.

POETRY

Poetry pays attention to the otherwise taken-for-granted scenes of young adult life. For example, Tom (Bean, 1970) wrote this free verse piece growing up in Hawai'i near the beach where long walks along the shoreline near Diamond Head offered time to reflect on nature.

Sand Crab

Blending with the seascape

yet rasping defiance at its changing immensity

He tows the Marlboro butt

away from his already crumbling home

In addition to short stories, poetry for young adults is now flourishing like never before. Partly because of the popularity of hip hop culture, the teachers we work with tell us that their teen students look favorably on poetry as a genre they can embrace. The explosion of blogging sites for sharing poetry, open mics, and poetry slams seems to be contributing to poetry's popularity (Albaugh, 2010). Fifty years ago, some 300 literary journals published poetry worldwide. Now, more than 2,000 online websites accept poetry and offer as many as 100 poems-per-issue (Albaugh, 2010). For example, *Poetry Daily* received millions of hits each month, reprinting a poem a day from books and journals.

Free-verse poems have overcome many of the barriers to students' enjoyment of this genre. Indeed, poet Georgia Heard's (2009) chronicle of her work with struggling readers in an 8th-grade urban setting shows the transformational power of poetry writing for urban youth. Heard noted,

One of the reasons to invite poetry into the lives of our students is to meet our invisible guests—grief, joy, anger, doubt, and confusion. We read poetry from this deep hunger to know ourselves and the world. (p. 9–10)

In her work with students in this school site, Heard gets to know a student named Celestino who comes to regard poetry reading and his own free-verse creations as a refuge from the gangs that prowl his neighborhood. Poetry lends itself to a social justice stance, and a number of websites support this effort (Ciardiello, 2010). For example, student poetry dealing with human rights issues can be found at the ePals Global LearningCommunity website: www.epals .com/content/humanrights.aspx.

Multicultural poetry collections like *Cool Salsa: Bilingual Poems on Growing Up Latino in the United States* edited by Lori Carlson (1994) show the double-edged emotions that accompany leaving one's home and first language behind. For example, in Gina Valdez's poem, "English con Salsa," the sardonic voice in the poem notes

> In four months you'll be speaking like George Washington,
>
> in four weeks you can ask, More coffee?
>
> In two months you can say, May I take your order?
>
> In one year you can ask for a raise, cool as the Tuxpan River. (p. 3)

A newer collection of bilingual poems in both Spanish and English, Lori Carlson's (2005) anthology *Red Hot Salsa: Bilingual Poems on Being Young and Latino in the United States* includes some teen poets as well as established figures.

Although written primarily by established authors like Sandra Cisneros and Luis J. Rodriguez, there are also poetry collections that feature up-and-coming teen poets. For example, the short story and poetry anthology we mentioned previously, *When We Were Countries: Poems and Stories by Outstanding High School Writers* (Pawlak, Lourie, & Hershon, 2010), features teen voices and hard scrabble coming-of-age scenes.

Solid Ground edited by Judith Tannenbaum (2006) is another anthology that features strong teen poet voices schooled by English teachers in the San Francisco, California Writers Corp project of the San Francisco Arts Commission. In 16-year-old poet Michelle Vail's poem "This is the Year," she declares hopefully,

One reason to invite poetry into the lives of our students is to give voice and experience to a variety of emotions.

> This is the year that my friends won't die.
>
> They will last as long as the trees reach toward the sky.
>
> There will be no guns or bullets to shoot people in the head. (p. 135)

Other poetry collections featuring young poets include Naomi Shibab Nye's (2010) *Time You Let Me In: 25 Poets Under 25*. Many of the poems deal with diasporas and immigration issues where the authors find themselves not fitting into their homeland or their new home and culture.

In Case 8.1, we look in on Macy Garth's high-school literature class again as her students culminate a poetry unit.

CASE 8.1: Ms. Garth's Students Write Poetry

Ms. Garth has been concluding her poetry unit for the past few years with a culminating activity where her students write, edit, and archive their original poetry in an online anthology. She uses previous class examples to frame this project and encourages her students to incorporate media into their online compositions.

James: Okay, Ms. Garth. I want to write about my neighborhood and all the graffiti on our fences and walls. Some of its colorful murals people have painted to make our neighborhood better.

Ms. Garth: Great, James. Why don't you focus your poem and photos on that? Include how a particular mural looks, what emotions it produces, and take digital photos to go along with your poem.

James: Yeah, I got it. It's going to be good.

Ultimately, James creates a poem around a mural that depicts Latino emigration journeys into the Los Angeles basin from Mexico. Hot and dry with the sun beating down, the characters in the mural are bent over but moving toward California, leaving their homes behind.

In addition to traditional anthologies that feature poetry by or for adolescents, several online resources offer yet another venue for teens interested in having their work read by others. For example, poetry addressing critical human rights issues is flourishing and includes civil rights, ethnic exclusion, and language discrimination. Multimodal digital poems combining text and media including iMovies offer students a powerful medium for tackling human rights issues (Gainer & Lapp, 2010). For example, you can learn more about digital storytelling at the website (www.storycenter.org/cook book.html).

Visual approaches to poetry that involve video creation and production ramp up students' interest in the poetry genre (Stuart, 2010). Websites offer guidance in how to analyze multimedia texts and progress to creating an original project. For example, the ReadWriteThink site that follows provides instruction in how to create an original multimedia project (Stuart, 2010: see) (www.readwrite think.org/lessons/lesson_view.asp?id=1088).

The National Writing Project website (www.nwp.org/cs/public/print/resource/1785) offers numerous articles and teaching ideas for incorporating poetry into your classroom.

In addition, state writing projects like the University of California Irvine Writing Project and others have a wealth of resources, workshops, and university-supported course offerings to support the infusion of student poetry reading and writing.

In the final section of this chapter, we take a look at a genre that serves to balance the serious nature of many young adult coming-of-age novels, short stories, and poems. Humorous novels abound and take the edge off of adolescent life.

HUMOR

"Humor is the Rodney Dangerfield of literary forms: It gets no respect!" notes young adult author and literature analyst Michael Cart (1995, p. 1). Yet scholar Don Nilsen (1993) believed that "Humor is a very important aspect of much of children's and adolescent literature" (p. 262). Despite some teachers' initial reluctance to situate humor as a legitimate genre in literature, Matthew D. Zbaracki (2003) argued for the vital nature of humor in the classroom, especially when engaging reluctant readers: "It is time for humorous literature to receive more respect. **Humor** is a genre that can engage children in reading. It motivates them, requires them to use various reading strategies, and encourages social interaction so they can share what they have read. By combining humorous literature with reading engagement a teacher may reach all readers" (p. 122). Moreover, research by Zbaracki and others suggests that humor may indeed motivate adolescent boys and prevent their disengagement from reading. As a means of promoting reading engagement through humor as well as other genres, Zbaracki and classroom teacher Charlie McCarthy created the website *Educating Zombies* (www.educatingzombies.com). In this cleverly tongue-in-cheek and inviting website, teachers, librarians, administrators, and parents can explore various titles and topics related to keeping readers engaged. In the section that follows, we offer a peek into the website and some of the recommended titles you may find there.

In *No More Dead Dogs* (2002), author Gordon Korman takes a deadly aim at the "heroic dog meets tragic end" genre. Sure to

Humorous literature may increase reading engagement and pleasure.

appeal to teens who resist such sentimentality, the protagonist in this book, Wallace Wallace, has written a hilarious yet unfavorable book report on *Old Shep, My Pal*. Despite the English teacher's displeasure, Wallace will not tell a lie—he hated every minute reading that book! Why does the dog in every classic novel have to die at the end? After refusing to do a rewrite, Wallace is forced to go to the rehearsals of the school production of the book as punishment. Although Wallace does not change his mind, he does end up changing the play into a rock-and-roll rendition.

Author and master of the macabre, David Lubar returns with 35 more warped and creepy tales in *The Battle of the Red Hot Pepper Weenies: And Other Warped and Creepy Tales* (2009). Similarly to the three previous *Weenie* collections—*In the Land of the Lawn Weenies: And Other Misadventures* (2003), *Invasion of the Road Weenies: And Other Warped and Creepy Tales* (2005), and *The Curse of the Campfire Weenies: And Other Warped and Creepy Tales* (2008)—he reveals the inspiration behind each story at the end of the book.

Prolific and popular author Gary Paulsen (2004) uses his experiences as a 13-year-old boy in *How Angel Peterson Got His Name: And Other Outrageous Tales of Extreme Sports*. To stave off boredom and impress girls, Gary and his friends engaged in the following:

- Shooting waterfalls in a barrel
- Breaking the world record for speed on skis by being towed behind a souped-up car, and then . . . hitting gravel
- Jumping three barrels like motorcycle daredevil Evel Knievel, except they only have bikes
- Wrestling . . . . a bear?

This book is sure to appeal to anyone who is 13, has been 13, or had a crush on a 13-year-old.

Although these titles are a tiny sample of titles of various genres that use humor, the website given above as well as resources such as *Best Books for Boys* (Zbaracki, 2008) or websites such as www.boysread.org and author Jon Scieszka's site www.guysread.org will provide you with many more titles as well as strategies for engaging reluctant readers.

Humor is also a common element in romance novels, often serving to defuse tensions around developing relationships and awkward moments. For example, in *A Novel Idea* (Friedman, 2005), Norah, an avid reader, starts a book club where James, her potential boyfriend, remains standoffish, so she decides to act like a heroine in a romance novel. Norah's missteps in this role create an endearing romantic comedy with numerous references to other young adult novels.

Perfect Strangers (Malcolm, 2004) pits classmates Madison and Jeremy running against each other for junior class president. Madison hates Jeremy because, in their freshmen year, he played a nasty prank on her. She talks regularly about Jeremy with her e-pal she has never met, and he seems to really understand her. Of course, as the novel unfolds, they will eventually meet.

Nick and Norah's Infinite Playlist (Cohn & Levithan, 2006) features dual points of view, alternating between Nick's and Norah's voices in a single night as they go to punk clubs to hear music, deal with the ups and downs of friendships, and cope with the growing affection they feel for each other. In another novel with a couple on a road trip home from Oregon to Kansas, *From Bad to Worse: A Novel (with Girls)* (Hafer & Hafer, 2007), characters Griffin and Amanda share their deepest secrets surrounding Griffin's dysfunctional family and his feelings for Amanda, just a friend when they start the drive east.

In a similar, sardonic vein, Sarah Dessen's (2002) *This Lullaby* features Remy, a girl who, on the heels of her mother's multiple marriages, simply does not believe in love. Her cynical view of romance is challenged by a rocker named Dexter, who is in love with Remy for the long haul. Humorous and biting, this popular romance novel is followed by *Lock and Key* (Dessen, 2008).

As suggested by these titles and others that you will encounter, humor is a vital and vibrant means of engaging adolescent readers and should be given the same respect as other genres. Indeed, humor may reach students that were previously disenfranchised from literature and literacy. asks you to visit either www .educatingzombies.com or www.guysread.com to explore how you can use humor in your own classroom.

ACTIVITY 8.3: Professional Reflection and Discussion

With a partner, visit either of the above websites. What resources are available? What titles recommended would you add to your library? Visit the "technology" page on Educating Zombies and talk with your partner about some of the creative uses for integrating technology into the classroom, especially as a means for students to create their own literary works.

MULTIMEDIA TEXT SET

This multimedia text set is drawn from the Educating Zombies website, and many of the books listed can be found directly linked from the website to an Amazon booklist. The aim of this text set is to provide a starting point for developing a collection of books and other texts to engage even the most reluctant reader. As Zbaracki and McCarthy state on their website

> Buy some or even all of the books below this drivel, then put those books on a high shelf in your room (classroom, library, bookstore, conservatory with a wrench . . .), then pull a book from the shelf for a student. Tell them it can't go home because you'd hate to lose it . . . Make sure eavesdropping children are present. Soon you'll have a small cluster of kids begging to borrow your "special" books. (Retrieved May 31, 2012 from http://www.educatingzombies.com/Books.html)

1. Keller, L. (YEAR). *Arnie the doughnut*. New York, NY: Henry Holt.

This is a rather silly story about a doughnut who narrowly escapes his doughnut fate. Arnie is proud to be chocolate covered, with bright-colored candy sprinkles. His first day on the planet is a big one. He is (a) cut into a ring, (b) deep fried, (c) cooled, (d) iced, (e) sprinkled, and (f) named Arnie. What he does not realize is that step (e) is being eaten by a human. So, when a customer, Mr. Bing, starts to put him in his mouth, he screams, "What are you doing?" Arnie is further crushed when he calls the bakery to warn the others only to discover that all the other pastries are aware of this arrangement.

2. Katz, A. (2008). *The flim-flam fairies*. Philadelphia, PA: Running Press Kids.

Say the word "fairies" and it conjures up images of little winged beings made of gossamer and light, exquisitely dressed in shimmering gowns or twirly, little bejeweled skating costumes. Well, you have not met The Flim-Flam Fairies.

3. Moore, A. (1995). *Watchmen*. New York, NY: DC Comics.

This Hugo Award-winning graphic novel chronicles the fall from grace of a group of superheroes plagued by all-too-human failings. Along the way, the concept of the superhero is dissected as the heroes are stalked by an unknown assassin. One of the most influential graphic novels of all time and a perennial bestseller, *Watchmen* has been studied on college campuses across the nation and is considered a gateway title, leading readers to other graphic novels such as *V for Vendetta*, *Batman: The Dark Knight Returns*, and *The Sandman* series.

4. Scieszka, J. (2008). *Knucklehead: Tall tales and almost true stories of growing up Scieszka*. New York, NY: Penguin.

How did Jon Scieszka get so funny, anyway? Growing up as one of six brothers was a good start, but that was just the beginning. Throw in Catholic school, lots of comic books, lazy summers at the lake with time to kill, baby-sitting misadventures, TV shows, jokes told at family dinner, and the result is *Knucklehead*. Part memoir, part scrapbook, this hilarious trip down memory lane provides a unique glimpse into the formation of a creative mind and a free spirit.

5. The Chronicles of Harris Burdick

http://www.youtube.com/watch?v=M3kpYep7EQw&list=PLE0282 62F81694192

Author Lemony Snicket interviews famous children and young adult litera-ture authors about Chris Van Allsburg's book *The Mystery of Harris Burdick* (1981) and their participation in the YA book for which they each wrote a story based on the intriguing illustrations.

6. Brief History of Comic Books

http://www.youtube.com/watch?v=zcgSQ-9AAnI&list=PLE028262F81694192

This short YouTube video offers a brief history of comic books and their place in American literature.

SUMMARY

In this chapter, we considered established genres of young adult literature including short stories, poetry, and humor. We also introduced websites that can support students' reading, discussion, and writing across each of these literary genres.

DISCUSSION QUESTIONS

1. What are some of the criteria for selecting texts in the genres discussed, and how do they relate to Common Core Standards?

2. Consider your own experiences as an adolescent. Was there a book that helped you to relate or cope with events in your life? Why is it important for students to have access to literature that reflect circumstances they may have encountered in their own lives?

3. Thinking of your own or future classroom, how might you use technology to help your students write and "perform" poetry or explore social issues?

4. How can genres such as humor engage disenfranchised readers? Do you see any drawbacks to using humor in the classroom?

KEY TERMS

Humor   159   Short Stories   153

Poetry   156

SMALL GROUP ACTIVITY: TEACHING SHORT STORIES, POETRY, AND HUMOR WITHIN A MULTIMEDIA FRAMEWORK

Directions: Read one of the selections within the genres treated in this chapter (short stories, poetry, and humor). Think about how you would teach this selection through a multimedia framework. Look over the websites listed in the chapter, and create a plan for a two-week unit centered on the genre you have selected. Share this unit in your small group, including assessment approaches.

RECOMMENDED READINGS

Ciardiello, A. V. (2010). "Talking walls": Presenting a case for social justice poetry in literacy education. *The Reading Teacher*, 63(6), 464–473.

This author uses the example of young Chinese immigrants who wrote wall poetry to protest their imprisonment at the Angel Island Detention Center in San Francisco Bay during the early 1900s. The article offers several websites and lists of social justice poetry by Gary Soto and others.

Heard, G. (2009). Celestino: A tribute to the healing power of poetry. *Voices from the Middle*, 16(3), 9–14.

This article features poet Georgia Heard's (2009) chronicle of her work with struggling readers in an 8th-grade urban setting. It shows the transformational power of poetry reading and writing for urban youth.

Stuart, D. H. (2010). Cin(E)-poetry: Engaging the digital generation in 21st century response. *Voices from the Middle*, 17(3), 27–35.

Students can create digital literacy productions that truly capitalize on the rich array of media available including music, color, sound, graphics, and so on.

RECOMMENDED YOUNG ADULT LITERATURE FEATURED IN THIS CHAPTER

Carlson, L. M. (1994). *Cool salsa: Bilingual poems on growing up Latino in the United States*. New York, NY: Fawcett Juniper.

This poetry anthology captures the double-edged emotions that accompany leaving one's home and first language behind. The poems are powerful and offer a model for teen authors interested in chronicling their own transnational lives.

Carlson, L. M. (2005). *Red hot salsa: Bilingual poems on being young and Latino in the United States*. New York, NY: Henry Holt.

A newer collection of bilingual poems in both Spanish and English, Lori Carlson's (2005) anthology includes some teen poets as well as established figures.

Cast, P. C. (2008). *Immortal: Love stories with bite*. Borders Books.

This collection features short stories by the horror genres major authors.

Dessen, S. (2002). *This lullaby*. New York, NY: Viking.

This popular and humorous novel features Remy, a girl who, on the heels of her mother's multiple marriages, simply does not believe in love. Her cynical view of romance is challenged by a rocker named Dexter, who is in love with Remy for the long haul.

Flake, S. G. (2005). *Who am I without him? Short stories about girls and the boys in their lives*. New York, NY: Hyperion.

This short story collection gets at the tensions arising in relationships where the characters' sense of self sometimes gets lost in love. These are realistic accounts of the complex trials of love and longing.

Gallo, D. (Ed.). (1984). *Sixteen: Short stories by outstanding writers for young adults*. New York, NY: Delacorte.

This early short story collection began a wave of new anthologies. Editor Donald Gallo moved the field of short stories for teens in a new direction with this anthology. The stories in this collection remain powerful and engaging.

Gallo, D. (Ed.). (2007). *First crossings: Stories about teen immigrants.* Cambridge, MA: Candlewick.
   These 10 stories get at the heart of teenage diaspora where characters have been wrenched out of the comfort zone of their native language and homeland. Transnationalism is more often than not the norm in our classrooms where students represent multiple ethnicities and languages mixing in a hybrid form of cross-cultural practices.

Hafer, T., & Hafer, J. (2007). *From bad to worse: A novel (with girls).* London, UK: Think.
   Main character Griffin Smith must confront his fragmented family after a trip home from Oregon with his high school sweetheart, Amanda Mac.

Korman, G. 2002. *No more dead dogs.* New York, NY: Hyperion.
   Wallace writes an unfavorable book report of *Old Shep, My Pal* questioning the need for dogs always dying in classic novels, propelling him into a school play on *Old Shep.*

Lubar, D. (2009). *The battle of the red hot pepper weenies: And other warped and creepy tales.* New York, NY: Tom Doherty Associates, LLC.
   In this macabre collection, the father of a girl who does not have a date for a school dance makes one in his laboratory and each of the titles that follow feature twisted tales.

Lubar, D. (2003). *In the land of the lawn weenies: And other misadventures.* New York, NY: Starscape.

Lubar, D. (2005). *Invasion of the road weenies: And other warped and creepy tales.* New York, NY: Starscape.

Lubar, D. (2008). *The curse of the campfire weenies: And other warped and creepy tales.* New York, NY: Starscape.

Mazer, A. (1993). *America street: A multicultural anthology of stories.* New York, NY: Persea Books.
   Older multicultural short story collections like this one continue to offer powerful pictures of families struggling with new social mores as they immigrate to the United States. This collection features well-known authors including Langston Hughes, Lensey Namioka, and Gary Soto, along with stories capturing the challenges of leaving one's homeland and grappling with new and often disturbing cultural norms.

Nye, N. S. (2010). *Time you let me in: 25 poets under 25.* New York, NY: Greenwillow.
   This collection features young poets reacting to a host of cultural and ethnic issues. Many of the poems deal with cultural displacement and immigration issues where the authors find themselves not fitting into their homeland or their new home and culture.

Paulsen, G. (2004). *How Angel Peterson got his name: And other outrageous tales of extreme sports.* New York, NY: Yearling.

Pawlak, M., Lourie, D., & Hershon, R. (Eds.)., (2010). *When we were countries: Poems and stories by outstanding high school writers*. Brooklyn, NY: Hanging Loose Press.

The fourth in this series of anthologies features teen voices and issues of coming of age, living and caring for aging grandparents, special moments with a mom or dad, and accentuating the taken-for-granted moments in daily life. This collection can serve as a model for teen short story and poetry writing aimed at real audiences.

Soto, G. (1990). *Baseball in April and other stories*. San Diego, CA: Harcourt Brace.

This early multicultural short story collection for teens offers ethical dilemmas that lend themselves to discussion. Characters are immersed in situations where multiple choices are possible.

Tannenbaum, J. (2006). *Solid ground*. San Francisco, CA: Aunt Lute Books.

This teen poet anthology features strong teen poet voices schooled by English teachers in the San Francisco, California, Writers Corp project of the San Francisco Arts Commission. Poems deal with gang violence, homelessness, immigration issues, and a host of other topics relevant to urban teens.

Van Allsburg, C. (1981). *The mysteries of Harris Burdick*. New York, NY: Houghton Mifflin.

RECOMMENDED WEBSITES

Young Adult Books

Teen Libris: Your Link to Teen Lit, www.teenlibris.com, offers reviews, interviews, book lists, and a forum and blog for book discussion.

Young Adult Short Stories

Another site, www.authors4teens.com, includes prominent young adult authors being interviewed by Donald Gallo. The site displays authors' biographical information, lists of their works, and other material.

Young Adult Literary Magazines and Online Resources

An excellent website for learning about *Hanging Loose* a literary magazine that regularly includes teen's creative writing alongside established authors, http://hangingloosepress.com

Young Adult Poetry Resources

Student poetry dealing with human rights issues can be found at the ePals Global Learning Community website: www.epals.com/

The National Writing Project website offers numerous articles and teaching ideas for incorporating poetry in your classroom. The site can be found at the following URL: www.nwp.org/cs/public/print/resource/1785

Young Adult Multimedia Resources

Learn more about digital story telling at the following website: www.storycenter.org/cookbook.html

The ReadWriteThink site that follows provides instruction in how to create an original multimedia project (Stuart, 2010): www.readwritethink.org/lessons/lesson_view.asp?id=1088

Other resources encompassing video poetry include www.bloomingtonlibrary.org/see_&d_do/videos

REFERENCES

Albaugh, D. (2010, February 6). The new math of poetry. *The Chronicle Review*, B12–B14.

Bean, T. W. (1970). *Strays*. Hilo, HI: Sandwich Island Printing.

Cart, M. (1995). *What's so funny? Wit and humor in American children's literature.* New York, NY: Harper Collins.

Ciardiello, A. V. (2010). "Talking walls": Presenting a case for social justice poetry in literacy education. *The Reading Teacher*, 63(6), 464–473.

Cohn, R., & Levithan, D. (2006). *Nick and Norah's infinite playlist.* New York, NY: Knopf.

Dessen, S. (2008). *Lock and key.* New York, NY: Viking.

Friedman, A. (2005). *A novel idea.* New York, NY: Simon & Schuster/Simon Pulse.

Gainer, J., & Lapp, D. (2010). *Literacy remix: Bridging adolescents' in and out of school literacies.* Newark, DE: International Reading Association.

Heard, G. (2009). Celestino: A tribute to the healing power of poetry. *Voices from the Middle, 16*(3), 9–14.

Malcolm, J. (2004). *Perfect strangers.* New York, NY: Simon & Schuster/Simon Pulse.

Nilsen, D. (1993). *Humor scholarship: A research bibliography.* Westport, CT: Greenwood Press.

Stuart, D. H. (2010). Cin(E)-poetry: Engaging the digital generation in 21st century response. *Voices from the Middle, 17*(3), 27–35.

Zbaracki, M. D. (2003). *A descriptive study of how humor in literature serves to engage children in the reading* (Unpublished dissertation). The Ohio State University, Columbus.

Zbaracki, M. D. (2008). *Best books for boys: A resource for educators.* Westport, CT: Greenwood.

Chapter 9

Nonfiction, Biographies, Information, and Self-Help

Nonfiction material for young adults spans a huge array of titles that can accommodate virtually any interest. Self-help books, informational websites, blogs, editorials, nature writing, sports, travel, medicine, science, fashion, how-to books, and magazines are just a few examples of this voluminous genre. *Biographies* continue to flourish and capitalize on teens' interest in other people's lives and possible futures. In this chapter, we touch on just a few of the titles available in this genre and suggest other resources you may want to consult.

Learning Objectives

- Understand the criteria for selecting texts in the genres discussed and how they relate to Common Core Standards.

- Consider and be able to discuss the ways in which students can use nonfiction genres to explore issues in their lives, communities, and world.

- Develop an understanding of various response strategies to use with students as they engage in nonfiction works.

- Know how to guide students in their use of a wide variety of nonfiction texts (including those available on the Internet) to determine trustworthy and valid sources.

- Continue to create a database of young adult literature that includes the genres discussed in this chapter.

Vignette: Michael Taack's Middle School Classroom

Students in Mr. Taack's class come to this urban middle school from many different neighborhoods, in some cases where poverty renders school a refuge from crowded conditions and gang-infested streets. Nestled in the old part of a southwestern city, Mr. Taack's students are predominantly from proud, hard-working Latino immigrant families. His class has a significant number of English Language Learners (ELLs). Mr. Taack views nonfiction and biographies as a way to tap students' interests. Before engaging students in writing their own autobiographies and reading biographies, he has them create their own graphic biography in the form of a pie chart depicting their lives and interests (Capacchione, 2008). The idea for this assignment came from a book on journal writing titled, *The Creative Journal for Teens,* by art therapist, Lucia Capacchione. This book combines art and writing in ways students find exciting and interesting. Their pie chart becomes a vehicle for writing an **autobiography** in draft form to be peer edited and developed into a larger term portfolio of their work.

Following an introduction to autobiography and biography using an example from an online biography of Latino young adult author and poet Gary Soto in the *Encyclopedia of World Biography* (www.notablebiogra phies.com/news/Sh-Z/Soto-Gary.html), Mr. Taack models the "My Life as a Pie" activity using his own life as a graduate student, dad, and husband. Once his students have a good grasp of the process, he gives them time to create their own autobiographical pie charts. Students indicate in a short essay why they have selected particular colors for their chart composition and what each color represented. The completed pie charts formed the basis for more extensive autobiographical writing and for reading **biographical essays** of young adult nonfiction and author biographies like that of Gary Soto.

Figure 9.1 shows Michael Medina's autobiographical pie chart and his essay on what each color represents.

Michael's essay explains his rationale for each section of the pie and its particular color. (Reprinted with permission.)

FIGURE 9.1

Source: Michael Medina.

My Life as a Pie

Blue: Blue represents friends! I chose blue because it's my second favorite color and its for friends. Blue is bigger than every slice in my pie excepy for family because mv family is more important than my friends. Some of my friends are Ricky, Ever, and Elijah.

Pink: *Pink represents music. I chose pink cause pink was one of the last colors there was. Pink is smaller than all the others except places because I spend more time listening to music than I do going to places like California. One of my favorite bands is Job for a Cowboy.*

Yellow: *Yellow represents School. I chose yellow because it's my third favorite color and it's for School. Yellow is the third biggest piece in the pie because that's where I see most of my friends and I allways have a great time at school. The best thing that I like to do at school is play guitar in Mariachi.*

Purple: *Purple represents family. I chose purple because its my favorite color and its for family. Family is the biggest piece on the pie because my family is the most important thing to me ever. My family members are Rufina (mom), Juan (dad), Arlet, Marilyn, and Adali.*

Orange: *Orange represents hobbies. I chose orange because it's my fifth favorite color and it's for hobbies. Hobbies is the fifth biggest piece because it's what I do when I'm bored and it really gets me going. Some of my hobbies are playing guitar and drawing.*

Brown: *Brown represents places. I chose brown because its my least favorite color and its for places. Places is the least biggest piece in the pie because I really never spend time traveling. Some of the places I've been to are Utah and California.*

Red: *Red represents sports. I chose red because red is my fourth favorite color and it's for sports. Sports is my fourth biggest piece in the pie because I love to do sports and I love to be active. Some of the sports I love to do are Skateboarding, and Football.*

Mr. Taack uses a **rubric** to evaluate each student's creation, and then he guides his students into reading autobiographies and biographies as a prelude to writing their own. The fact that this writing flowed from students' rich experiential lives helped get them excited about reading other people's stories, particularly those that describe struggles, hardship, and overcoming adversity.

Common Core Standards

The following standards are addressed in this chapter.

RI.6.1-10.1 Cite textual evidence to support analysis of what the text says explicitly as well as inferences drawn from the text.

RI.6.2-10.2 Determine a central idea of a text and how it is conveyed through particular details; provide a summary of the text distinct from personal opinions or judgments.

(Continued)

(Continued)

RI.6.3-10.3 Analyze in detail how a key individual, event, or idea is introduced, illustrated, and elaborated in a text (e.g., through examples or anecdotes).

RI.7.7 Compare and contrast a text to an audio, video, or multimedia version of the text, analyzing each medium's portrayal of the subject (e.g., how the delivery of a speech affects the impact of the words).

RI.7.8 Trace and evaluate the argument and specific claims in a text, assessing whether the reasoning is sound and the evidence is relevant and sufficient to support the claims.

RI.7.9 Analyze how two or more authors writing about the same topic shape their presentations of key information by emphasizing different evidence or advancing different interpretations of facts.

RI.8.7 Evaluate the advantages and disadvantages of using different mediums (e.g., print or digital text, video, and multimedia) to present a particular topic or idea.

RI.8.8 Delineate and evaluate the argument and specific claims in a text, assessing whether the reasoning is sound and the evidence is relevant and sufficient; recognize when irrelevant evidence is introduced.

RI.8.9 Analyze a case in which two or more texts provide conflicting information on the same topic and identify where the texts disagree on matters of fact or interpretation.

RI.9-10.4 Determine the meaning of words and phrases as they are used in a text, including figurative, connotative, and technical meanings; analyze the cumulative impact of specific word choices on meaning and tone (e.g., how the language of a court opinion differs from that of a newspaper).

RI.9-10.5 Analyze in detail how an author's ideas or claims are developed and refined by particular sentences, paragraphs, or larger portions of a text (e.g., a section or chapter).

RI.9-10.6 Determine an author's point of view or purpose in a text, and analyze how an author uses rhetoric to advance that point of view or purpose.

RI.11-12.4 Determine the meaning of words and phrases as they are used in a text, including figurative, connotative, and technical meanings; analyze how an author uses and refines the meaning of a key term or terms over the course of a text (e.g., how James Madison defines faction in Federalist No. 10).

RI.11-12.5 Analyze and evaluate the effectiveness of the structure an author uses in his or her exposition or argument, including whether the structure makes points clear, convincing, and engaging.

RI.11-12.6 Determine an author's point of view or purpose in a text in which the rhetoric is particularly effective, analyzing how style and content contribute to the power, persuasiveness, or beauty of the text.

WORKING WITH ESTABLISHED GENRES OF YOUNG ADULT LITERATURE

Both nonfiction and biography genres have award-winning titles available. In this chapter, we profile a few of these selections and indicate where others may be found. Although the mainstream bookstores and online resources like Amazon and Barnes and Noble can be useful, we recommend considering your particular teaching context as well as your students' backgrounds and interests. Your school media specialist can be especially helpful in searching topics and titles in this wide-ranging genre.

As a way to get started on your exploration of nonfiction and biography, Activity 9.1 asks you to interview another person in your class to inventory his or her particular nonfiction and biography reading experiences.

ACTIVITY 9.1: Professional Reflection and Discussion

Directions: Interview another class member about his or her reading experiences and preferences in nonfiction and biography. List the specific titles mentioned, and then exchange roles and include your own titles and preferences in nonfiction and biography. Share these lists in small groups and consider how you, as a teacher, might accommodate a range of interests that your students are likely to express.

NONFICTION

How do we define nonfiction? At its most basic level, **nonfiction** is prose writing about real people and their experiences. However, Bonnie S. Sunstein (2010) takes a nuanced view of nonfiction, noting,

> I define nonfiction writing as simply this: the mix of art, craft, and information, put together by writers who let readers know they are interested in a topic, and who speculate about what that interest might mean. (p. 13)

When you search nonfiction titles, the best writing in this genre often taps what has gone unnoticed in accounts of famous people and events. For example, Charles Darwin's theory of evolution published in *The Origin of*

The best writing in the nonfiction genre often taps what has gone unnoticed in other accounts of people and events.

Species in 1859 is an integral part of the history of science. However, Darwin's romance with his religious wife Emma and the tensions that surrounded his devotion to science go unnoticed. In The National Book Award Finalist selection, *Charles and Emma: The Darwins' Leap of Faith* (2009) author Deborah Heiligman takes the reader into the private lives of the Darwins to explore how the couple negotiated profound differences in their beliefs about human origins amid a life-long loving relationship:

All the observations he made—on himself, his children, the animals And plants around him—were in service to his theory of natural selection. Looking at each organism he studied, he tried to work out how that species had been formed. He always thought, too, about the objections people would raise. (p. 121)

Darwin's wife Emma read his drafts against her foundation of religious beliefs, offering a counterpoint to his theories without damaging their close bond.

As you begin searching and reading nonfiction selections, we recommend considering the following criteria. High-quality nonfiction does the following:

- Explores in depth the taken-for-granted accounts of people and events
- Offers the reader new insights and experiences for discussion
- Avoids clichés and simplistic conclusions
- Is believable and credible
- Is engaging

Several media accounts of war in the Middle East casually use the terms *democracy* and *freedom*. But these taken-for-granted terms take on a more nuanced meaning when the reader's lens looks through the eyes of a teenager living in a war zone (Bean & Harper, 2006). In the nonfiction selection, *Thura's Diary: My Life in Wartime Iraq* (Al-Windawi, 2004), we gain an insider's understanding of the gut-wrenching days and nights that accompanied the fall of Saddam Hussein's regime. Thura is a 19-year-old Iraqi student living in Baghdad. At the onset of war and the closure of her college, she notes in her diary,

Last night we didn't sleep. The air was full of fumes from the bombs. My head was on the pillow but I was not comfortable inside the room. Sleeping together, there is no space and we were all looking around and listening for each bomb. How far away are they? How near? It makes me terrified, always thinking, am I going to live or am I going to die? (p. 65)

Topics in nonfiction stretch to the horizon and should depend, in part, on your particular teaching context. As you engage students in responding to young adult nonfiction, consider the following guidelines (Lamb, 2010):

- Draw the reader's attention to the author's purpose for writing a selection (e.g., to inform, persuade, or sell something)
- Consider the period and social context of the writing (e.g., a war zone, a high school in the United States, or an urban or rural setting)

A number of possible response approaches are available (Lamb, 2010) You can have your students do the following:

- Keep a reflective journal
- Write a letter to the author
- Write a dialogue with the author taking an opposing viewpoint
- Write an annotation summarizing the work

If you decide to have your students do annotation writing based on their reading of a nonfiction selection, then you may want to consult the ReadWriteThink website on "Teaching Student Annotation: Constructing Meaning Through Connections" (www.readwritethink.org/lessons/lessons-view.asp?id=1132).

In addition to the rich annotation guidelines offered in the ReadWriteThink material, you may want to consider a four-part annotation approach called "iREAP" (Manzo, Manzo, & Albee, 2002). This approach can be used with traditional print-based nonfiction and the increasingly widespread array of e-books and online nonfiction.

Essentially, iREAP is an acronym denoting a four-part annotation that progresses hierarchically from a simple rendering of the author's message to a critical reading of the author's motives for writing the piece. For example, the following informational nonfiction paragraph describes how to sail a windsurfing board upwind. The article was posted online with a photo of the author tacking a windsurfer to windward. The informational text and an example of iREAP annotations follow.

SAILING UPWIND

Just like a sailboat, a windsurfer cannot sail directly into the wind. You must go upwind in a zigzag fashion with your sail close hauled near your body and the mast angled back a bit. When you tilt the mast toward the tail of the board, the board's nose edges farther into the wind, increasing your ability to go at an angle that maximizes your movement toward your intended goal. My custom windsurfing boards are designed to sail close to the wind and be very fast off the wind. You can order one of my custom boards at: VegasDude.com but be prepared to pay more than the factory pop-out boards most people buy.

The four iREAP annotation types that can be used to deconstruct and respond to this short online nonfiction piece are as follows (Manzo et al., 2002):

R = Read to get the authors message

E = Encode the message in your own words while reading

A = Annotate your analysis of the message by writing a summary response

P = Ponder the author's motivation to write this piece (persuade, sell something, argue a position) and critique the author's position by choosing to agree or disagree with it.

Here's an example of a student's iREAP annotation for this online passage:

I am a windsurfer and, while I agree with the instructions for sailing upwind, the process is a lot more complicated than simply moving the sail to the correct position. You have to hook yourself into the wishbone shaped boom and make constant adjustments for the wind velocity and water conditions. The board matters a bit but it's really the foil of the sail that creates a center of effort force as the energy travels through your body to the board. So, while I agree with some of the instructions offered by this author, much more is needed. Frankly, this looks like a hook to get readers to think about buying one of the author's custom windsurfing boards. Without endorsements and testimony from users of this equipment and comparisons to other boards, we really don't know if this product is worth the money (about twice the cost of a conventional factory mold produced board).

Critical reading of nonfiction material whether in traditional print form or online is crucial. Indeed, Manzo et al. (2002) noted that iREAP is designed to help students "think more precisely and deeply about what they read" (p. 43). Modeling this process initially will help your students develop a critical stance in their reading of nonfiction that should transfer to other sources they read.

As you search for high-quality nonfiction sources, websites like the American Library Association's (ALA's) annual Best Books for Young Adults (www.ftrf.org/ala/mgrps/divs/yalsa/booklistsawards/bestbooks) and the ALA's Young Adult Reading List should be helpful.

In addition to online informational material, the history subcategory of nonfiction features a rich array of sources. For example, *Far From Home: Latino*

Baseball Players in America (Wendel & Villegas, 2008) chronicles the history of Latino baseball players and their communities.

The stories of war survivors are chronicled in *War Is . . . Soldiers, Survivors, and Storytellers Talk About War* (Aronson & Campbell, 2008). This collection includes interviews, stories, memoirs, and blogs offering multiple perspectives on war.

Middle Ground: Exploring Selected Literature From and About the Middle East (Finkle & Lilly, 2008) is yet another collection that provides students with a richer understanding of people in this region. Lesson plans are included with this collection to engage students in critical discussion.

In addition to nonfiction material geared for average and above-average readers, a number of high-interest, low-vocabulary selections are available for struggling/striving readers in your classroom. For example, Hampton-Brown's *Edge Series* (National Geographic, 2010) includes nonfiction selections leveled to accommodate students' needs. Similarly, Artesian Press offers several titles organized by themes (e.g., natural disasters). These books are typically short (60 pages) but maintain the appearance of a longer, novel-sized paperback. For example, within the Natural Disaster Series, Anne Schraff's (2004) *Earthquakes* uses examples of devastating quakes to introduce the Richter scale. In the nonfiction selection *Fashion* (Schraff, 2006), the author traces the history of fashion and styles of dress from prehistoric times to the present.

Biography is another genre category that captivates students' interests in how other people cope with challenges. Magazines like *Teen People* capitalize on the general interest in celebrities, heroes, and fallen heroes. In the next section, we explore this genre and consider some of the selections that you may want to use with your students.

BIOGRAPHIES

Biographies offer students a window on difference and diversity (Singer & Shagoury, 2006). These often compelling accounts of others' lives give your students insight into multiple perspectives on issues that are meaningful to adolescents. The life trajectories of famous people give students a sense of possible futures. For example, actor Michael J. Fox's (2010) short autobiography, *A Funny Thing Happened on the Way to the Future,* traces his journey to full-time acting from a less than stellar, and ultimately incomplete, high school experience:

> In the outright creative subjects (drama, music, creative writing, other art electives, drawing, painting, and printmaking) I'd bring home A's. But any subject based on fixed rules, like math or chemistry or physics, sent my grades into free fall. (p. 20)

Finding his way as an actor occurred partly because of a special mentor and advocate, providing readers with a sense that one cannot go it alone and life's mentors are important. Michael J. Fox noted, "Gary David Goldberg who, in his role as creator and executive producer of *Family Ties*, rescued me from poverty, plucked me from obscurity, and in many ways, helped to prepare me for the challenges and opportunities I never saw coming" (2010, p. 87).

As you think about selecting autobiographies and biographies for your students, consider the following advice from Donelson and Nilsen (2005, p. 269): "For biographies to ring true, the author must become immersed in the subject's life so that he or she can write with passion and commitment." The criteria for selecting high-quality biographies parallel that for nonfiction; it must ring true and be an authentic rendering of the subject's life.

Case 9.1 illustrates a way to introduce your students to autobiography and biography readings by starting with students' unique voices and experiences.

CASE 9.1: Phyllis Olana's 9th-Graders' Autobiographical Writing

Ms. Phyllis Olana has her 9th-graders engage in an autobiographical writing assignment before they begin reading biographies about people who, through their social justice activism, changed the world. She begins with a focus on students' language, including dialects, native language, and Internet forms of communication like texting (text messages). Phyllis learned about this approach and its related online lesson plan in a professional development workshop in her district. Her students represent multiple native languages and cultures, including Spanish, Hawai'ian, and Filipino.

The huge volume of biographies available for your students is both exciting and daunting.

Issues of language and identity can be explored through an activity using author Amy Tan's autobiographical essay "Mother Tongue." In a ReadWriteThink lesson developed by teacher Renee Shea, Amy Tan talks about writing stories in "All the Englishes I grew up with." This lesson can be found on the ReadWriteThink website (www.readwrite think.org/classroom-resources/lesson-plans/exploring-language-identity-mother-910.html).

Phyllis begins by brainstorming with her students the various languages her students use.

Phyllis: Let's talk about some of the different languages we use.

Milan: Texting! I got that down.

Kawika: Dakine pidgin! Dats how I like talk!

Grace: Tagalog. I talk to my Manong that way.

Phyllis: Okay, those are some good examples. We're going to read an essay by author Amy Tan called "Mother Tongue" where she talks about "All the Englishes I grew up with." Then we will write in our journals about a time when someone viewed you a certain way, either positively or negatively, based on your language. Our diverse languages say a lot about us, who we are, and how we feel. It's a good way to start thinking about biography before you choose a specific biography to read and discuss.

As her students begin reading their chosen biography, Phyllis introduces them to an online resource called *Bio Maker: The Biography Maker* (http://bellingham schools.org/department-owner/curriculum/bsd-bio-maker-biography-maker). This resource guides students through a step-by-step process for writing a biography, and Phyllis wants her students to pair up and create classroom biographies based on what they learn about other class members using their biography reading as a model for this activity.

The huge volume of biographies available for your students is both exciting and daunting. We profile a few titles in the following section, and more can be found at the American Library Association site and commercial sites like Amazon and Barnes and Noble.

Well-known author Mark Twain's (Samuel Clemens's) travels and adventures are chronicled in *The Trouble Begins at 8: A Life of Mark Twain in the Wild, Wild West* (Fleishman, 2008). Biographies and autobiographies illuminate literary figures and the hidden elements of their lives in ways not possible in typical expository textbook summaries.

African American author Walter Dean Myers's (2002) autobiography, *Bad Boy: A Memoir,* takes the reader into the author's home in Harlem in the 1940s during his high school years. He did poorly in school while secretly reading literature at home, fighting rival gang members, and finally dropping out of high school to enlist in the Army. Writing was Walter Dean Myers's way out of poverty and despair, ultimately leading to a huge catalog of award-winning young adult works.

INFORMATION

Informational books and online resources cover virtually every subject imaginable including health, science, sports, the arts, technology, and so on. Informational books should be the following:

- Easily searchable
- Up-to-date
- Include research notes and additional informational resources (e.g., websites)
- Feature attractive layout and design elements that support reader comprehension
- Feature friendly, readable writing

Case 9.2 provides an example of a self-selected informational book on a famous Hawai'ian big wave surfer and North Shore (O'ahu-lifeguard) Eddie Aikau.

CASE 9.2: Phil Frank's Middle School Reading Class With Struggling Readers and Self-Selected Readings

Students in Mr. Phil Frank's middle school reading class can self-select books from their various hobbies and athletic interest areas to read and develop posters representing elements of the book they select. Mr. Frank teaches reading with a focus on struggling readers in a rural Hawai'ian middle school located on Kauai.

In this case, one of Mr. Frank's students, Phillip Jardine, was an avid Hawai'ian surfer, competing in contests at Hanalei Bay on the windward side of Kauai. He was very interested in surfing's history, and he was fully immersed in learning the

Hawai'ian language as part of the island's Hawai'ian immersion program. He heard about a surfer named Eddie Aikau who was lost at sea on a 1978 maiden voyage of the Hokule'a double canoe when it swamped in the Molokai Channel. Eddie volunteered in the middle of the night to paddle toward the island of Molokai for help in windy conditions in large seas amid one of the most treacherous channels in the world.

Eddie was a powerful North Shore surfer and lifeguard at Waimea Bay, a renowned big wave spot on O'ahu. Phillip, an 8th-grader was reading at a 4th-grade level and struggling with textbook material in his content area classes. Mr. Frank used students' self-selected books to help them learn reading strategies that would improve their comprehension and potentially transfer to other reading assignments.

Phillip chose a Hawai'ian/English bilingual book about Eddie Aikau titled *We Called Him Ryon: The Story of Eddie Aikau* (2010). The book was written by Jonathan A. Ibanez, a student at St. Anthony's Junior-Senior High School in Wailuki, Maui. The author was the winner of the 2010 annual Eddie Aikau Essay Contest. The book is a high-interest, low-vocabulary account of Eddie's bravery that could partner with the advanced reading biography *Eddie Would Go: The Story of Eddie Aikau, Hawaiian Hero* (Coleman, 2001). Phillip's dad had this book and surfed with Eddie during the Hawai'ian Surfing Association North Shore contest days in the 1960s. The book Phillip selected about Eddie is written at a 3rd-grade level with striking illustrations by Big Island artist and Hawai'ian language immersion teacher Henani Enos. At 96 pages, this chapter book appeals to struggling readers interested in surfing heroes. Phillip devoured the book and created a large poster of Eddie Aikau paddling in huge waves to save his friends on the floundering Hokule'a. The informational book genre is huge and easily searchable on the Internet.

For example, if students are interested in other uses for French fries, they can consult green inventor Greg Melville's (2008) *Greasy Rider: Two Decades, One Fry-oil-powered Car, and a Cross-country Search for a Greener Future.*

Students interested in the stars might select Camille Flammarion's (2010) *Astronomy for Amateurs* or, for a trip back in technology time, Michael Woods and Mary B. Woods' (2011) *Ancient Communication Technology: Sharing Information with Scrolls and Smoke Signals.* Other books about the natural world include the 2009 American Library Association Robert F. Siebert

Informational Award Honor Book, *Bodies from the Ice: Melting Glaciers and the Recovery of the Past* (Deem, 2008), describing frozen mummies from around the world with striking photos.

The category of informational books is voluminous, and we would urge you to tap into students' diverse interests, use the American Library Association awards, and search Amazon.com for an extensive array of captivating books. In addition to this nonfiction collection, the category of self-help books is equally voluminous and appeals to adolescents' interest in relationships, dieting, coping with family issues, and a host of other topics that fall under this label.

SELF-HELP

Numerous series aimed at the teen self-help market have been around for some time. Using buzz words like "effective," "successful," "chicken soup for the (fill-in) soul," and so on, this category aims to offer teens advice and mentoring to avoid pitfalls related to diet, drugs, finances, relationships, sex, drinking, and other addictions. Often written by physicians, psychologists, religious leaders, and professors, many of these books do offer step-by-step guidelines for surviving life's challenges.

Like informational books, self-help books should be the following:

- Easily searchable
- Up-to-date
- Include research notes and additional informational resources (e.g., websites)
- Feature attractive layout and design elements that support reader comprehension
- Feature friendly, readable writing
- Offer strategies for change

A few titles are mentioned here, and many more problem-specific titles can be located online and in commercial bookstores. For example, *You Don't Have to Learn Everything the Hard Way* (Saul, 2007) offers specific teen advice on making choices, dealing with failure, drug and alcohol abuse, and nurturing healthy relationships.

In a more recent book, Josh Shipp's (2010) *The Teen's Guide to World Domination: Advice on Life, Liberty, and the Pursuit of Awesomeness* adopts a more contemporary tone while offering critical life advice. Helping teens navigate their social spheres is taken up by Michelle Garcia Winner and Pamela Crooke (2011) in *Socially Curious, Curiously Social: A Social Thinking Guidebook for Bright Teens & Young Adults.*

Other books like *The Young Adult's Guide to Breaking Food Addiction: Recover from Emotional Eating Today* (2012) address common coping addictions in teens including anorexia and other issues. Therapists and social workers are other good sources of potential titles that offer coping strategies for teens trying to survive cancer, family break-ups, bullying, and a host of other life challenges.

Self-help texts offer coping strategies for teens trying to survive a host of life challenges.

MULTIMEDIA TEXT SET

In this text set, we return to Mr. Frank's classroom to further explore the resources available when using informational text. Although this set focuses on the life of Eddie Aikau, it can be used as a model for other sets on a variety of topics.

1. Ibanez, J. (2010). *We called him Ryon: The story of Eddie Aikau.* Honolulu, HI: One Voice Publications and the Eddie Aikau Foundation.

This book was written by Jonathan A. Ibanez, a student at St. Anthony's Junior-Senior High School in Wailuki, Maui. The author was the winner of the 2010 annual Eddie Aikau Essay Contest. The book is a high-interest, low-vocabulary account of Eddie's bravery.

2. Coleman, S. H. (2001). *Eddie would go: The story of Eddie Aikau, Hawaiian hero.* Honolulu, HI: Mind Raising Press.

This biography offers an in-depth look at the life of Eddie Aikau. Deeply engaging and moving, this biography will captivate adolescent readers.

3. Lyman-Mersereau, M. (2008). *Eddie Wen' Go: The story of the upside-down canoe.* Honolulu, HI: Watermark Publishing.

In this picture book, one of Eddie's crew members, Marion Lyman-Mersereau, imagines what may have happened after Eddie left that fateful night. Although it is not an informational text, it provides a creative counterpoint to the biographies listed previously.

4. *Eddie's Day* (2010).

In this brief documentary of the 25th Annual Quicksilver Eddie Aikau Event at Waimea Bay, surfers from around the world, including Eddie's brother Clyde, talk about what it is like to surf one of the most famous spots in the world.

5. Peralta, S. (Director). (2004). *Riding giants* [Motion picture]. United States: Sony Pictures Classics.

Riding Giants is a superb documentary on the history of big wave surfing, directed and co-written by Stacy Peralta. It is a dynamic account of the history of the surfing subculture, starting centuries ago, but focusing on the past 55 years, which saw surfing explode into mainstream culture and become extraordinarily athletic and increasingly daring.

SUMMARY

Nonfiction selections, biographies, information, and self-help books abound in print and online forms. In this chapter, we examined nonfiction and its application in the English classroom. Criteria for selecting high-quality nonfiction were offered, along with titles and approaches to teaching nonfiction (e.g., iREAP, journals, and summaries). Autobiographies and biographies were introduced with example titles and teaching approaches that capitalize on Internet resources. In addition, we considered the voluminous array of information and self-help books for teens.

DISCUSSION QUESTIONS

1. What are the criteria for selecting texts in the genres discussed, and how do they relate to Common Core Standards?

2. Reflecting on your own or future classroom, what are some ways your students can use nonfiction genres to explore issues in their lives, communities, and world?

3. Of the various response strategies presented, which would you use with students as they engage in nonfiction works? What other response strategies might also be appropriate?

4. As you guide your current or future students in their use of a wide variety of nonfiction texts (including those available on the Internet), how will you help them develop criteria for evaluating trustworthy and valid sources?

KEY TERMS

Autobiography 170

Biography 177

Biographical Essay 170

Nonfiction 173

Rubric 171

SMALL-GROUP ACTIVITY: YOUNG ADULT NONFICTION AND BIOGRAPHY ANNOTATED BIBLIOGRAPHY

Directions: In your small group, brainstorm some young adult nonfiction topics or potential young adult biographies you would like to explore. Have your group members search for high-quality titles, read a few, and annotate at least three titles you can share with your group to create an annotated bibliography of nonfiction and biography resources for your classroom. Compile your combined annotated bibliography in an online list.

RECOMMENDED READINGS

Bean, T. W., & Harper, H. J. (2006). Exploring notions of freedom in and through young adult literature. *Journal of Adolescent & Adult Literacy, 50* (2), 96–104.

This article troubles simplistic notions of freedom and several nonfiction and fiction young adult selections set in the Middle East and other war zones. In addition, the article includes a critical literacy teaching framework for guiding student discussion of nonfiction and fiction selections.

Capacchione, L. (2008). *The creative journal for teens: Making friends with yourself* (2nd ed.). Pompton, NJ: New Page/Career Press.

Authored by an art therapist, this book combines drawing and writing in ways students find exciting. As an alternative to traditional journal writing, it offers English teachers a powerful resource to explore with students.

Lamb, M. R. (2010). Teaching nonfiction through rhetorical reading. *English Journal, 99* (4), 43–49.

The author offers a number of reader response strategies for nonfiction that range from a response journal to annotation and summary writing. Each one is carefully illustrated, and additional teaching resources are offered.

Manzo, A., Manzo, U., & Albee, J. J. (2002). iREAP: Improving reading, writing, and thinking in the wired classroom. *Journal of Adolescent & Adult Literacy*, *46* (1), 42–47.

The authors provide a step-by-step process to engage students in critical reading of material, including online nonfiction. The process encourages deep reading and a careful examination of an author's motives for writing a piece.

Singer, J., & Shagoury, R. (2006). Stirring up justice: Adolescent reading, writing, and changing the world. *Journal of Adolescent & Adult Literacy*, *49* (4), 318–339.

This article includes an extensive listing of biographies of people who changed the world for the better, for example, the Dalai Lama, Helen Keller, Martin Luther King, and others.

Sunstein, B. S. (2010). Tucking pigeons up your sleeve: Ten personae teach one nonfiction course. *English Journal*, *99* (4), 13–21.

This article offers one of the best discussions of nonfiction teaching we have encountered. The author moves beyond simplistic definitions of nonfiction to offer an interesting account of contemporary essayists and personalized writing in this genre. This particular themed issue of the *English Journal* is devoted to nonfiction teaching and writing.

RECOMMENDED YOUNG ADULT LITERATURE FEATURED IN THIS CHAPTER

Al-Windawi, T. (2004). *Thura's diary: A young girl's life in war-torn Baghdad*. New York, NY: Puffin.

This account traces the onset of war in Baghdad from the perspective of an Iraqi citizen, Thura, a 19-year-old college student. Ultimately, she flees the city for the United States and a chance to continue her college studies. Her diary traces this journey away from the bombings and strife in her homeland.

Aronson, M., & Campbell, P. (2008). *War is . . . soldiers, survivors, and storytellers talk about war*. New York, NY: Candlewick Press.

This collection offers multiple perspectives on war including memoirs, interviews, and blogs.

Atlantic Publishing Group. *The young adult's guide to breaking food addiction: Recover from emotional eating today*. (2012). Ocala, FL: Atlantic.

This comprehensive look at unhealthy approaches to food includes compulsive eating, the role of the brain in this process, food addiction as an unhealthy stress reducer, and various eating disorders. Most importantly, the guide offers specific, doable strategies for change.

Coleman, S. H. (2001). *Eddie would go: The story of Eddie Aikau, Hawaiian hero*. Honolulu, HI: Mind Raising Press.

This is a superb biography of Eddie Aikau, a famous but humble Hawai'ian big wave surfer and North Shore lifeguard. Eddie lost his life trying to paddle for help in the stormy Molokai Channel after the voyaging canoe Hokule'a was swamped in the night amid driving winds and large ocean swells.

Deem, J. M. (2008). *Bodies from the ice: Melting glaciers and the recovery of the past*. Boston, MA: Houghton Mifflin Co.

Melting alpine glaciers are unearthing corpses and clues to the Earth's ancient past. In one of these discoveries, a 5,300-year-old man, now called Otzi, was found. This book takes the reader into the archeological exploration of glaciers and the clues they are revealing to our past.

Edge Series (2010). Washington, DC: Hampton-Brown and National Geographic.

This series includes nonfiction selections leveled to accommodate students' needs. The selections are from major young adult authors, and support material is included.

Finkle, S. L., & Lilly, T. J. (2008). *Middle ground: Exploring selected literature from and about the Middle East*. Urbana, IL: National Council of Teachers of English.

Numerous lessons and materials are included with this collection cutting across nonfiction and films aimed at developing students' understanding of geopolitical issues in a global society.

Flammarion, C. (2010). *Astronomy for amateurs*. Memphis, TN: General Books, LLC.

This famous volume provides detailed descriptions of the constellations and a host of other topics for students interested in astronomy.

Fleishman, S. (2008). *The trouble begins at 8: A life of Mark Twain in the wild, wild, west*. New York, NY: Green Willow Press/HarperCollins.

This biography traces the adventures of young author Samuel Clemens (aka Mark Twain) as he journeys from coast to coast.

Fox, M. J. (2010). *A funny thing happened on the way to the future*. New York, NY: Hyperion.

Well-known actor Michael J. Fox offers readers a short autobiographical look at his journey from reluctant high school student to struggling actor, to major star and advocate for Parkinson's disease patients. Witty and light, Fox's writing is easily accessible for teens.

Heligman, D. (2009). *Charles and Emma: The Darwins' leap of faith*. New York, NY: Henry Holt.

This account of Charles Darwin and his wife Emma takes the reader into the couple's home to witness the at times thorny debates surrounding their very different notions of evolution. The relationship is enduring, despite their differences.

Ibanez, J. (2010). *We called him Ryon: The story of Eddie Aikau*. Honolulu, HI: One Voice Publications and the Eddie Aikau Foundation.

This bilingual Hawai'ian/English chapter book was written by 8th-grade Maui student Jonathan Ibanez for an essay contest sponsored by the Eddie Aikau Foundation. Centered on the ill-fated 1978 voyage of the double sailing canoe, Hokule'a, the book will appeal to struggling readers interested in surfing and voyaging culture.

Myers, W. D. (2002). *Bad boy: A memoir*. New York, NY: Amistad.

This contemporary biography takes the reader into the author's home in Harlem in the 1940s during his high school years. He did poorly in school while secretly reading literature at home, fighting rival gang members, and finally dropping out of high school to enlist in the Army.

Saul, L. A. (2007). *You don't have to learn everything the hard way*. Denver, CO: Kadima Press.

This powerful self-help book is based on the author's background in applied psychology and adolescents' requests for advice on sensitive topics including drugs, sex, peer pressure, abuse, and other tough topics young adults must face.

Schraff, A. E. (2004). *Earthquakes*. Buena Park, CA: Artesian Press.

This short (60-page) book is designed to accommodate reluctant and struggling readers' interests. This is one nonfiction title that is part of a larger, thematic emphasis on natural disasters. Other titles include

Schraff, A. E. (2006). *Blizzards (natural disaster)*. Buena Park, CA: Artesian Press.

Schraff, A. E. (2004). *Wildfires*. Buena Park, CA: Artesian Press.

Schraff, A. E. (2004). *Tornadoes (natural disaster)*. Buena Park, CA: Artesian Press.

Schraff, A. E. (2004). *Hurricanes and floods (natural disaster)*. Buena Park, CA: Artesian Press.

Schraff, A. E. (2006). *Fashion*. Buena Park, CA: Artesian Press.

The author traces the history of fashion and styles of dress from prehistoric times to the present. As part of the eXtreme Custom Series, this title traces fashion from prehistoric times to the present. Other titles include *Tattoos*, *Food*, and *Body Modification*.

Shipp, J. (2010). *The teen's guide to world domination: Advice on life, liberty, and the pursuit of awesomeness*. New York, NY: St. Martin's Griffin.

This engaging self-help book by renowned speaker Josh Shipp takes on bullies, phonies, negative influences, and addictions with humor and helpful strategies for change.

Wendel, T., & Villegas, J. L. (2008). *Far from home: Latino baseball players in America*. New York, NY: National Geographic.

This book chronicles the history of Latino baseball players in the United States with attention to Latino communities.

Winner, M. G., & Crooke, P. (2011). *Socially curious, curiously social: A social thinking guidebook for bright teens & young adults.* Great Barrington, MA: North River Press.

The authors offer teens practical strategies for navigating their social worlds including dating, texting, and engaging in caring relationships.

Woods, M. B., & Woods, M. (2011). *Ancient communication technology: Sharing information with scrolls and smoke signals.* Minneapolis, MN: Twenty-First Century Books.

This book looks at the communication vehicles in ancient times including smoke signals, scrolls, painting, writing systems, and early libraries with an eye toward the evolution and dynamic nature of communication.

RECOMMENDED WEBSITES

American Library Association's annual Best Books for Young Adults: http://www.ftrf.org/ala/mgrps/divs/yalsa/booklistsawards/bestbooks

Bio Maker: The Biography Maker: http://bellinghamschools.org/department-owner/curriculum/bsd-bio-maker-biography-maker

This resource guides students through a step-by-step process for writing a biography.

ReadWriteThink: Teaching student annotation: Constructing meaning through connections: http://www.readwritethink.org/lessons/lesson-view.asp?id=1132

ReadWriteThink: Lesson by Renee Shea on Amy Tan's "Mother Tongue": http://www.readwrite think.org/classroom-resources/lesson-plans/exploring-language-identity-mother-910.html

REFERENCES

Bean, T. W., & Harper, H. J. (2006). Exploring notions of freedom in and through young adult literature. *Journal of Adolescent & Adult Literacy, 50*(2), 96–104.

Capacchione, L. (2008). *The creative journal for teens: Making friends with yourself* (2nd ed.). Pompton, NJ: New Page/Career Press.

Darwin, C. (1859). *The origin of species.* London, UK: John Murray.

Donelson, K. L, & Nilsen, A. P. (2005). *Literature for today's young adults* (7th ed.). Boston, MA: Allyn & Bacon.

Lamb, M. R. (2010). Teaching nonfiction through rhetorical reading. *English Journal, 99*(4), 43–49.

Manzo, A., Manzo, U., & Albee, J. J. (2002). iREAP: Improving reading, writing, and thinking in the wired classroom. *Journal of Adolescent & Adult Literacy, 46*(1), 42–47.

Singer, J., & Shagoury, R. (2006). Stirring up justice: Adolescent reading, writing, and changing the world. *Journal of Adolescent & Adult Literacy, 49*(4), 318–339.

Sunstein, B. S. (2010). Tucking pigeons up your sleeve: Ten personae teach one Nonfiction course. *English Journal, 99*(4), 13–21.

Chapter 10

Comics, Manga, Graphic Novels, Zines, and Street (Urban) Literature

In this chapter, we consider and challenge more traditional notions about genres and the literary canon. Indeed, we argue that contemporary text forms offer interesting bridges to the traditional literary canon or the classics. *Comics, manga, graphic novels, zines,* and *street literature* all offer engaging forms of literature that appeal to a wide range of students. In particular, we examine contemporary forms of young adult literature and the influences of digital literacies and rapidly evolving text forms offered in cyberspace. In general, we observe these newer text forms coexisting with older, traditional print forms and offering students unparalleled opportunities to develop intertextual connections across a broad range of texts.

Learning Objectives

- Understand the evolving nature of texts and the ways in which genre lines may "blur" with older, more traditional texts, especially as they relate to the Common Core Standards.

- Consider and be able to discuss the importance of students having access to contemporary literature especially in relationship to canonical texts.

- Develop an understanding of the nature of contemporary forms of young adult literature such as zines and street literature and the ways they have given voice to marginalized groups.

- Know how to use the variety of genres presented in this chapter to engage disenfranchised/marginalized readers.

- Continue to create a database of young adult literature that includes the genres discussed in this chapter.

Vignette: Victoria Mancini's American Literature Class

Victoria Mancini's American literature class includes an emphasis on various historical contexts. In the example that follows, she has her students self-select a particular comic book superhero and research its origins using local bookstores, the media center, Internet resources, and interviewing family members who may have read a particular superhero comic in the past.

Mrs. Mancini walks over to one of the small groups to see how they are doing with this assignment.

Mrs. Mancini: Okay, Phillipe, you said that you plan to gather information about your superhero, Silver Surfer. What have you found out so far?

Phillipe: A lot on the Internet, but I also found a book at Barnes and Noble that talks about when this comic started. It got started in 1966. I had no idea it was that old. Now there are films and video-games based on the comic.

Mrs. Mancini: That's great because your particular superhero is one of the less well-known ones compared to Superman and Wonder Woman, but there is a Hollywood film out as well. How do you plan to share this information with your other small group member?

Phillipe: I want to create a slide show using Photostory to narrate the show and display transitions.

Common Core Standards

The following standards are addressed in this chapter:

RL.6.9, 7.9 Compare and contrast texts in different forms or genres (e.g., stories and poems; historical novels and fantasy stories) in terms of their approaches to similar themes and topics.

RL.8.2, 9-10.2 Determine a theme or central idea of a text, and analyze its development over the course of the text, including its relationship to the characters, setting, and plot; provide an objective summary of the text.

RL.8.3, 9-10.3 Analyze how particular lines of dialogue or incidents in a story or drama propel the action, reveal aspects of a character, or provoke a decision.

RL.9-10.5 Analyze how an author's choices concerning how to structure a text, order events within it (e.g., parallel plots), and manipulate time (e.g., pacing and flashbacks) create such effects as mystery, tension, or surprise.

RL.11-12.6 Analyze a case in which grasping a point of view requires distinguishing what is directly stated in a text from what is really meant (e.g., satire, sarcasm, irony, or understatement).

WORKING WITH CONTEMPORARY GENRES OF YOUNG ADULT LITERATURE

The position statement of the International Reading Association's Adolescent Literacy Commission advanced several principles aimed at improving instruction for teenage readers (Moore, Bean, Birdyshaw, & Rycik, 1999; Sturtevant et al., 2006). One of the most important principles supports the use of a variety of text forms with adolescents. Specifically, "[a]dolescents deserve access to a wide variety of reading material that they can and want to read" (Moore et al., 1999, p. 4). More recently, the adolescent literacy policy document *Reading Next* noted that the use of diverse texts constituted one of the "promising elements of effective adolescent literacy programs with a substantial base in research and/or professional opinion" (Biancarosa & Snow, 2006, p. 12).

Adolescents' out-of-school leisure reading interests cut across a wide spectrum of genres (Smith & Wilhelm, 2002). In an effort to get a better picture of adolescents' leisure reading habits, researchers queried 584 urban minority middle school students (Hughes-Hassell & Rodge, 2007). Students in this study were mainly Latino and African American with 86% of the students in this school setting qualifying for free or reduced-cost lunches. The reading scores at this school were among the lowest in the district. Nevertheless, when students were asked to describe their out-of-school leisure reading habits, 72% of the students said they enjoyed reading as a leisure activity in the evening and on weekends. In terms of genre preferences, both males and females indicated a strong preference for magazines over traditional books. However, 69% of these students reported reading more than two books each month outside of school. Girls often read material offering new fashion tips, and boys looked to hip hop artist profiles. Within the magazine-related genre, sports, videogames, and music information topped the list for boys. Girls sought out music magazines, videogame information, and fashion or beauty tips. Comic books were also popular with these students, while books accounted for about a third of their reading material. Importantly, students' main sources of reading material were the school library, the public library, and the classroom. Because print-based materials like books and magazines can be costly, these students looked to free resources, but 43% of this group visited bookstores, particularly Spanish–English bookstores in their local neighborhood.

The authors of this study suggested that magazines be better represented in school library settings, particularly magazines like *Black Beat*, *Jet*, *Latina*, *Slam*, *Urban Latino*, and others (Hughes-Hassell & Rodge, 2007). Comics also need to be featured more, particularly for reluctant readers as many have

The boundaries between traditional and contemporary genres sometimes blur as a result of multiple forms of text.

DVD support with additional artwork and large character text. Graphic novels and manga were also high on these students' list of preferred leisure reading materials. Graphic novels consist of book-length stories published in a comic-book style with short sentences and substantial visual cues that help struggling readers. Manga consists of stylized characters based on Japanese print conventions, sometimes in black and white. Each of these text forms is engaging for urban adolescent readers with good support for selecting graphic novels offered by the *School Library Journal, Booklist,* and *Voice of Youth Advocates.* Clearly, genre categories continue to evolve and expand to include multimedia forms of text heavily supported by visuals. More is discussed about graphic novels and Internet text forms later in this chapter.

As newer forms of text develop and constitute new genres within young adult literature, the boundaries between traditional and contemporary genres sometimes blur. For example, much like a Web Quest, novels can easily send a reader on a web-based journey, similar to the older Choose Your Own Adventure Series books that offered multiple pathways to reading and navigating a story. Contemporary students are accustomed to channel switching across multiple text forms including their cell phone text messages, MP3 files, and more static, print-based material. Thus, like all category systems, genres are a social construct, in constant flux. As we explore genres, we consider gender issues and other driving forces that influence reader interest and engagement. Naturally, wild generalizations are not helpful as we consider reading preferences. Adolescents as individuals have diverse interests that resist and challenge simplistic recommendations (Alvermann et al., 2007).

Canonized, well-known genres currently coexist with an ever-evolving array of new genres that challenge older notions of who can author a work and how it gets distributed. For a fairly sophisticated look at these expanding genres of young adult literature, we call on work by Gunther Kress (2003). In a brief history of the term *genre,* Kress noted it means "kind" and it has historical roots in Aristotle's approach to distinguishing major literary forms (e.g., epic, tragedy, and so on). Genre also served to distance high-culture forms from popular or low-culture forms.

Today, these divisions are fast disappearing, and a contemporary view of genre reflects this more socially grounded stance. For example, Kress viewed contemporary genres from a literacy-as-social practice point of view. Although he recognized the value of learning more traditional genres, Kress raised several important questions at the heart of emerging and often student-authored genres. For example, "[a]re the genres which are most powerful in a society to be taught in preference to others?" (Kress, 2003, p. 85). And, "[a]re the genres of marginal groups—whatever the reasons for their marginality—also to be included in the curriculum?" (p. 85). What genres might fit into this category?

We explore various examples of contemporary genres including long-standing examples like comics that now include manga and graphic novels, as well as "street" literature with its connection to African American hip-hop culture (Young, 2006). Each of these expanding genres is well represented in mainstream bookstores (Beach, 2007). For example, if you visit a Barnes and Noble store, you are likely to find multiple rows of manga based on the Japanese comic form that is read back to front. Kress (2003) observed that we are already in a period in which many of the formerly stable genres are morphing into hybrid forms where categories blend and merge.

During this exciting time for young adult literature and its related genres, the potential to engage students in reading across a wide array of entry points has never been better. It simply means thinking about ways to integrate new media and traditional texts in creative ways, and we will have more to say about various response strategies in future chapters (e.g., Photostory). Activity 10.1 asks you to consider your own experiences with contemporary genres of young adult literature.

ACTIVITY 10.1: Professional Reflection and Discussion

Directions: Take a moment to brainstorm your own encounters with contemporary forms of young adult literature (e.g., manga, zines, and street literature). Share these titles with others in your small group to continue developing a resource list you can use with your students. Share the list in a wiki with others or via Google documents to integrate everyone's ideas.

Many young adult novels blend elements of diary, court transcripts, and instant messaging to take the reader into otherwise hidden dimensions of characters' lives. In addition, authors may include website URLs that direct the reader to online material related to the novel. For example, the popular Scholastic series *The 39 Clues* (Riordan, 2008) includes a website where middle school readers can ferret out keys to the Cahill family mystery (www.the39clues.com).

The whole notion of how a work of literature is written now also includes issues of design that encompass visual layout, ancillary material (e.g., a website or video clip), and other multimodal elements used to communicate with a reader/viewer. Thus, a contemporary definition of genre offered by Kress (2003) noted that "Genre is a social category: [I]t is made by people in their social encounters, and when it has become text it gives us insight into the make-up of the social world in which it was made" (p. 100).

Underlying all of this natural tension surrounding traditional and emerging genres is creativity and the tendency for new text forms to break down barriers from the past. Comics, long a staple in teen reading, offer a good example of how this long-standing genre has morphed into very contemporary forms.

COMICS

Comic books have been a mainstay in adolescents reading since their inception in 1896 and the 1930s onset of Action Comics including *Superman* (Bucher & Manning, 2006). Because comic books are visually engaging with film versions that are hugely popular (e.g., *Spiderman, Wonder Woman,* and others), they offer a great way to hook adolescent readers into exploring story lines, character development, visual design analysis, and, ultimately, the creation of their own comics in various forms. Apple's Comic Life and other websites offer online resources to construct original comic story frames (Beach, 2007). Comic Life can be found on the Apple website, and it supports creating and publishing original comic book frames and stories to iWeb. It offers an excellent student resource for expanding on students' natural interest in reading comics and developing their own creativity.

The Comic Book Project (Bitz, 2004) guided students through the process of writing, drawing, and producing their own comic books (www.comic bookproject.org). Students' comics are then featured on a website art gallery for others to read and enjoy.

Lesson plans incorporating comics are archived and available through the ReadWriteThink website co-sponsored by the International Reading Association and the National Council of Teachers of English. For example, *The Comic Book Show and Tell* website offers students a window on commercial comic book creators that illustrates how a comic is developed (Reid, 2007). This website, created by lesson author James Carter, has a wealth of resource material and related standards to incorporate the use of comic books in the classroom. Using the website, students then have an opportunity to revise original scripts on the website URL (www.readwritethink.org/lessons/lessons_view.asp?id=921).

In addition, a related link to Comic Books for Young Adults offers an excellent listing of comics by age and interest level, as well as those that would appeal to students based on gender. The link can be accessed through the Comic Book Show and Tell website.

Leisure reading across various text forms outside of school, including comics and magazines that appeal to adolescents, has been shown to increase reading achievement in vocabulary, reading comprehension, verbal fluency, and content knowledge (Hughes-Hassell & Rodge, 2007). Comics continue to reign, along with magazines, as the favored out-of-school reading material for teens with Marvel and other publishers offering DVD collections that include original comic book art (Hughes-Hassell & Rodge, 2007).

More recently, comics are viewed as nicely aligned with notions of multimodal literacy necessary for complex, contemporary reading in both print and online environments (Jacobs, 2007). Comic pages unfold in multiple panels where readers must make inferential connections across panels to construct meaning. These multimodalities include "images of people, objects, animals, and settings, word balloons, lettering, sound effects, and gutters all come together to form page layouts that work to create meaning in distinctive ways and in multiple realms of meaning making" (Jacobs, 2007, p. 21). For example, a comic book author's use of line and white space, as well as what objects are central (e.g., a pirate ship) in an opening panel, may signal elements of plot and forward movement in the story. These multimodal features, along with narration and dialogue, are all open to class discussion within the comic genre.

In teaching with comics, Jacobs (2007) recommended helping students develop their knowledge of linguistic, audio, visual, gestural, and spatial conventions to deconstruct the underlying "grammar" of this genre. He noted that "By teaching students to become conscious and critical of the ways in which they make meaning from multimodal texts such as comics, we can also teach students to become more literate with a wide range of multimodal texts" (p. 24).

Comics are merely one form of visually stimulating story material amid many evolving forms. Manga is closely related to the comic book in its layout, with multiple panels, white space, and elements common to traditional comic book structures (Xu, Perkins, & Zunich, 2005). Case 10.1 is based on a university young adult literature class where the instructor asks his students to go to a local bookstore and explore the features of manga that stand out for them (e.g., reading from back to front).

CASE 10.1: Avery Monroe's Classroom and Manga

To introduce his students to manga, teacher Avery Monroe takes his students on a field trip to the school media center where they spend time in the stacks looking at manga selections. Norene, one of Mr. Monroe's students, gravitates toward a manga titled, *Future Diary* (Esuno, 2008). This is new territory for Norene, and she is captivated by this novel. Daryl locates *Fullmetal Alchemist* (Arakawa, 2009) with its action-packed pages. Both students sign out these books and quickly become hooked on these serial stories, anxiously awaiting the next installments.

MANGA

Going to the local bookstore and library will also reveal a wealth of titles with multiple shelves devoted to this popular genre.

Manga is a Japanese word denoting amusing drawings, and indeed, manga are comic book like in their appearance and layout (Schwartz & Rubinstein-Avila, 2006). While related to its Japanese and very popular animated cartoon anime cousins (e.g., *Dragon Ball Z*), manga is print based and more closely related to the format of graphic novels with its familiar book look. Manga may lead to related film-based and video-game spin-offs, and anime also feeds the development of related manga in reciprocal fashion (Schwartz & Rubinstein-Avila, 2006). Much like comics, accomplished manga reading requires a multimodal approach that is sensitive to various font and script styles, as well as to the interplay between text and visual elements. Unlike reading in traditional Western text, Japanese manga needs to be read in a right-to-left, back-to-front fashion. In addition, even this convention gets disrupted in manga's hypertext design (Schwartz & Rubinstein-Avila, 2006). Manga occupies a powerful niche in the United States with growing sales, shelf space in major bookstores, and a format that requires sophisticated reading skills consistent with the demands of reading Internet websites. In addition, gender is treated more fluidly than in Western comics (Schwartz & Rubinstein-Avila, 2006).

A good way to get a sense of the vast array of manga available to students is to ask students interested in this genre about particular titles they read. Going to the local bookstore and library will also reveal a wealth of titles with multiple shelves devoted to this popular genre. Many of the manga offerings are in series that follow characters on their journey with the books numbered in the series. For example,

Red River Vol. 10 (Shinohara, 2005), finds Yuri, a Japanese school girl, magically transported to the ancient Hittite empire where she is rescued by the handsome but arrogant Prince Kail. However, problems arise when Queen Nakia, an evil sorceress, seeks her son's succession to the throne. Much like a medieval knight's tale, swords and jousting spears coexist with brief, romantic interludes. The vocabulary is rated with a symbol on the book indicating it is for the older teen and the dialogue is peppered with polysyllabic words (e.g., "investigation") well supported by visual images.

Rebirth Vol. 20 (Woo, 2006) is a violent quest against evil with the action taking place in the vampire lord's tournament fortress where Rett, one of the good guys, attempts to assist Deshwitat in a duel with the evil Mr. Grey. This action-packed manga fantasy appeals to teen boys. Because this manga was published in the United States, it is set up to read front to back for Western readers. At the end of the story, author Kang-Woo Lee sketches a brief cartoon commentary to his fans, commenting on problems with his health and smoking, assuring his millions of readers that he is on the mend.

Subgenres of manga focus on audience dimensions that differentiate manga for boys (*shonen;* e.g., *Rebirth*) and girls (*shojo;* e.g., *Red River*) with competitive sports a focal point for boys' manga and other more technologically based stories. Girls' manga, while still dealing with love and romance, also balances a difficult blend of the strong and powerful female with compliant caretaker responsibilities in the family (Schwartz & Rubinstein-Avila, 2006). In the classroom, manga offers much the same venue for critique and analysis mentioned by Jacobs for comic books. This is especially true for the inequities noted with respect to male and female depictions in manga. For additional resources, Adam Schwartz and Eliane Rubenstein-Avila (2006) recommended consulting Gilles Poitras's website on manga and anime (www.koyagi.com).

GRAPHIC NOVELS

Graphic novels offer readers an extended, comic art form that resembles the typical length of a young adult novel (Beach, 2007). Generally running from 100 to 200 pages, graphic novels are available on a variety of topics and genres including the classics, nonfiction historical accounts, historical fiction, science fiction, fantasy, and political satires and critiques. The edited book *Building Literacy Connections with Graphic Novels: Page-by Page, Panel by Panel* (Carter, 2007) is a great teacher resource on using graphic novels in the English classroom. Each chapter offers guidance in pairing award-winning graphic novels with the classics as a natural, multiple text bridge that supports students' interest in visual media. For example, well-established graphic novels like Spiegelman's (1996) *The Complete Maus: A Survivor's Tale* takes the reader into the world of a Polish–Jewish ghetto during World War II. This Pulitzer Prize-winning account is an excellent resource for units in world history.

Similarly, *Persepolis: The Story of a Childhood* (Satrapi, 2003) is a powerful autobiography of a young girl growing up in Tehran, Iran, during the Islamic revolution of 1979. Reading this novel alongside other thematically related novels like Graham Salisbury's (2005) *Eyes of the Emperor* with Eddie Okubo's account of Japanese American soldiers during the attack on Pearl Harbor allows for powerful, intertextual connections about the conditions of war, racial discrimination, and other social justice issues (Harris, 2007). Graphic novels that critique stereotyping like *Fagin the Jew* (Eisner, 2003) can be read as a counterpoint to anti-Semitism in Charles Dickens's *Oliver Twist* (Webb & Guisgand, 2007). The graphic novel *Malcolm X: A Graphic Biography* (Helfer & Duburke, 2006) can be paired with Malcolm X's original work or excerpts from this account.

In addition to these more serious graphic novels, a host of other graphic novels can be found on Amazon.com and the American Library Association websites. These range from science fiction, to superhero offerings like *Firestorm: The Nuclear Man-Reborn* (Moore, Champagne, & Igle, 2007) where superhero Firestorm must prevent a deadly nuclear accident using atomic forces, to series graphic novels like *Puffin Graphics: Dracula* (Reed & Cloonan, 2006).

The American Library Association also features annual lists of recommended graphic novels for adolescents (www.ala.org/yalsa/booklists). The next form of young adult contemporary literature seeks to critique and satirize societal problems and issues while avoiding commercial exploitation.

ZINES

Zines and e-zines are handmade publications centered on the unique interests of their creators. Often made with scissors and glue, these publications satirize, critique, or entertain the reader by providing unique views of contemporary topics. In electronic form, e-zines capitalize on desktop publishing software and the Internet for distribution.

Zines, along with their related forms (e.g., blogs or weblogs and podcasts), are a form of social commentary. For example, zines can range from treatises about lost pets, teen angst and love, problems with drugs and alcohol, the environment, racism, and other issues (Jacobi, 2007). While often in the form of out-of-school productions, zines can connect to school-based projects in English class, and they may offer an interesting reader response form to young adult novels.

In an innovative use of zines, Jacobi (2007) saw an opportunity to link community literacy practices with in-school composition curriculum. Because zines are iconoclastic and exist outside mainstream canonical texts, it is crucial not to domesticate this individualistic form of commentary. Jacobi noted that "As countercultural artifacts, they are often situated in direct opposition to canonical literature and dominant discourse and work to celebrate difference through multigenre creative expression" (p. 44).

Zines have enjoyed a long history, initially as fanzines in the 1930s and merging with underground political movements in the 1960s and 1970s (Jacobi, 2007). Often written by teenage girls in protests surrounding **homophobia**, dieting, rape, and other issues, zines can serve democratic purposes (Guzzetti & Gamboa, 2004). The Zine Project developed by Jacobi combined a writing workshop approach to zine creation with students in a college upper division writing course offering guidance to community groups (e.g., Boys and Girls clubs) interested in doing writing that is not necessarily academic in nature. Issues of homelessness, poverty, and health care are all community-based topics of interest to teen zine writers. In essence, zines provide a critical space to challenge pat assumptions about teens and communities. A valuable resource where The Zine Project author Tobi Jacobi discusses how to use zines in and out of the classroom can be found online (www.readwritethink.org/lessons/lesson_view.asp?id=915).

Other expanding genres include a growing body of street literature from non-mainstream authors addressing gritty life stories set in urban contexts. Although well outside mainstream young adult literature, this body of work is, like the popular A-list books, gaining an enthusiastic audience of adolescent girl readers.

STREET LITERATURE

Street literature consists of a body of work featuring powerful African American female characters actively resisting abuse and the controlling behaviors of their male counterparts. If you visit your local chain bookstore and go to the African American literature section, you will encounter street literature nestled amid classic authors like Langston Hughes. Street literature has a close affinity with hip hop culture and its often gritty, in-your-face vibe. Street literature (or "street lit") is often the product of grassroots self-taught writers, self-publishing their works. It is important to note that this is a rough, counterpoint literature that has parallels with the work of multicultural young adult authors like Sharon Flake, Walter Dean Myers, and Matt de la Pena, among others.

Students should consult multiple sources to provide several resources across these genres.

Street lit authors' novels deal with violence, sex, and survival in the ghetto. For example, well-known early titles in this genre include *Project Chick* (Turner, 2002) and *Thugs and the Women Who Love Them* (Clark, 2004). Much like the A-list books discussed in Chapter 4, street lit lends itself to discussion and critique. Main characters are young African American women usually lorded over by powerful African American men. These women struggle with a strong desire to detach themselves from abusive power relationships, and themes of escape and street survival underpin each of the novels. Often read outside of school, this emerging genre seems to be very popular with African American girls. Indeed, mainstream bookstores have picked up on the popularity of street lit with African American teens, and since early 2000, a growing array of titles is emerging.

As you search for young adult novels in various genres, we recommend consulting multiple sources including regular book review columns like that of James Blasingame (2007) in the *Journal of Adolescent & Adult Literacy*, as well as online sources like the American Library Association, International Reading Association, National Council of Teachers of English, and other websites. One strategy that works for us, given the sheer volume of novels coming out each year, is to consult the most recent work by an author, read it, and work backward to the earlier works. We also receive great leads on new works from other teachers and attending conferences where authors are featured (e.g., International Reading Association and the National Council Teachers of English conventions).

MULTIMEDIA TEXT SET

This multimedia text set was constructed by classroom teacher Grace Yi. It uses poetry, comic books, and informational texts and websites to expand on and further explore teen issues such as those in Sharon Flake's (2005) *Who Am I Without Him? Short Stories About Girls and the Boys in Their Lives*. In the following, Grace shares her multimedia text set and her rationale for including the sources for the set.

I tried to choose my text set based on a variety of perspectives including a Latin American perspective. I also think a theme about my text set is the power of your voice and the importance of having one and treating each other fairly.

1. Carlson, L. M. (1994). *Cool salsa: Bilingual poems on growing up Latino in the United States*. New York, NY: Fawcett Juniper.

This book is about growing up Latino in America and how that means speaking two languages and essentially living two lives. It celebrates this double life.

2. Duffy, D. (2010). *Black comix: African American independent comics, art and culture*. Brooklyn, NY: Mark Batty.

This is a collection of comics from African American artists. Japanese and American artists have largely dominated the world of comics, until now. This book is a great starting point to finding out more about comics created from an African American perspective.

3. Holyoke, N. (2001). *A smart girl's guide to boys*. Middleton, WI: Pleasant Company.

The great part about this book is that its focus is not on dating. Although it is a guide to boys, it focuses mostly on the inner girl and gaining your own independence. *Who Am I Without Him?* (Flake, 2005) is geared toward girls and giving them a voice. This book does something similar and is written just for girls. This book also has comic-book graphics, friendly fonts, and colors that teens could appreciate.

4. Macavinta, C. (2003). *Respect: A girl's guide to getting respect & dealing when your line is crossed*. Minneapolis, MN: Free Spirit Publishing.

This book helps empower teen girls and helps them attain and hold on to the respect they deserve. The book includes tips, activities, writing exercises, and quotes from real teens. This book has a splashy, magazine-style layout that has lots of pictures.

5. www.brainpopjr.com/health/besafe/bullying/
www.brainpop.com/socialstudies/culture/bullying/preview.weml

This brainpop video is about bullying, and I believe that my students could make a connection to this now, before gender divides and gender-based opinions take over. There is a brainpopjr version of this video as well, which approaches children from the viewpoint of someone who does not have any clue what bullying is. I want to expose my students to bullying so that they know the difference between right and wrong. Finally, the video advertises that students will find out about when it's right to confront the person who's bullying you, and who you can talk to if you need an adult to intervene.

6. www.teenink.com/

This is a website to give teens a voice. This is a literary magazine and website for teens. There are eight major categories that this magazine includes poetry, fiction, nonfiction, celebrity interviews, opinion, reviews, art/photos, and college articles. The articles are written by teens and voted and ranked by users. I think older students would enjoy going on this website and finding out what other teens are writing about.

SUMMARY

This chapter began with a discussion of research and findings about adolescents' reading preferences. The chapter then explored contemporary genres, including (a) comics, (b) manga, (c) graphic novels, (d) zines, (e) street literature, and (f) sources of contemporary young adult literature and the ways in which each speak to the literate lives of adolescents today.

DISCUSSION QUESTIONS

1. In what ways do you see genre lines "blur" between contemporary young adult literature discussed here with older, more traditional texts? How can you use canonical and contemporary young adult literature to meet the requirements of the Common Core Standards?

2. Consider your current or future classroom. How will you integrate the genres discussed in this chapter into your curriculum? Do any seem more challenging than others? Why?

3. How can you incorporate contemporary forms of young adult literature such as zines and street literature to engage disenfranchised/marginalized readers?

4. Discuss how you would justify the use of contemporary young adult literature such as graphic novels and zines to parents and administration at your school website?

KEY TERMS

Graphic Novels   199   Street Literature   201

Homophobia   201   Zines   200

SMALL-GROUP ACTIVITY: EXPLORE ONE OF THE WEBSITES IN THIS CHAPTER AND JIGSAW THE CONTENTS

Directions: Select one of the websites listed in this chapter (e.g., Comic Life) and become familiar enough with it that you can share its key features and teaching possibilities in a jigsaw small group session with other class members. How would you use this material in the classroom, integrated with more traditional young adult literature?

RECOMMENDED READINGS

Beach, R. (2007). *Teaching media literacy.com: A web-linked guide to resources and activities.* New York, NY: Teachers College Press.

This resource book spans contemporary topics including digital media literacy, visual literacies, and multiple, expanding genres. Most importantly, this 133-page book features teaching recommendations incorporating critical literacy dimensions teachers and their students can use to view and construct films, comics, graphic novels, and so on.

Carter, J. B. (2007). *Building literacy connections with graphic novels: Page by page, panel by panel.* Urbana, IL: National Council of Teachers of English.

This book is a great teacher resource on using graphic novels in the English classroom. Each chapter offers guidance in pairing award-winning graphic novels with the classics as a natural, multiple text bridge that supports students' interest in visual media.

Harris, M. (2007). Showing and telling history through family stories in *Persopolis* and young adult novels. In J. B. Carter (Ed.), *Building literacy connections with graphic novels: Page by page, panel by panel* (pp. 38–53). Urbana, IL: National Council of Teachers of English.

This author provides a wealth of examples on how to pair graphic novels with young adult literature, particularly historical novels surrounding issues of war and displacement.

Hughes-Hassell, S., & Rodge, P. (2007). The leisure reading habits of urban adolescents. *Journal of Adolescent & Adult Literacy, 51* (1), 22–33.

These authors conducted a study aimed at determining the leisure reading interests and habits of 584 urban minority middle school students. In addition to charting students' views about leisure reading, the authors offer recommendations for teaching, particularly with respect to the use of magazines, the Internet, and developing genres like manga.

Jacobi, T. (2007). The Zine Project: Innovation or oxymoron? *English Journal, 96* (4), 43–49.

This author argues that zines are unique forms of democratic communication ideally suited for critiquing social practices in community settings. As highly iconoclastic, individually created publications, these handmade creations offer a strong counterculture look at a variety of topics including drug addiction, poverty, health care, and so on. Issues of social difference including racism, homophobia, extreme dieting, and other often ignored community topics can be taken up in the zine genre.

Schwartz, A., & Rubinstein-Avila, E. (2006). Understanding the manga hype: Uncovering the multimodality of comic-book literacies. *Journal of Adolescent & Adult Literacy, 50* (1), 40–49.

This is a very comprehensive look at manga's history and development as a genre, which is now very popular in the United States. In addition, the authors explore how to use manga in the classroom to help students develop strong multimodal reading and critical deconstruction of manga.

Webb, A., & Guisgand, B. (2007). A multimodal approach to addressing anti-Semitism: Charles Dickens's *Oliver Twist* and Will Eisner's *Fagin the Jew*. In J. B. Carter (Ed.), *Building literacy conversations with graphic novels: Page by page, panel by panel* (pp. 113–131). Urbana, IL: National Council of Teachers of English.

These authors provide a concrete model and example lessons aimed at using a graphic novel to critique anti-Semitism in a classic work of fiction.

Xu, S. H., Perkins, R. S., & Zunich, L. O. (2005). *Trading cards to comic strips: Popular culture texts and literacy learning in grades K-8*. Newark, DE: International Reading Association.

This resource book offers concrete teaching guidelines and plans for working with comics, graphic novels, and other media-based texts. Numerous lesson plan examples and websites are provided to help educators incorporate popular culture texts into their teaching.

RECOMMENDED YOUNG ADULT LITERATURE FEATURED IN THIS CHAPTER

Arakawa, H. (2009). *Fullmetal alchemist*. San Francisco, CA: Viz Media.

This manga work follows Edward Elric on a quest to locate the Philosopher's Stone. Featuring abundant conflict and battle scenes, this text is an engaging read.

Eisner, W. (2003). *Fagin the Jew*. New York, NY: Doubleday.

This graphic novel lends itself to a critique of anti-Semitism in both Dickens's classic *Oliver Twist* and a critique of stereotypical elements in Fagin as well. Norah remains standoffish so she decides to act like a heroine in a romance novel. Norah's missteps in this role create an endearing romantic comedy with numerous references to other young adult novels.

Esuno, S. (2008). *Future diary*. Los Angeles, CA: Tokyopop.

This manga work features nail-biting action as the main characters find a giant sink hole they are compelled to explore.

Flake, S. G. (2005). *Who am I without him? Short stories about girls and the boys in their lives*. New York, NY: Hyperion.

This short story collection gets at the tensions arising in relationships where the characters' sense of self sometimes gets lost in love. This collection contains realistic accounts of the complex trials of love and longing.

Helfer, A., & Duburke, R. (2006). *Malcolm X: A graphic biography*. New York, NY: Farrar, Straus & Giroux.

This graphic novel format provides a readable version of Malcolm X's biography that can be paired with the original work or excerpts from the longer account.

Moore, S., Champagne, K., & Igle, J. (2007). *Firestorm: The nuclear man-reborn*. New York, NY: DC Comics.

This graphic novel features a superhero trying to prevent a nuclear accident by using atomic forces. The main character, Firestorm, is actually a hybrid combination of a male college student and a female politician.

Reed, G., & Cloonan, B. (2006). *Puffin graphics: Dracula*. New York, NY: Puffin.

This graphic novel and its related tales of Frankenstein and other classics offer a very readable introduction to their longer, more dense canonical novels. These graphic novels can easily be paired with their older, full-length originals.

Salisbury, G. (2005). *Eyes of the emperor*. New York, NY: Wendy Lamb Books.

This young adult historical novel chronicles the racism and displacement experienced by Japanese American soldiers after the Japanese bombing of Pearl Harbor and the onset of war. It can be paired with graphic novels like *Persepolis* and others set in war zones.

Satrapi, M. (2003). *Persepolis: The story of a childhood*. New York, NY: Pantheon.

This graphic novel is a powerful autobiography of a young girl growing up in Tehran, Iran, during the Islamic revolution of 1979. It can be read and discussed alongside other young adult novels dealing with war issues.

Schinohara, C. (2005). *Red River* (Vol. 10). San Francisco, CA: VIZ Media.

Yuri, a Japanese school, is girl magically transported to the ancient Hittite empire where she is rescued by the handsome but arrogant Prince Kail. However, problems arise when Queen Nakia, an evil sorceress, seeks her son's succession to the throne.

Spiegelman, A. (1996). *The complete Maus: A survivor's tale*. New York, NY: Pantheon.

This Pulitzer Prize-winning graphic novel takes the reader into the world of a Polish–Jewish ghetto during World War II. It can serve as an excellent resource for units dealing with themes of discrimination and displacement in world history and English.

Turner, N. (2004). *A project chick*. Columbus, OH: Triple Crown.

In this African American "street" lit novel, main character Teresa sets out as a single mom after leaving Lucky, her baby's rich but deranged daddy. Teresa ends up on public assistance and runs through a daily grind of one obstacle after another. She is tough and persevering. While not part of the in-school canon of African American literature, street lit is widely popular with African American teen girls, in particular, because of its themes of women expressing independence and power in the face of ghetto life.

Woo. (2006). *Rebirth* (Vol. 20). Los Angeles, CA: Tokyopop.

This male-oriented manga features a violent quest against evil with the action taking place in the vampire lord's tournament fortress where Rett, one of the good guys, attempts to assist Deshwitat in a duel with the evil Mr. Grey. This action-packed manga fantasy appeals to teen boys, and its sequel is profiled at the end of the book.

RECOMMENDED WEBSITES

American Library Association annual recommended graphic novels list: http://www.ala.org/yalsa/booklists

Bitz, M. (2004). *The comic book project*. New York, NY: The Comic Book Project: http://www.comicbookproject.org

Comic Life (see the Apple website).

Jacobi, T. (2007). The Zine Project: Innovation or oxymoron? *English Journal, 96* (4), 43–49: http://www.readwritethink.org/lessons/lesson_view.asp?id=915

Poitras, G. (2006). Website on Manga and Anime: http://www.koyagi.com

Riordan, R. (2008). *Book one: The maze of bones, the 39 clues*. New York, NY: Scholastic: http://www.the39clues.com

REFERENCES

Alvermann, D. E., Hagood, M. C., Heron-Hruby, A., Hughes, P., Williams, K. B., & Yoon, J. C. (2007). Telling themselves who they are: What one out-of-school Time study revealed about underachieving readers. *Journal of Literacy Research, 28*(1), 31–73.

Beach, R. (2007). *Teaching medialiteracy.com: A web-linked guide to resources and activities*. New York, NY: Teachers College Press.

Biancarosa, C. & Snow, C. E. (2006). *Reading next: A vision for action and research in Middle and high school literacy: A report to Carnegie Corporation of New York* (2nd ed.). Washington, DC: Alliance for Excellent Education. Retrieved from http://www.all4ed.org/publications/Reading Next/ReadingNext.pdf

Blasingame, J. (2007). Books for adolescents. *Journal of Adolescent & Adult Literacy, 51* (1), 280–291.

Bucher, K., & Manning, M. L. (2006). *Young adult literature: Exploration, evaluation, and appreciation*. Upper Saddle River, NJ: Pearson.

Carter, J. B. (2007). *Building literacy connections with graphic novels: Page by page, panel by panel*. Urbana, IL: National Council of Teachers of English.

Clark, W. (2004). *Thugs and the women who love them*. Brooklyn, NY: Black Print.

Dickens, C. (1837–1838). Oliver Twist. *Bentley's Miscellany*.

Guzzetti, B. J., & Gamboa, M. (2004). Zines for social justice: Adolescent girls writing on their own. *Reading Research Quarterly, 39*(4), 408–436.

Harris, M. (2007). Showing and telling history through family stories in *Persopolis* and young adult novels. In J. B. Carter (Ed.), *Building literacy connections with graphic novels: Page by page, panel by panel* (pp. 38–53). Urbana, IL: National Council of Teachers of English.

Hughes-Hassell, S., & Rodge, P. (2007). The leisure reading habits of urban adolescents. *Journal of Adolescent & Adult Literacy, 51*(1), 22–33.

Jacobs, D. (2007). More than words: Comics as a means of teaching multiple literacies. *English Journal, 96*(3), 19–25.

Kress, G. (2003). *Literacy in the new media age.* London, England: Routledge.

Moore, D. W., Bean, T. W., Birdyshaw, D., & Rycik, J. A. (1999). *Adolescent literacy: A position statement.* Retrieved from http://www.reading.org/downloads/positions/ps1036_adolescent.pdf (Also published in the *Journal of Adolescent & Adult Literacy, 43,* 97–112).

Reid, L. (2007). ReadWriteThink connection. *English Journal, 96*(3), 25.

Schwartz, A., & Rubinstein-Avila, E. (2006). Understanding the manga hype: Uncovering the multimodality of comic-book literacies. *Journal of Adolescent & Adult Literacy, 50*(1), 40–49.

Smith, M. W., & Wilhelm, J. D. (2002). *"Reading don't fix no Chevys:" Literacy in the lives of young men.* Portsmouth, NH: Heinemann.

Sturtevant, E. G., Boyd, F. B., Brozo, W. G., Hinchman, K. A., Moore, D. W., & Alvermann, D. E. (2006). *Principled practices for adolescent literacy: A framework for instruction and policy.* Mahwah, NJ: Lawrence Erlbaum.

Webb, A., & Guisgand, B. (2007). A multimodal approach to addressing anti-Semitism: Charles Dickens's *Oliver Twist* and Will Eisner's *Fagin the Jew.* In J. B. Carter (Ed.), *Building literacy conversations with graphic novels: Page by page, panel by panel* (pp. 113–131). Urbana, IL: National Council of Teachers of English.

Xu, S. H., Perkins, R. S., & Zunich, L. O. (2005). *Trading cards to comic strips: Popular culture texts and literacy learning in grades K-8.* Newark, DE: International Reading Association.

Young, E. (2006, September–October). Urban lit goes legit. *Black Issues Book Review,* pp. 1–23.

Chapter 11

Postmodern Forms of Young Adult Literature

In the previous chapters, we alluded to various genres and the notion that genres are ever changing and expanding to reflect contemporary times and issues. Nowhere is this more apparent than in the increasing array of young adult literature featuring *postmodern elements*. So, what is *postmodernism,* and how has this movement and viewpoint influenced young adult literature? Moreover, what does this form allow us to do in our ongoing work with young adult literature and adolescent readers?

Learning Objectives

- Understand the tenets of **postmodernism** as they relate to young adult literature, especially the underlying notion of multiple meanings and interpretations.

- Consider and be able to discuss how postmodern young adult literature invites critical literacy perspectives and rejects grand narratives or "one-size-fits-all" interpretations.

- Develop an understanding of the nature of teacher and student creativity as it relates to the exploration of postmodern texts.

- Know the elements of postmodern texts and various strategies for exploring the genre with students.

- Continue to create a database of young adult literature that includes some of the titles discussed in this chapter.

Vignette: Mr. Sergio Ramirez's Contemporary Literature Class

Mr. Ramirez:	We've been reading **postmodern picture books** like Istvan Banyai's (1995a) *Zoom* where the initial image of a rooster's red top knot takes up the whole frame before zooming out to reveal a whole rooster, two children looking at the rooster, and so on. Now that you have read some postmodern picture books, we are going to create our own versions in your small groups. You can use the *Brushes* iPad Edition (www.brushesapp.com) to create the images and artwork for your postmodern picture book. As a guideline, follow the structure of *Zoom* where the viewer's perspective moves out, or you can have pages that increasingly zoom in on objects, people, and so on.
Ramon:	Mr. Ramirez, what are we going to do with these?
Mr. Ramirez:	Thanks for asking, Ramon. I almost forgot. I will be judging your work with a rubric I'll share with you shortly. But the real point of this activity is to create some postmodern picture books we can share with students down the street at Arroyo Elementary, so have fun with this. We'll be going there early next month.

Students begin brainstorming their story boards for this activity based on what they have learned in think alouds with Mr. Ramirez in the somewhat challenging genre of the postmodern picture book.

Common Core Standards

The following standards are addressed in this chapter:

RL.6.9, 7.9 Compare and contrast texts in different forms or genres (e.g., stories and poems, historical novels, and fantasy stories) in terms of their approaches to similar themes and topics.

RL.8.2, 9-10.2 Determine a theme or central idea of a text and analyze its development over the course of the text, including its relationship to the characters, setting, and plot; provide an objective summary of the text.

RL.8.3, 9-10.3 Analyze how particular lines of dialogue or incidents in a story or drama propel the action, reveal aspects of a character, or provoke a decision.

RL.9-10.5 Analyze how an author's choices concerning how to structure a text, order events within it (e.g., parallel plots), and manipulate time (e.g., pacing and flashbacks) create such effects as mystery, tension, or surprise.

RL.11-12.6 Analyze a case in which grasping a point of view requires distinguishing what is directly stated in a text from what is really meant (e.g., satire, sarcasm, irony, or understatement).

DEFINING POSTMODERNISM

In this chapter, we take up emerging forms of young adult literature character-ized by postmodern features that bend the boundaries of traditional, sandwich-like story structures. Postmodern picture books and novels generally include font shifts, point-of-view shifts, mixed genres within a single novel, and so on. These works have pedagogical value because they unsettle conventional notions of reading and writing practices. Moreover, they offer models to stimulate stu-dent creativity in the production of their own postmodern stories. These works encourage *critical literacy* and expand the possibilities for multiple interpreta-tions and multiple layers of meaning within a single text. In addition to novels with postmodern features, we include genres featured earlier in Chapter 10: graphic novels, mixed media works, comics, zines, and even satiric YouTube creations in this category. But before looking at young adult literature represen-tative of this growing trend, some basic background on postmodernism as a movement is crucial. We might add that this topic is voluminous, spanning many disciplines, and the brief foray into postmodern definitions offered here is merely an introduction.

In many ways, postmodernists would reject the whole notion of a nice, neat definition of the field. Rather, because postmodernism has influenced art, archi-tecture, media, history, economics, politics, ethics, theology, and literature, we can point most easily to its common features as a starting point. First, postmod-ernism in fields like architecture served as a kind of backlash to the boring, egg-crate building designs of the modern era (Cahoone, 1996). If you think for a moment about various school buildings you have been in, as both a student and a teacher, most adhered to a kind of cookie-cutter design that, in its uniformity, saved taxpayer construction dollars but often resulted in a bland sort of struc-ture. As a result, most teachers creatively dress up their classrooms to counter the dull institutional walls and a potentially stultifying atmosphere that is unlikely to stimulate students' learning.

If you take the architecture boat tour in Chicago, just off Michigan Avenue by the Wrigley building, you can get a dramatic feel for the shift from modern-ism to postmodernism in architecture. Similarly, the art of pop culture icons like Andy Warhol in the 1960s blurred the distinction between high- and low-brow art by elevating the lowly Campbell soup can to a position alongside classical art in major galleries in New York and elsewhere. These examples show a con-scious shift away from the assembly line uniformity and predictability that drove the industrial age. Postmodernists reject this "one-size-fits-all" mentality on a number of fronts. So for our purposes, as teachers of literature working with young adults, what features of postmodernism are important to know?

First, there is a lack of blind faith and belief in grand narratives, and a concomitant effort to look at any event from multiple viewpoints and positions (Lyotard, 1996). For example, if we read in a history of Hawai'i that "Captain Cooke discovered the islands," we could say this is a pro-Western, pro-colonizer point of view. What about the Hawai'ians who were there? What about their navigational prowess sailing double canoes across thousands of miles of ocean to settle the Sandwich Islands, well before Cooke? Indeed, the ongoing renaissance in Hawai'ian culture and language stands in marked contrast to the years of colonial rule that nearly extinguished this group of people. Contemporary young adult literature set in Hawai'i documents ongoing resistance to the past colonizing forces of the missionaries, tourism, and efforts to domesticate the locals (Bean, 2008). Thus, a postmodern perspective complicates and illuminates any grand narrative event by critiquing whose voices were heard and whose voices were silenced.

A postmodern perspective critiques grand narratives.

What is critical for discussions of postmodern literature is the underlying notion of multiple meanings and interpretations. "A text can be read in an indefinitely large number of ways, none of which provides the complete, or true meaning" (Cahoone, 1996, p. 15). For example, the now well-known young adult novel, *Monster* (Myers, 1999) follows Steve, a teen who has been incarcerated in a county detention center after a convenience store robbery where the owner was shot and killed. The novel combines elements of a screenplay Steve is writing, his diary entries chronicling the screams and sleepless nights he experiences in jail, and court transcripts of his trial. In addition, his guilt or innocence, as well as the degree to which this is a documentary or simply a screenplay, remains an enigma throughout the novel. Indeed, *Monster* can serve as a model for students to write their own postmodern multilayered stories, as well as a forum to critique Steve's treatment as a young African American male in the court system.

As we explore this genre, you may want to consider how postmodern books open spaces for teacher and student creativity with multimedia, as well as the opportunity this genre affords for critical literacy. Urban educator Ernest Morrell (2004) notes that

In effect, postmodern criticism calls attention to the shifting boundaries related to the increasing influence of the electronic mass media and information technology, the changing nature of class and social formations in postindustrial capitalist societies, and the growing transgressions of boundaries between life and art, high and popular culture, and image and reality. (p. 30)

As a teacher, postmodern young adult literature can be a powerful vehicle for developing students' *critical literacy* and *creativity* in responding to this genre. At an advanced level, students may create parodies of traditional forms (Beach, 2007). For example, the B action movie *Snakes on a Plane*, starring Samuel L. Jackson, spawned numerous spoofs by teens who offered these multimedia productions on YouTube. These satires explored the absurdity of the movie's premise with parodies of the emergency page in the seat pocket of the plane, superimposing snakes in each frame and step-by-step instructions for what to do if this unlikely event happens. Similarly, media literacies have been satirized, most notably, in a European YouTube production, "The First Help Desk Call (www .youtube.com/watch?v=OelFoz-Tjf8), that shows the trouble early book reading caused as it replaced traditional scrolls. Popular films like *Crash* also experiment with time and space constraints to explore racism and other contemporary topics.

In summary, postmodernism and postmodern books open teaching space for multiple reader response possibilities (Morrell, 2008), including the following:

- Questioning ultimate, unified truth
- A view that knowledge is socially constructed
- Multiple viewpoints and interpretations
- Creation of counternarratives
- Critiques of power and agency

Activity 11.1 illustrates how these elements operate in a question-based discussion of the young adult novel *Shooter* (Myers, 2004). The novel is based on the Columbine High School shooting and deals with bullying and masculine power relations. Structured around a series of texts, including the school counselor's notes, diaries, and other text forms, *Shooter* offers the potential for multiple viewpoints and interpretations.

ACTIVITY 11.1: Professional Reflection and Discussion

Directions: Using Walter Dean Myers's (2004) young adult novel *Shooter* in your small group, develop three questions that explore who has power and who does not in this story. Consider cultural dimensions that influence the distribution of power in high schools, and think about a counternarrative that might have avoided the tragic outcome in this story.

Because the postmodern genre holds so much promise for boundary breaking and creativity, we take a brief look at what we know about teacher and student creativity as a prelude to exploring postmodern picture book and novels.

TEACHER AND STUDENT CREATIVITY

Creativity can serve as a welcome antidote in a world driven by narrow, high-stakes assessments. Indeed, some scholars writing in this often-neglected area of curriculum design see creativity as essential to our future. For example, Ambrose (2003) argued that "Those who will lead us in the 21st century must learn to operate within an environment that is open-ended, complex, chaotic, and unpredictable" (p. 23). Oddly enough, these are the very characteristics that operate in postmodern fiction, making this genre an ideal vehicle for stimulating teacher and student creativity.

Most definitions of creativity allude to novel elements or interpretations as key ingredients. For example, Weisburg (2006) noted that "Creative thinking refers to processes underlying production of creative products, which are novel works—or—innovations—brought about through goal-directed activities" (p. 7). If we apply the key ingredient of novelty to teaching, we can define teacher creativity as *the development of unusual or novel lessons and units likely to serve as a jumping off point for student productions (e.g., multimedia, songs, YouTube video clips, and so on).* Postmodern books, including postmodern picture books, offer a powerful starting point for engaging students in their own creative productions. In addition, postmodern books, precisely because of their unusual structures and treatment of characters, lend themselves to critical literacy questions and discussion.

To explore some of the postmodern literature that is available, we start by looking at a few key postmodern picture books and their potential as sites for critical literacy discussion.

POSTMODERN PICTURE BOOKS AND CRITICAL LITERACY

Readers accustomed to the simple, linear progression of a traditional story sometimes struggle with *postmodern picture books* and their use of nonlinear plots, narrators who directly address the reader, multiple narrators, blending of genres, as well as time and space bending (Serafini, 2005). For example, the postmodern picture book, *Voices in the Park* (Browne, 2001), chronicles four different individuals on their outing with two pet dogs in a city park with each of the four telling a story from their individual perspective. The first voice is the mother with her son Charles and their Labrador retriever, Victoria. The second voice is an unemployed dad and his daughter Smudge who also go for a walk to the city park along with their dog. The two dogs and children, Charles, from an upscale family, and Smudge, whose dad is unemployed, encounter each other, and Charles's mother gets upset. "I saw him talking to a very rough-looking child" (Browne, 2001, p. 6). This story goes to the heart of prejudice as we see in the final two voices. The third voice is Charles back at home, bored and recounting his chance meeting with Smudge at the park. He thinks she's nice and looks forward to seeing her again, even though his mom was clearly against it. The final voice is Smudge, and she recalls her visit to the park and playing on the equipment with Charles until his mother made him leave. She observed that he was sad when his mom took him away, but he gave her a flower and she put it in water at home and made her dad some cocoa.

Each voice is important and separate, but the voices are interconnected across the narrative to deal with class issues, prejudice, and hope. Both the dogs and the children cross socioeconomic boundaries and differences to enjoy each other's company while Charles's mom personifies disapproval and prejudice. The author interleaves this picture book with a number of surrealistic images including Santa Claus, Mona Lisa, the Queen of England, a Victorian clad couple dancing in the park, and other incongruous images in marked contrast to the somber mood of the adult characters in the story. *Intertextuality* where an author calls upon the reader's background knowledge (e.g., of Victorian times, Santa Claus, and other images) to make sense of otherwise confusing elements is crucial to reading and interpreting postmodern picture books. For example, this story makes sense in light of what we know about class differences and status characteristic behavior. The mother in the story disapproves first of the dog she regards as scruffy, and her view of Smudge is similar. Smudge's dad is feeling down, looking unsuccessfully for a job in the classified ads while his daughter enjoys the park. The contrasts are stark and jarring as this children's book unfolds.

Time bending is common in this narrative with each voice presented sequentially, yet describing an event that was simultaneous (Serafini, 2005). In a study of students' responses to *Voices in the Park*, students commented that this time bending element was "weird" (Serafini, p. 48). In general, postmodern picture books need multiple readings in order to pay attention to the diverse elements supporting the narrative. In particular, illustrations and discussions about why an author used specific ones are crucial to working through the ambiguity inherent in these stories. The cover of *Voices in the Park* invites the reader along on this

Postmodern books offer a powerful starting point for engaging students in their own creative productions.

journey with a pathway and two of the characters (the children from two families) that draw the reader's eye into the scene.

USING THINK ALOUDS TO INTRODUCE POSTMODERN PICTURE BOOKS

As you engage your students in some of the postmodern picture books and young adult novels highlighted in this chapter, it will be important to model some of the navigational strategies you used to read and reread these highly creative works. You may want to do a think aloud that illustrates how you approach a first reading of books like *Voices in the Park* and others profiled in this chapter. By walking students through your own challenges reading and rereading this complex genre, you can make your students more comfortable with the process of suspending quick judgments about a book.

For example, Case 11.1 shows one of the authors, Tom, in a think aloud as he first attempted to navigate artist Istvan Banyai's (2005) postmodern picture book *The Other Side*. It follows Tom, page by page, on a first reading of this visually striking and challenging look at the other side of things. You may want to get a copy of the book to follow along.

CASE 11.1: Tom's Think Aloud Example

The Book Cover: I look at the title, and it moves from black lettering against a taxi cab yellow background, flowing into backward silver lettering against a black background. The black part must be a curtain to the other side because a boy in red shorts with a red baseball cap is on his knees peeking under the black curtain.

Page 1: Shows numbered, step-by-step directions for making a paper airplane.

Page 2: Has a strange array of images including a girl practicing a cello while standing on a chair facing out an open window. A paper airplane can be seen aloft just outside the window, bordered by curtains in what appears to be an old house. It has wood floors and an old-style wall heater. On the couch nearby rests an iPod with ear buds, a CD, and a hat. Just below the couch is a stuffed teddy bear facing the window with stitching all along his back. On the opposite wall is a framed portrait in silhouette of a little girl holding what appears to be a cell phone. An old-style, antique-framed black music note graces the opposite wall. In other words, there's a lot of stuff packed into this single page, and I suspect the paper airplane is going to take me on a journey.

Page 3: The view is now from the outside (or other side) looking at the small boy with the baseball hat throwing paper airplanes out the building window. It's an older city building like those in New York, Chicago, or Toronto. The next, facing page has a large jet liner with the red hat boy in one of the windows. A relief map of a city is below, looking very small.

Remainder of the Book: As I continue reading, trying to make sense out of the various angles, the little boy is seen from inside the plane, heading on holiday to the Bahamas and a beach. Later, it's fall and he's in a wooded park wearing a warm jacket. Further on, there's an image of a classroom and a geography lesson. It's an old-style classroom with desks in rows, and the little boy and another girl launching paper airplanes. An image of the Earth from space is on the blackboard with a male teacher in a tie using a pointer to direct students' attention. The desks are so old they have inkwells! There are 28 children, elementary age, and four African American students. The students appear bored, and the room looks chaotic.

The End: There is an image of the little boy's room in the same building as the girl at the start of the book. His room is filled with guy things of that era, maybe 1950s, including a bike, train set, a moon orbit poster, and an old-style clock on a fireplace mantel. A model airplane hangs from the ceiling. In the last two images, we see the little girl leaning out her window looking up at the little boy who waves to her. Finally, the building is dark except for two yellow lights in the two characters' units and a view of their heads asleep on the window sills. I need to read this again to really get a feel for the multiple views of "the other side." I think we could use this book as a model to make our own books exploring the other side of things.

TEACHING CHALLENGES AND POSSIBILITIES WITH POSTMODERN PICTURE BOOKS

In thinking about other teaching approaches to postmodern picture books, each of the multiple points of view needs to be addressed. In addition, the illustrations matter in framing a story in this genre and it is crucial to consider what they mean and why particular images are included. For example, *Black and White* (Macaulay, 1990) chronicles an interruption in commuter train service and the effect this had on people's lives (Antsey, 2002). Multiple stories emerge in this postmodern picture book where a train is delayed because of cows on the track. The first story is narrated by a boy who as a passenger on the train spotted the cows. The second story within a story is by a teenage girl recounting how difficult parents can be. The third story consists of loudspeaker announcements in the railway public address system. Finally, in the fourth story, a narrator offers a treatise on the Holstein cows (Antsey, 2002). Because these books are complex, they "require the reader to actively process various representational forms, cope with the unexpected in both format and text structure, and consider multiple meanings, readings, and intents (Antsey, 2002, p. 456).

To get a feel for the surprises and uniqueness of postmodern picture books, try Activity 11.2 with a small group of your classmates.

ACTIVITY 11.2: Professional Reflection and Discussion

Directions: Locate a postmodern picture book you have not read before. Using a recording device (e.g., iPod with an iTalk microphone), do a think aloud as you read the book for the first time. Then, in a small group, share your recorded think aloud experience with others and brainstorm the challenges and possibilities with each of the books in your group. In essence, how would you introduce and use this book in your classroom?

As you begin to work with postmodern picture books in your classroom, there are some good resources available. For example, the lesson plan website ReadWriteThink features an excellent teaching plan for *Black and White* (Macaulay, 1990). It introduces the use of a Plot Summary Graphic Organizer (Antsey, 2002).

PLOT SUMMARY GRAPHIC ORGANIZER

Based on Antsey's (2002) use of this strategy, students read a multiple voice postmodern picture book like *Voices in the park*. You can review the steps for this strategy at the ReadWriteThink lesson plan website (www.readwrite think.org/).

The following steps are based on the ReadWriteThink lesson plan for using postmodern picture books in the middle school (Antsey, 2002) with David Macauley's (1990) *Black and White* (www.readwritethink.org/lessons./lesson_view.asp?id=66).

Plot Summary Organizer Steps

1. Form five small groups of students.

2. Four groups are asked to each attend to one of the four story lines.

3. The fifth group attends to all story lines (i.e., all four story lines in the book).

4. Each group completes a plot summary graphic organizer that includes setting, characters, and events. Figure 11.1 displays the template for a plot summary graphic organizer.

5. When each group has finished reading and preparing a plot summary, mix the groups such that one student from each of the previous groups meet to share their plot summaries (see Figure 11.3).

6. Students can discuss how each story line is related by comparing their summaries with the one created by group 5 (who read the whole story).

7. Finally, have a whole-class discussion of the book as a stimulus for writing their own postmodern picture book with small groups each developing and integrating story lines.

FIGURE 11.1 Plot Summary Graphic Organizer

Group 1	Group 2	Group 3	Group 4	Group 5
setting	setting	setting	setting	setting
characters	characters	characters	characters	characters
events	events	events	events	events

One student from each of the five groups forms a new, mixed group to summarize the whole story line

---

APPLYING THE PLOT SUMMARY GRAPHIC ORGANIZER TO OTHER STORIES

Voices in the Park, like *Black and White*, also features multiple viewpoints and story lines. Using the steps described for this strategy, each group of students follows and summarizes one of the four overlapping stories with the fifth group reading the whole book. For example, group 1 might follow the mother who takes the family Labrador for a walk in the park along with her son Charles. Group 2 might follow the father and daughter team headed to the park. Each group records setting, characters, and events. The first event in the first story panel involves the Labrador getting bothered by a scruffy mutt that ties Charles to the other family walking this dog in the park. Once this step is completed, groups can then intermix and share key information following the steps for creating an integrated plot summary graphic organizer. Finally, they can create their own postmodern picture book using the current book as a model.

POSTMODERN PICTURE BOOKS OF NOTE

Because postmodern picture books rely on artistic visuals rather than on words to convey meaning, they can be particularly attractive to struggling adolescent readers (Carr, Buchanan, Wentz, Weiss, & Brant, 2001). Unlike conventional picture books, the number of postmodern picture books is relatively small but growing. Well-known artists like Istvan Banyai have created some classics within this evolving genre. For example, *Zoom* (Banyai, 1995a) and *Re-Zoom* (Banyai, 1995b) take the reader on a journey that features close-up views morphing to wide-angle panoramas of farms and cities. When you share these novels with students, the message is that rereading of complex text, even texts consisting of pictures and no print, is crucial. In an effort to guide students' initial reading of books like *Zoom* and *Re-Zoom*, Leigh Van Horn (2008) recommends having students verbalize their reactions to instances where an illustrator surprises or fools the reader. For example, in *Zoom*, the first page is filled with a red plant-like image that turns out to be a rooster's head.

Because of their surrealistic features, postmodern picture books are best read and discussed in groups in order to gain the multiple interpretations possible in this genre. The following progression is helpful as you engage your students in an initial read aloud with a postmodern picture book like *Re-Zoom* (Banyai, 1995b). Although based on reading conventional wordless picture books to adolescents (Albright, 2002), the instructional sequence will be helpful in tackling the twists and turns of postmodern picture books. In essence, this is a co-reading of the book where each page is displayed and talked about by the teacher and students with the caveat that the first reading is just a beginning because multiple readings are necessary to revise initial hunches. Reading postmodern works is akin to figuring out a puzzle or playing a multilayered video game.

READ ALOUD STEPS AND *RE-ZOOM* EXAMPLE

1. Display the cover and title, and ask students what they think about when they see the word *Re-Zoom*?

2. Go to page 3 with its image of a hunter shooting a bow and arrow. The image is mottled with dots. Comment on this, and ask students what they see in this image.

3. On the next two pages, the camera lens zooms out to reveal the hunter as an image on a wristwatch with the next page pulling back further to show an image of a boy's hands doing a rubbing of an ancient Egyptian icon. There is a lot going on in this frame, and it includes a blend of the ancient wall art with a jarring Felix the cat t-shirt worn by the boy doing the rubbing.

4. At this point, students and the teacher can co-construct meaning through analogies to films (e.g., *Indiana Jones*), what they currently know about hieroglyphics, anthropology, and so on. As the image morphs into a pyramid, then a spire in a city square in Paris, along with other convoluted images that ebb and flow, ultimately into darkness, encourage students to make and revise their interpretations as you read the book together.

5. Talk about students' feelings as they wrestle with books like *Re-Zoom*. These are often disturbing, disruptive, and challenging texts to undertake, departing radically from traditional story structures. Nevertheless, their visual appeal is similar to video clips on YouTube and video game structures. Most importantly, postmodern picture books are a good jumping off point to creating their own biographies, neighborhood chronicle of a single event, and so on.

If you were an astronaut, gazing down at Earth from afar, Steve Jenkins's wordless picture book, *Looking down* (1995), might capture your wide-angle view. Created with paper cutout illustrations, *Looking down* slowly zooms toward Earth, much like Google Earth where the Earth's surface becomes more distinct in each frame. The oceans become visible, then an aerial view of a city on a coastal inlet, homes with backyard swimming pools, and finally a little boy kneeling on the sidewalk, looking at an insect through a magnifying glass. His close-up view of a bright red and black-spotted lady bug dominates the last page. We have journeyed from outer space to suburbia.

Looking down offers a model for students to use in doing their own paper cut collage pieces that might reflect an aerial view zooming into their neighborhood. Similarly, David Wiesner's (2006) award-winning wordless picture book

Flotsam takes the reader to the shoreline where a boy is digging in the tide line next to the surf, initially finding a sand crab and then an old box underwater camera with film still in it. He takes the role to be developed at a one-hour photo, and the illustrations chronicle what fish might photograph if they had an underwater camera. Later, photos of other children from around the world emerge, following the lineage of this camera's voyages and adventures. This picture book could become a jumping off point for creating student-authored books based on their own trips to the beach with a lens on how creatures there might see their worlds.

In David Wiesner's (2001) *The Three Pigs*, the nice, neat flow of the original story of the wolf blowing down the first pig's straw house is completely turned on its head. Rather, in this postmodern version, the three pigs escape into the pages of other fables including the cat and the fiddle. The three pigs in this version are footloose and able to fly on a paper airplane to other stories where they talk to each other and the other characters. The narrow, defined space of the original story is blown apart in this postmodern version. And, this story can serve as a spinning off point for students to take other fables and create new twists and turns on older classics.

There are numerous other postmodern picture books available, and a search on the Internet will reveal lists of titles you may want to explore. In addition to postmodern picture books, a growing array of young adult novels contain features that include multiple fonts, interleaved story lines, time bending, and other meta-fictive postmodern characteristics. Earlier in the chapter we mentioned Walter Dean Myers's novel *Monster* (1999). In the section that follows, we introduce some additional novels by Myers and others that fit within the category of postmodern young adult novels. It is important to note that many graphic novels, manga, and other emerging genres also contain many of the features we might label as postmodern.

POSTMODERN YOUNG ADULT NOVELS

To some extent, categorizing certain young adult novels as "postmodern" is a bit arbitrary. For example, are graphic novels, teen zines, and novels that mimic text messaging like *ttfn* (Myracle, 2006), profiled in the genre chapter earlier postmodern young adult novels? For our purposes, young adult novels in this category should contain many of the features found in postmodern picture books. Ultimately, it boils down to what you plan to do as a teacher with these novels, especially in terms of reader response questions and critical literacy discussions that move students beyond the level of personal response.

For example, a novel like *Criss Cross* (Perkins, 2005) follows four 14-year-olds in small-town America, each poised for a change. Using haiku, dialogue, split-screen scenarios, and an aura of randomness, this postmodern novel invites the reader on a journey of self-discovery with the four main characters. The chapters are short, multigenre gems that adolescents resonate with in a world of text messaging and rapid-fire communication.

Although this genre is growing in popularity, we introduce a few titles and focus on how you might engage students in critical discussion of some representative novels using various strategies including reader response (Rosenblatt, 1978), critical literacy (Bean & Stevens, 2007), and a strategy called **Dinner Party** (Bean, Readence, & Baldwin, 2008; Vogt, 2002).

Much like postmodern picture books, postmodern young adult novels typically bend time conventions, vary fonts, and include other meta-fictive elements to shed light on characters' actions and issues. For example, Walter Dean Myers's well-established novel *Monster* (1999) alluded to earlier in this chapter, includes a diary, screenplay, and transcripts of main character Steve's ongoing trial for his involvement in a convenience store robbery. Myers leaves room for reader speculation about Steve's innocence or guilt, and some readers find this amorphous element disturbing, much like the open-endedness of many postmodern picture books. On the other hand, this very element makes postmodern young adult literature ideal for critical literacy discussions, exploration of silenced characters, and issues of power. For example, in the postmodern Australian young adult novel *Fighting Ruben Wolfe* (Zusak, 2000), the two protagonists, Cameron and Ruben Wolfe, spend their Sunday afternoons boxing in illegal fights to contribute money for their out-of-work dad and mom. The novel portrays the brothers as tough, urban teens, but when the font shifts to cursive writing at night, that shift signals conversations between the two boys that are sensitive and devoid of masculine posturing. Although this novel relies on font shifts for effect, time bending and other meta-fictive features are absent.

In Myers's *Shooter* (2004), loosely based on the Columbine High School shooting, we gain insight into the psyche of main characters Cameron Porter, a 17-year-old African American student, and Leonard Gray, an Anglo student found dead of a self-inflicted wound at Madison High School following the shooting and death of classmate and football star, Brad Williams. Other students were wounded in the shooting, and the novel begins with a psychologist's interview transcript of his conversation with Cameron Porter about the incident. Various text forms and fonts are used throughout the novel, including newsprint, signature blocks on official documents, and a disturbing diary section from the shooter, Leonard Gray. In his diary, he notes, "Nothing is working. I am on the wrong end of eternity and I've got to leave this tired world behind. Cameron is still together" (Myers, 2004). Even the cover of the novel centers on the crime scene with a yellow-and-black "do not cross" crime tape draping the gray cover with a bullet hole in the middle.

In the section that follows, we introduce various ways in which students can respond to a postmodern novel like *Shooter*. Traditional reader response questions engage the reader in a personal, individual response to the characters and their plight, whereas critical literacy discussion requires students to collaborate and, more often than not, disagree on their interpretations. We admit to a preference for collaborative, collective novel discussion through critical literacy but also value reader response.

READER RESPONSE AND CRITICAL LITERACY QUESTIONS

Reader Response

Generally, reader response (Rosenblatt, 1978) asks for personal reactions to events in a novel. The intent is to engage the reader in a transaction with the text that goes beyond some predetermined interpretation. For example, the generic questions that follow represent some possible reader response items:

- How would you have responded to a situation like the one in the novel?
- In your view, how well did the character handle this situation?
- What are your experiences with situations like this one?

Although reader response overcomes the limitations of the New Criticism, with its emphasis on particular meanings and interpretations, often owned by the text and teacher alone, reader response has some limitations, In particular, it is highly personal and may ignore the many ways in which the social world impacts reading and reader identity (Cherland, 2002). For example, instances of racism chronicled in young adult novels are not simply individual experiences but also socially driven, collective acts. Thus, using a blend of reader response questions and critical literacy discussion in the guides you develop will help balance individual and collective contributions to interpreting postmodern and other young adult novels. The guides introduced in this section are equally applicable to more traditional novel structures, not just to postmodern young adult novels.

Critical Literacy

Critical literacy engages the reader in close scrutiny of power relationships among characters in a novel. In addition to their artistic and aesthetic elements, critical literacy positions novels and other texts as social constructions open to multiple interpretations (Bean & Stevens, 2007). The constructed world of the novel can be deconstructed when students consider critical questions about power, gender, race, and class stereotyping (Bean & Moni, 2003).

Critical literacy goes beyond personal reactions to events in a novel to consider wider angle social issues including (a) the historical and cultural context of any text, (b) the notion that no text is neutral in its subject and reader positioning (e.g., how are characters positioned regarding race, class, and gender?), and (c) gaps and silences (i.e., who is represented in the novel or text, and who lacks voice and power?).

Although there are many possible critical literacy questions you might pose, the following general categories offer some possibilities:

- Who has a voice in the novel? Why?
- Who does not have a voice? Why?
- What are the power relationships involved?
- What race, class, and gender issues are highlighted?
- What ideologies are operating to shape this novel?
- How could it be shaped differently?
- If you were going to rewrite (a passage or section), how would you change it?

Clearly, you do not want to incorporate all of these questions into a single discussion guide. In the example that follows, a few reader response and critical literacy questions are included to engage students in a rich discussion.

Critical literacy positions novels and other texts as social constructions open to multiple interpretations.

DISCUSSION GUIDES: COMBINING READER RESPONSE AND CRITICAL LITERACY

At the most basic level, discussion guides consist of a series of questions designed to offer a close reading of a novel that may help students move beyond their own individual interpretations. That is not to say that simply reading one of these novels for the pleasure derived from its story line, characters, and their dilemmas is not important, in and of itself. But the value of close reading and interpretive discussion is its potential to offer new insights and broaden discussion to include multiple viewpoints. In addition, the more students become adept at close, deep reading, the more that foundation is likely to impact their reading of other texts (Sumara, 2002). Notice in the discussion guide examples that follow how both reader response questions and critical literacy questions can be combined to move students into a critique of events in a novel like *Shooter* that frame larger social issues in the lives of teens and their teachers in American high schools. The first discussion guide example took place early in the reading of *Shooter*, while the second example occurred later in the novel.

Discussion Guide 1: Shooter

Author Biography

Walter Dean Myers has authored more than 70 books for youth. He has received numerous awards for his books including the Michael L. Printz award for *Monster*. Born in West Virginia and raised by foster parents in Harlem, New York, he wants his writing to make connections—touching the lives of his readers. In *Shooter*, the novel we are reading, Myers takes up the subject of bullying in secondary schools. As you consider the following reading response and critical literacy questions in your small-group discussion, keep this fact in mind. Once your group has recorded your responses on the sticky notes at your table, we will talk about these issues as whole group.

Reader Response Questions

1. Early in the novel, Cameron Parker goes to a target shooting range. At the shooting range, there is a target with Martin Luther King Jr. holding a gun. It is quickly shot down by one of the target shooters. Upset at this racist target and act, Cameron tells his father about it and his father tells him to stay focused and not "go off on some civil-rights kick" (p. 20). *How would you have responded to the situation at the range? How would you have responded to Cameron's father?*

2. Currently, there are numerous sites on the Internet and projects at various school districts aimed at reducing bullying. *In your opinion, to what extent do you think these efforts are working? Why or why not?*

Critical Literacy Questions

3. To what extent do you think Cameron, a shy, intelligent African American student, and Len, an angry, slightly built Anglo teen, capture some of the power dimensions of high school (e.g., jocks rule and being nerdy is associated with being feminine)?

4. In the opening part of the novel, Cameron is being interviewed by Dr. Richard Ewings, Senior County Psychologist. The tensions with Cameron's father emerge as he describes the pressures to achieve at athletics. (Recall that his dad fixed it so he could get on the basketball team, despite not making the tryouts.) To what extent can an "official" like Dr. Ewing elicit the truth about what happened with Cameron and Len leading up to the shooting?

As the novel progresses, we learn more about the bullying and harassment experienced by Len and his conversations with Cameron where he reveals his feelings of isolation. In the Discussion Guide that follows, larger issues of how masculinity is constructed in high schools emerge.

Discussion Guide 2: Appendix 4 Len's Journal (pages 167–198)

Background

In this section of the novel, Len begins to write in a diary (or what he calls a "die-ary"). Starting in January, Len chronicles his feelings of being alone, his mom and dad's abusive and dysfunctional relationship, and his growing alienation at school where he is harassed by Brad Williams, a popular jock. "I told Cameron that I felt isolated" (p. 174).

As the entries progress from January until April 22, Len's interest in guns and killing escalates. He even tries volunteering for the Army.

Reader Response Question

1. In your view, would it have helped if Len's mom were able to read Len's diary? And what are the moral and ethical dilemmas surrounding reading another person's private diary?

Critical Literacy Questions

2. On page 181, Len and Cameron go to their high school principal to express their concerns about Brad's harassment. The principal tells them to "ignore the creatures from the Planet of the Apes. They are EXPRESSING themselves."

3. This response portrays Len and Cameron as the ones who are outsiders and at odds with others. *What would an alternative rewriting of this section about bullying look like?*

Although discussion guides offer a good deal of scaffolding for readers, other strategies move the teacher a bit more into the background. For example, Dinner Party (McLaughlin & Vogt, 2000) is a strategy that relies heavily on students dramatizing an episode from a young adult novel. Generally used at the close of reading a novel, Dinner Party involves students taking on character roles, including characters who have been silenced, killed, or simply not part of the original novel but created by the teacher for this activity (Bean et al., 2008).

DINNER PARTY

The original purpose for Dinner Party is for students to dramatize and role-play characters in novels, short stories, biographies, material about historical figures, scientists, artists, politicians, and other key figures (McLaughlin & Vogt, 2000). This activity may deal with social justice issues expressed in the work, including prejudice, gender bias, disability, sexual preference, and so on. Although scripts may be written, improvisations are generally more interesting and fun. It is important to have students develop a well-grounded knowledge of the characters they are portraying. Accomplishments, flaws, and works or writings may be used to inform the performance. Costumes are optional, and it is a good idea to videotape a Dinner Party performance for students to view later.

In addition to portraying the main and supporting characters in a young adult novel, we advocate infusing a strong element of critical literacy in any rendering of Dinner Party. This adaptation of the original strategy involves including characters who were positioned as silent or absent, along with other supporting figures integral to the production of the text (e.g., the author, publisher, teacher, parents, and so on). The example that follows is based on *Money Hungry,* Sharon Flake's (2001) award-winning young adult novel for middle grades students. The novel directly confronts a family's experience with homelessness, assistance policies, and neighborhood prejudices.

Dinner Party Example

Background

In Sharon Flake's (2001) novel *Money Hungry,* the main character, Raspberry, is a 12-year-old African American girl obsessed with hoarding money she has made selling goods to her classmates. She hides the money in old coffee cans in her project apartment room where she lives with her mother. Early in the novel, Raspberry sells her classmates stale candy that results in mass stomachaches and nausea. She also cuts school to work cleaning car windshields on the busy city street near her home. Raspberry and her mom lived in a car before getting a project apartment, and she fears they will someday have to go back to living on the street. Her dad is a homeless alcoholic. Homelessness haunts Raspberry and drives her entrepreneurial spirit:

> I wake up screaming and crying. In the dream, we're back on the streets. This time, we ain't in a van. We're walking up and down the streets pushing a cart. Begging. Always begging people for something. The weird thing is that in the dream, I have money. I have a whole cart full of cash, but nobody lets me use it to buy anything. (p. 81)

Scenario

Raspberry must attend a required parent meeting with her principal and school counselor in this scene because she has been cutting school. It is important to have a moderator who acts as a gatekeeper and question asker. In the example that follows, the school counselor is the moderator.

Characters

The following list of characters and the abbreviations for the dialogue that follows should illustrate how Dinner Party operates.

- School Counselor (SC)
- Principal (P)
- Raspberry (R)
- Her Mom (M)
- Her Middle School Core English Teacher (E)
- A Community Activist and Business Leader (CA)

Example

Students in Ms. Ballantine's middle school language arts class read Sharon Flake's *Money Hungry*, responding to discussion guides, and as a culminating activity, six students played the various roles including that of the moderator (School Counselor). The following scene illustrates a fairly typical Dinner Party exchange, in this case, based on a required parent conference.

SC: Thank you for coming in (Raspberry and her mom).

M: I know Raspberry hasn't been coming to school. She's been out making money washing car windshields on the street with Oddjob, a friend of our family. She's

(Continued)

(Continued)

been very worried about having enough money to survive. This is because we had to live for a while in our car after her dad ran out. But now we have an apartment in the projects and I'm working and taking classes to get ahead.

R: I have nightmares about living on the street again, and the project isn't safe either. When I sold some stale candy by accident at school, you called me in and it's been downhill since then.

P: (Principal's cell phone rings). I'm sorry, I've got an emergency in the parking lot. SC can let me know what you all decide (Principal leaves the meeting).

E: May I say something? In my experience, Raspberry is one of the best writer's I've had in class. She's creative and interested in the young adult novels we read. But lately, Raspberry has been missing class and she's falling behind in her reader response journal. I even have that set up as a blog so we can all comment on our readings, but Raspberry hasn't posted anything for two weeks.

R: Are you kidding? We don't have a computer in our project apartment! It would be stolen right away!

CA: Raspberry, we have a computer center nearby where you can get online and complete these assignments. I'll show you where it is. Also, since you have such a good business mind, we could probably use your help with our fundraising efforts. In exchange, the center has laptop computers that we can loan out. How does that sound?

R: Okay, if I can leave it with Mrs. E so it doesn't get stolen.

E: That's fine until you get another place where you feel your things will be safe.

M: We're on the list for section 8 housing in a nice neighborhood where Raspberry's best friend lives. Her dad is a doctor, and he's helped us out from time to time.

SC: Okay, I think we have a plan. Raspberry agrees to make up the assignments in Mrs. E's class and CA will provide computer access and a loaner laptop. That's great. Welcome back, Raspberry. With your business sense, I think you'll have a great future. Thanks for coming in M.

In summary, Dinner Party offers students a dramatic way to respond to a novel, and in our experience, students become fairly animated and creative when offered this opportunity. They enjoy videotaping these scenarios and watching the end result in an iMovie.

MULTIMEDIA TEXT SET

This text set is designed to explore the various aspects of postmodern text discussed in this chapter. As such, it is not focused around a particular theme; rather, it allows for discussion and multiple interpretations of the included texts.

1. Mon Seul Desir: A Post Modern Fairy Tale
   www.youtube.com/watch?v=Yv5HJvF95S0&feature=related

In this short video, the producer's recreate the traditional fairy-tale genre in a way that invites multiple interpretations of the story.

"Moe talks about postmodernism" from *The Simpsons*
   www.youtube.com/watch?v=QdO9orWQ-Nk

This short clip from the popular series *The Simpsons* plays with the notion that postmodernism is "weirdness for weirdness's sake." Students can take up Moe's position and discuss what elements of postmodern expression are evident in the clip.

2. Taun, S. (2001). *The red tree*. Sydney, Australia: Lothian.

The Red Tree is a picture book that treats the very serious issues of childhood loneliness and depression with compassion, and it offers hope to the reader that help is available to those affected by these problems. Tan uses images such as a giant fish and ships, cityscapes, and landscapes to minimize the girl and reinforce her feelings of insignificance and disconnection to the world. He emphasizes certain words such as *darkness* and *troubles* by the size of the font used, to underscore the emotions the girl is experiencing.

However, throughout the book, the author offers a symbol of hope to the girl (and the reader), if they search for it. Amid the complexity of the visual images, there lies a tiny red leaf that appears in all the illustrations.

3. Taun, S. (2000). *The lost thing*. Sydney, Australia: Lothian.

This book is written from a child's perspective and is reminiscent of a boy's carefully constructed scrapbook. The plot is fairly simple—a young boy living in a treeless city in the future finds a lost red thing. When he takes it home, he is not permitted to keep it, so he eventually finds a new home for it. Apart from one page that is totally blank, the pages are totally covered, there are no white areas, and all the pages consist of a collage of scientific and technical blueprints. Layered onto these images are verbal texts that have been neatly handwritten onto blue-lined paper, cut out, and then glued in place.

(Note: This book has been made into an award-winning short film. For more information and to view the trailer, please visit the following website: http://www.thelostthing.com/)

4. Sis, P. (1996). *Starry messenger*. New York, NY: Farrar, Straus and Giroux.

This Caldecott Honor picture book tells the story of Galileo Galilei's discoveries, rise to prominence, and imprisonment by the church. Sis expresses the wonder of Galileo's celestial observations in a multipaneled arrangement across pages: in the center, Galileo trains his telescope on the moon; surrounding panels replicate Galileo's notes about and sketches of the lunar surface. Other paintings take inspiration from maps and treatises; still others borrow historical imagery to convey the loneliness of the censored scientist. Handwritten passages from Galileo's own works are incorporated into the pages and supply information missing from the text.

SUMMARY

This chapter introduced postmodernism and its influence on the field of young adult literature. In addition, the often-neglected topics of teacher and student creativity were taken up, particularly around reading and developing postmodern picture books. Specific strategies for working with postmodern picture books included (a) think alouds and (b) plot summary graphic organizers. Profiles of postmodern picture books of note and read-aloud examples were introduced. Postmodern young adult novels and specific strategies for reading and responding to these works included (a) reader response questions, (b) critical literacy questions, (c) discussion guides encompassing both of these categories, and (d) a drama strategy, Dinner Party.

DISCUSSION QUESTIONS

1. How do the tenets of postmodernism as they relate to young adult provide for multiple meanings and interpretations?

2. Consider your current or future classroom. How can you use postmodern young adult literature to engage in critical literacy discussion and avoid "one-size-fits-all" interpretations?

3. How does engaging in the exploration of postmodern literature encourage creativity for both teachers and students?

4. Which of the strategies for engaging and responding to postmodern texts discussed in this chapter will you be the most likely to try with your current or future students? What other strategies might be appropriate?

KEY TERMS

Critical Literacy   227   Postmodern Elements   211

Dinner Party   225   Postmodern Picture Books   212

SMALL-GROUP ACTIVITY: READ A POSTMODERN YOUNG ADULT NOVEL AND ROLE PLAY IN A DINNER PARTY DISCUSSION

Directions: Locate and read a postmodern young adult novel like *Criss Cross* (Perkins, 2005), profiled earlier in this chapter. In a small group of four students, take up the roles of the four 14-year-olds in this novel in a Dinner Party discussion. Videotape the enactment, and share this with other students in your course.

RECOMMENDED READINGS

Albright, L. K. (2002). Bringing the Ice Maiden to life: Engaging adolescents in learning through picture book read-alouds in content areas. *Journal of Adolescent & Adult Literacy*, 45 (5), 418–428.

The author offers a list of picture books about Latin America, along with a step-by-step lesson example for social studies content based on a scientific discovery and analysis of a frozen Incan mummy.

Anstey, M. (2002). "It's not all black and white": Postmodern picture books and new literacies. *Journal of Adolescent & Adult Literacy*, 45(6), 444–457.

This author walks through the various elements of postmodern picture books, illustrating each one with reference to David Macaulay's (1990) postmodern picture book *Black and White*.

Carr, K. S., Buchanan, D. L., Wentz, J. B., Weiss, M. L., & Brant, K. J. (2001). Not just for the primary grades: A bibliography of picture books for secondary content teachers. *Journal of Adolescent & Adult Literature*, 45(2), 146–153.

The authors offer a wealth of picture books for read alouds centered on social studies and language arts. Although not postmodern picture books, the extensive bibliography is a valuable resource in working with struggling readers and English language learner (ELL) adolescents.

ReadWriteThink lesson plan: Postmodern picture books in the middle school. Retrieved from http://www.readwritethink.org/lessons/lesson_view.asp?id=66

This plan walks through how to have students in five groups develop a Plot Summary Graphic Organizer that will result in a discussion exploring the relationship between each subsection or voice in the story. Based on the article in the *Journal of Adolescent & Adult Literacy*, this strategy helps students deal with a small element of a complex postmodern picture book before tackling integrating multiple voices and elements. The postmodern picture book *Black and White* (Macaulay, 1990) is used to illustrate this process.

Van Horn, L. (2008). *Reading photographs to write with meaning and purpose, grades 4-12*. Newark, DE: International Reading Association.

This carefully crafted book guides educators toward the creation of lessons that engage students in critically analyzing photographs, ultimately to develop their own personal writing, biographies, and chronicling social issues in their neighborhoods and communities. The author illustrates critical reading of postmodern picture books like *Zoom* and *Re-Zoom*

POSTMODERN PICTURE BOOKS FEATURED IN THIS CHAPTER

Banyai, I. (1995a). *Zoom*. New York, NY: Penguin Puffin.

The world shrinks as the camera angle changes, miniaturizing the taken-for-granted images like a farm rooster, to the size of a child's farm toy model. Each image can be read and reread, front to back, or starting at the end of the book and moving forward.

Banyai, I. (1995b). *Re-zoom*. New York, NY: Penguin Puffin.

Undulating through multiple images where the increasingly wide-angle view of the artist intrudes to continually disrupt the stability of a figure and its ground, this book challenges the reader to continually revise (or re-zoom) initial interpretations.

Banyai, I. (2005). *The other side*. San Francisco, CA: Chronicle Books.

Look behind the curtain on the title page of this novel into a world that combines images of the 1950s with postmodern artifacts like the iPod as you follow the trajectory of a paper airplane and a little boy and girl looking out their city apartment windows.

Brown, A. (2001). *Voices in the park*. New York, NY: DK Publishing.

This powerful postmodern picture book features four different voices and views of a walk in a city park. There is an aura of depression and foreboding in the adult voices, pointing to urban crime and joblessness juxtaposed against happy dancers and a character in a Santa Claus suit. Nevertheless, the two children, a boy and a girl, enjoy the park when their dogs play in the fountain and they meet to go on the slide.

Jenkins, S. (1995). *Looking down*. New York, NY: Houghton Mifflin.

Created with paper cutout illustrations, *Looking down* slowly zooms toward Earth, much like Google Earth where the Earth's surface becomes more distinct in each frame.

Macaulay, D. (1990). *Black and white*. Boston, MA: Houghton Mifflin.

Multiple stories emerge in this postmodern picture book where a train is delayed because of cows on the track.

Wiesner, D. (2001). *The three pigs*. New York, NY: Clarion.

In this postmodern version, the three pigs escape into the pages of other fables including the cat and the fiddle. The three pigs in this version are footloose and able to fly on a paper airplane to other stories where they talk to each other and to the other characters.

Wiesner, D. (2006). *Flotsam*. New York, NY: Clarion.

The author takes the reader to the shoreline where a boy is digging in the tide line next to the surf, initially finding a sand crab and then an old box underwater camera with film still in it. He takes the role to be developed at a one-hour photo, and the illustrations chronicle what fish might photograph if they had an underwater camera.

POSTMODERN YOUNG ADULT NOVELS FEATURED IN THIS CHAPTER

Flake, S. G. (2001). *Money hungry*. New York, NY: Hyperion.

Sharon Flake earned the Coretta Scott King-John Steptoe Award for this young adult novel featuring main character 13-year old Raspberry Hill. Raspberry lives with her mom, and she fears being evicted from their small apartment to a life on the street. As a result, she sells items at school and hordes cash to ward off problems, but they find her anyway.

Myers, W. D. (1999*). Monster*. New York, NY: HarperCollins.

This award-winning novel exemplifies the elements of a postmodern young adult novel as it includes multiple genres (e.g., Steve's diary while in jail, courtroom transcripts, and a screenplay Steve is writing) and an indeterminate approach to his guilt or innocence in a corner convenience store robbery and murder.

Myers, W. D. (2004). *Shooter*. New York, NY: HarperCollins.

Based on the Columbine High School shooting, this novel features numerous font shifts and text types, chronicling the case against main characters Leonard Gray, Cameron Porter, and friend Carla. A football player and well-liked jock had been killed in the incident and other students wounded.

Perkins, L. R. (2005). *Criss cross*. New York, NY: Greenwillow HarperTrophy.

This 2006 Newbury Medal-winning book chronicles the lives of four 14-year-olds in a small town through mixed genres including haiku, song lyrics, and split-screen scenarios. The author creates a world where randomness capitalizes on the reader's creativity to make intertextual connections.

Zusak, M. (2000). *Fighting Ruben Wolfe*. New York, NY: Scholastic.

The main characters, Australian high school students, Cameron and Ruben Wolfe, survive by boxing on a weekend illegal fighting circuit that allows them to make money for their struggling urban home where their dad is out of work and their mom works part time. The novel contrasts their tough street personas with love of family through font shifts signaling public and private selves.

RECOMMENDED WEBSITES

Plot Summary Graphic Organizer Read-Write-Think Lesson Plan:
www.readwritethink.org/

And related postmodern picture book lesson plan:
www.readwritethink.org/lessons./lesson_view.asp?id=66

The First Help Desk:
A YouTube video spoof on technology help desks based on the shift from scrolls to books:
www.youtube.com/watch?v=OelFoz-Tjf8

REFERENCES

Albright, L. K. (2002). Bringing the Ice Maiden to life: Engaging adolescents in learning through picture book read-alouds in content areas. *Journal of Adolescent & Adult Literacy, 45*(5), 418–428.

Ambrose, D. (2003). Paradigms, mind shifts, and the 21st century Zeitgeist: New contexts for creative intelligence. In D. Ambrose, L. M. Cohen, & A. J. Tannenbaum (Eds.), *Creative intelligence: Toward theoretic integration* (pp. 11–31). Creskill, NJ: Hampton Press.

Anstey, M. (2002). "It's not all black and white": Postmodern picture books and new literacies. *Journal of Adolescent & Adult Literacy, 45*(6), 444–457.

Beach, R. (2007). *Teaching media literacy.com: A web-linked guide to resources and articles.* New York, NY: Teachers College Press.

Bean, T. W. (2008). The localization of young adult fiction in contemporary Hawai'i. *The ALAN Review, 35*(2), 27–35.

Bean, T. W., & Harper, H. (2007). Reading men differently: Alternative portrayals of masculinity in contemporary young adult fiction. *Reading Psychology, 28*(1), 11–30.

Bean, T. W., & Moni, K. (2003). Developing students' critical literacy: Exploring identity construction in young adult fiction. *Journal of Adolescent & Adult Literacy, 46*(8), 638–653.

Bean, T. W., Readence, J. E., & Baldwin, R. S. (2008). *Content area literacy: An integrated approach* (9th ed.). Dubuque, IA: Kendall/Hunt.

Bean, T. W., & Stevens, L. P. (2007). *Critical literacy: Context, research, and practice in the K-12 classroom.* Thousand Oaks, CA: Sage.

Beghetto, R. A., & Plucker, J. A. (2003). The relationship among schooling, learning, and creativity: "All roads lead to creativity" or "You can't get there from here?" In J. C. Kaufman & J. Baer (Eds.), *Creativity and reason in cognitive development* (pp. 316–332). New York, NY: Cambridge University Press.

Cahoone, L. (1996). *Introduction. From modernism to postmodernism: An anthology.* Cambridge, MA: Blackwell.

Carr, K. S., Buchanan, D. L., Wentz, J. B., Weiss, M. L., & Brant, K. J. (2001). Not just for the primary grades: A bibliography of picture books for secondary content teachers. *Journal of Adolescent & Adult Literature, 45* (2), 146–153.

Cherland, M. R. (2002). Criticisms of reader response. In B. J. Guzzetti (Ed.), *Literacy in America: An encyclopedia of history, theory, and practice* (pp. 115–118). Santa Barbara, CA: ABC-CLEO.

Lyotard, J. (1996). The postmodern condition: A report on knowledge. Reprinted in L. Cahoone (Ed.), *From modernism to postmodernism: An anthology* (pp. 481–513). Cambridge, MA: Blackwell.

McLaughlin, J., & Vogt, M. (2000). Dinner party. In M. McLaughlin & M. L. Vogt (Eds.), *Creativity and innovation in content area teaching* (pp. 91–103). Norwood, MA: Christopher-Gordon.

Morrell, E. (2004). *Becoming critical researchers: Literacy and empowerment for urban youth.* New York, NY: Peter Lang.

Morrell, E. (2008). *Critical literacy and urban youth: Pedagogies of access, dissent, and liberation.* New York, NY: Routledge.

Myracle, L. (2006). *ttfn.* New York, NY: Harry N. Abrams.

Rosenblatt, L. M. (1978). *The reader the text the poem: The transactional theory of the literary work.* Carbondale, IL: Southern Illinois University Press.

Serafini, F. (2005). Voices in the park, voices in the classroom. *Reading Research and Instruction, 44*(3), 47–65.

Sumara, D. J. (2002). *Why reading literature in school still matters: Imagination, interpretation, insight.* Mahwah, NJ: Lawrence Erlbaum.

Van Horn, L. (2008). *Reading photographs to write with meaning and purpose, grades 4-12.* Newark, DE: International Reading Association.

Vogt, M. (2002). Active learning: Dramatic play in the content areas. In M. McLaughlin & M. Vogt (Eds.), *Creativity and innovation in content area teaching* (pp. 73–90). Norwood, MA: Christopher-Gordon.

Weisberg, R. W. (2006). Expertise and reason in creative thinking: Evidence from case studies and the laboratory. In J. C. Kaufman & J. Baer (Eds.), *Creativity and reason in cognitive development* (pp. 7–42). New York, NY: Cambridge University Press.

Chapter 12

Global and Multicultural Literature for Young Adults

This chapter concerns young adult literature that involves or allows for a focus on the experience of social and cultural difference and diversity, locally, nationally, and most importantly globally. In the past we might have called this multicultural literature, or possibly international or world literature, but we prefer the more inclusive and comprehensive term **global literature**. Like multicultural literature, this category includes minority, indigenous, and other literature that highlights local or national culture, communities, and regions (e.g., Native American literature, African American literature, Asian American Literature, Anglo American literature, literature of the America South, and that of the Great Plains/Prairies), but unlike multicultural literature, it also includes historical and contemporary works from the international community, that is, from other countries, other regions, or specific global populations (e.g., pan-indigenous peoples: Native Americans, First Nations, Inuit, Aboriginal, Maori, Sami, etc.).

Learning Objectives

- Understand the distinction between multicultural and global young adult literature.

- Consider and be able to discuss how global young adult literature encompasses the international community from a variety of perspectives.

(Continued)

(Continued)

- Develop an understanding of cosmopolitan theory as it relates to the exploration of global texts.

- Know the elements of global young adult literature and various strategies for exploring the genre with students.

- Continue to create a database of young adult literature that includes some of the titles discussed in this chapter.

Vignette: Ms. Prine's Middle School Global Literature Class

Ms. Prine teaches in an international charter middle school. She has her students, many of whom have emigrated from various countries, read an award-winning young adult novel *Words in the Dust* (2011) by Trent Reedy. The novel chronicles Zulaikha's life in Afghanistan where she is teased incessantly for a facial deformity (cleft palate) in a culture that values women by their marriage prospects. Although the Taliban is no longer in power, they have taken her mother from her, and at 13, she is keeping house for a very busy and intolerant father and his nasty wife. All this begins to change as Zulaikha meets Meena, a former professor who wants to encourage Zulaikha's writing and teach her about poetry. Her life is altered forever by facial surgery arranged by the U.S. military presence in Afghanistan. Ms. Prine asks her students to create Body Biographies (Bean, Readence, & Baldwin, 2011) of one of the characters in the novel. Body biographies start with an outline of a student's body on butcher paper. Students search the Internet or develop their own drawing in the body outline that represents thoughts, feelings, and experiences the character has in the novel. Ms. Prine has her students do a gallery walk where they present their body biographies and explain how they depict the character's experiences.

Common Core Standards

The following standards are addressed in this chapter:

RL.6.9, 7.9 Compare and contrast texts in different forms or genres (e.g., stories and poems and historical novels and fantasy stories) in terms of their approaches to similar themes and topics.

RL.8.2, 9-10.2 Determine a theme or central idea of a text, and analyze its development over the course of the text, including its relationship to the characters, setting, and plot; provide an objective summary of the text.

RL.8.3, 9-10.3 Analyze how particular lines of dialogue or incidents in a story or drama propel the action, reveal aspects of a character, or provoke a decision.

RH.9-10.4 Determine the meaning of words and phrases as they are used in a text, including vocabulary describing political, social, or economic aspects of history/social science.

RH.11-12.8 Evaluate an author's premises, claims, and evidence by corroborating or challenging them with other information.

RH.11-12.9 Integrate information from diverse sources, both primary and secondary, into a coherent understanding of an idea or event, noting discrepancies among sources.

By including multicultural literature from within the country, as well as international or world literature, global literature is a much broader designation and neatly avoids isolating national from international works and authors. Such isolation is a problem. As noted by several scholars, students in world literature classes tend to come away from such courses perceiving "anything non-Western as 'other' or foreign, rather than with a stronger sense that we are the world; and, the world is us" (Qureshi, 2006, p. 34; Reese, 2002).

Moreover, global literature avoids the relativism inherent in the term *international literature* because what is international or foreign is related to one's location. What is international or world literature from the perspective of a reader in India might be different from someone from Canada or the United States.

The designation of international or world literature has other difficulties as well. In America, international literature at times refers to works written in other countries but published (in English) in the United States; in some cases, it refers to these books and to those written by immigrants in the United States about their home countries. In other instances, it is a broader category including any work regardless of the location of the publisher, the language of the text, and/or nationality or location of the author. In this sense, it is more closely aligned with our notion of global literature.

Global literature encompasses it all. In the rationale that is included in this chapter, we discuss why a category that includes national minority and multicultural literature along with works written from elsewhere may be particularly important and relevant for 21st-century students. Activity 12.1 taps into students' global and international experiences and funds of knowledge.

ACTIVITY 12.1: Professional Reflection and Discussion

Reflect alone and share with others the following. Consider your own global/international experience. What are the major global/international experiences or encounters you have had to date in your life? Name and discuss the ways in which the global world is implicated in your day-to-day life: food, music, film, clothing, transportation, services, work, and study. Consider the global literary texts you have read or films you have seen. List the literary texts or thematic units you have studied formally in the course of your secondary and postsecondary education that might fit the category of world or international or global literature.

YOUNG ADULT LITERATURE/GLOBAL LITERATURE

Although global literature is a very broad category, for the purposes of this textbook, we have some parameters. The focus on social and cultural diversity means that not every text would be included. Obviously, narratives where the social and historical circumstances of the context and/or the social and cultural background of the characters are relatively insignificant in the development of the plot or theme would not be included in global literature. For example, generic crime fiction or romantic fiction in which the setting or characters serve only to add a "colorful" or "exotic" backdrop for the narrative would not be considered in a unit on global literature. For us, this explanation is critical because the overriding intention with this literature is to expand students' understanding of themselves and others in the world through the critical study of social and cultural diversity and on how power has now and in the past defined social difference and its effects on individual and collective life.

Our focus is on adolescent literature, so we are concentrating in this chapter on global literature for young adults. While global literature is a relatively new term, global literature for young adults is even more recent, although we suspect teachers have been working with the idea for some time. Young adult literature as described in Chapter 2 includes works written specifically for adolescents that usually feature adolescent characters, with themes and narratives that adolescents generally find appealing. Global literature for young adults can be considered a subset of young adult literature. It includes works ideally written for adolescents that feature children or adolescent characters in narratives where race, ethnicity, or nationality, along with other forms of social difference (e.g., gender, religion, social class, language, or disability) are critical. In these stories, a focus on culture diversity and difference and social power is possible.

Well-known children and adolescent literature might be included in the category (e.g., *The Diary of a Young Girl* by Anne Frank [1952/1995]), but many contemporary works fit the category including such award-winning, young adult books as *Night* (1982) by Elie Wiesel, the testimony of a teenager transported with his family to Auschwitz; and *The Breadwinner* (2001), *Parvana's Journey* (2002), and *Mud City* (2003) by Deborah Ellis, all of which are set in Afghanistan during the 1990s and concern the efforts of a 12-year-old girl to help her family survive during the time of Taliban rule. Other award-winning examples include *The Other Side of Truth* (2001) by Beverley Naidoo, set in Nigeria and England; *Before We Were Free* (2002) by Julia Alvarez, set in the Dominican Republic in the 1960s; *Tasting the Sky: A Palestinian Childhood* (2007) by Ibtisam Barakat, set in Palestine; and American texts such as *The Absolutely True Diary of a Part-Time Indian* (2007) by Sherman Alexie; the graphic novel *American-Born Chinese* (2007) by Gene Luen Yang; and *Esperanza Rising* (2000) by Pam Munoz Ryan.

These and other texts will be discussed further in the chapter. In addition, there is an annotated bibliography, as well as a list of websites, that will provide readers with titles of the most recent and recognized works and various teaching resources that would fit the category.

We believe that these works written specifically for adolescents hold tremendous power to engage adolescent readers; however, we must acknowledge that not all cultures would name and recognize adolescents and young adult literature in the same way, if at all. Many cultures may not have texts specified for adolescents, nor will all adolescents, particularly older students, be enamored with what adults have designated and produced as "young adult literature." Also, several excellent contemporary works were not specifically written for adolescents but are popular with them and with their teachers, and these texts would seem to hold great promise for expanding students' understanding of themselves and others in the world in a unit on global literature. These texts include such works as *Persepolis: The Story of a Childhood* (2003) and *Persepolis 2: A Story of Return* (2004), best-selling graphic novels written about childhood in Iran by Marjane Satrapi; *Maus I: A Survivor's Tale: My Father Bleeds History* (1986) and *Maus II: A Survivor's Tale: And Here My Troubles Began* (1992), graphic novels written by Pulitzer prize winner Art Spiegelman; or *The Kite Runner* (2003) a novel and now a film written by Khaled Hosseini. We have included a small number of these texts in this chapter, but in general, we have focused on works that are specifically written for adolescents.

Global literature expands understanding of what it means to be a global citizen.

We should also note that although we concentrate on fictional texts in this chapter, specifically novels, the works could include other fictional forms: short stories, poetry, plays, and so on. In addition, although we have used the term *literature*, we encourage a loose definition of this term and ask teachers to consider, in addition, nonfiction and nonprint works, for example, oral and print histories and biographies, and media such as films, documentaries, television, music, and Internet websites.

Global literature is an inclusive, comprehensive, and dynamic category, and we recognize that it may create an organizing nightmare for school librarians and teachers, but it just means broadening the diversity of texts and authors made available to students in light of these new and changing times for 21st-century teens. The intention is to expand students' understanding of themselves and others in the world and of the issues of difference and diversity. By allowing them to cross local and national borders in their reading, they can experience, aesthetically and intellectually, the widest range of experiences and perspectives possible, and they can read and consider local and national literature in relation to the global literature they have read. Nonetheless, the logistics of organizing and framing global literature for students can be challenging, so we offer the following ideas for your consideration.

Some school jurisdictions offer a separate world literature course, which could with little effort be turned into a global literature course, along the lines of what we have outlined. But whether this exists at your school or not, we would support the efforts of any teacher or group of teachers to include more global literature as supplementary reading throughout their English/Language Arts program. Most importantly, we would recommend that a concentrated unit on a theme involving global literature be included in the curriculum.

One of the most common ways of organizing such a unit of study is by place and/or by time, mirroring the traditional organization in university English departments, for example, 18th-century French literature, Victorian (British) literature, 20th-century American literature, and so on. Alternatively multicultural units of study are often organized by the particular social, cultural, or ethnic groups, for example, women's literature, Native American literature, African American (Black) literature, and Hispanic literature. Because the focus in this chapter is on the broad and comprehensive category of global literature, we would recommend a thematic or multicultural unit.

Thematic units that have a global theme with local relevance for adolescents would be most appropriate. Teachers may want to survey their students to determine a specific theme for their study. Students might be interested in global young adult literature that focused on the general topic of war and conflict, the Holocaust, immigration and migration, intergenerational conflict, fantasy, or coming of age, but it will be important to solicit their ideas. Although we need to take into account their interests, the specific theme or question or emphasis that would frame the unit would be much more dynamic reflecting the specific issues, interests, and energies most prominent at the time.

Providing adolescents with choice and ensuring encounters with a wide range of reading materials is recognized as an element of good teaching according to various policy statements offered by the International Reading Association (www.reading.org), by the National Reading Conference (www.nrconline.org), and by the National Council for Teachers of English (www.ncte.org). Choice is important in motivating and engaging students in their reading, and the range of reading abilities and English language abilities in any one classroom will demand a wide range of reading materials with differing reading levels. More importantly, in a theme in a unit on global literature, a wide range of voices from any one population on any issue or theme is particularly important to avoid simple and stereotypical thinking. Not all texts need to be intensively studied. Although there may be only one or two core texts read intensively by all or by a group of students (literature circles), we suggest supporting texts of all sorts be read in any one unit.

"ADOLESCENT LIVES IN TIMES OF WAR AND CONFLICT": A SAMPLE UNIT

The process of developing a unit encompassing global literature can be illustrated with the following unit centered on conflict in the Middle East. In a unit on "Adolescent Lives in Times of War and Conflict," for example, chosen by the students from a list generated and organized by the class and their teacher, central inquiry might focus on the question of how adolescents understand and represent their experience of war. In the case of American students, the unit might begin with a project investigating local teens' knowledge and experience of the war in Iraq and Afghanistan, perhaps through personal or journalistic writing. Literary works that might serve to support and broaden this investigation to a global perspective, depending on the grade and reading levels of the students, might include Thura Al-Windawi's (2004) nonfiction text: *Thura's Diary: A Young Girl's Life in War-Torn Baghdad*. As suggested by the title, this book is an actual diary of an "average Iraqi teenager" during the bombing of Baghdad in 2003. In addition, other works to consider are Amal Rifa'i and Israelia Odelia Ainbinder's (2003) book of letters titled *We Just Want to Live Here*, which chronicles a friendship between a Palestinian and Israeli teenage girls following the Intifada of 2000, and Deborah Ellis's

(2004) nonfiction text *Three Wishes: Palestinian and Israeli Children Speak*, in which Israeli and Palestinian children offer their personal stories concerning the ongoing Middle East conflict. Mentioned previously in the chapter, Ellis's popular (2002) novel *Parvana's Journey*, and/or the graphic novel *Persepolis: A Story of a Childhood* by Marjane Satrapi, and/or the classic text *Diary of a Young Girl* by Anne Frank (1952/2005) and/or *Night* (1982) by Elie Wiesel. Teachers may also want to consider the powerful novel by Walter Dean Myers (2008) *Sunrise over Fallujah*, a fictional story of a young American soldier serving in Iraq.

One or two of these texts might serve as a core text and would read be intensively with their teacher and/or their classmates or a subsection of their classmates. The reading and writing done in this unit could be supported further by recent newspaper reports, magazine articles, film, documentaries, Internet sites, and United Nations documents (e.g., the Convention on the Rights of the Child, www.un.org). Certainly a teacher might offer students supplementary magazine articles focused on the issue of child soldiers (see *Time* Magazine*)*.

These literary material and texts offered in this unit will be, or certainly can be, emotionally difficult for students and teachers, although we think watching the evening news can be equally as difficult. A supportive and sensitive teacher is necessary for this unit and any unit that allows for deep engagement with traumatic local/global events and circumstances. Materials will need to be carefully selected as appropriate for the age and emotional maturity of the students involved. Class discussion will be a must.

Other challenges that this and any unit on global literature might present include the following. The wide range of texts and literature needed in any global literature unit might not be easy to secure. Some schools and departments with a strong focus on national and canonical works may not have a wide selection of classroom texts that fall under the category of global or international literature, particularly those that might also be considered contemporary young adult texts. In part, this may be because global literature is not a priority nor is it a well-known area of study for many teachers or administrators, who might be more inclined to go with what is familiar to them and their own educational history. Furthermore, there may be a prescribed list of approved texts that prevents new and alternative works from being considered, let alone purchased. This means that teachers, department heads, media specialists, and librarians will need to work together to expand the approved lists for all the reasons described previously.

Another challenge for some teachers is that they may feel uncomfortable teaching a literary work that they have not read before, situated in a place, about a population, and culture they themselves do not know. Fortunately, there are many resources for teachers, not the least of which are students, their parents, and communities. The involvement of parents and community members can provide some powerful learning experiences for everyone. In addition, the school librarian, literacy specialist/coach, and bookstore personnel might be able to assist in the selection of powerful, award-winning texts.

We would like to draw particular attention to an excellent list of such books: The Notable Books for a Global Society K-12 (www.tcnj.edu/~childlit/proj/nbgs).

An annotated bibliography of the books on this list is published each year in *The Dragon Lode*, the journal of the Children's Literature and Reading Special Interest Group of the International Reading Association. For a recent analysis of the list, see Nancy Hadaway and Marian McKenna's 2007 text *Breaking Boundaries with Global Literature: Celebrating Diversity in K-12 Classrooms*.

No teacher can have the breadth of knowledge that may be called on in a unit on global literature, so above all else, a teacher needs to acknowledge the limits of his or her own knowledge, even about cultures and circumstances that he or she may know intimately. Of course, no teacher or student should feel pressured to represent his or her cultural background(s) or for that matter share his or her family's history or circumstances if reluctant to do so.

A wide range of interpretations or voices is important on sensitive or difficult issues in any unit but particularly in a unit in global literature; for example, the issue of wearing the hyjab may arise in the reading of literature written by and about Muslim women and girls. A range of perspectives on this issue would seem in order. This does not mean that teachers need to include all perspectives and/or opinions, even those that might be offensive. Democratic principles and values and human rights doctrine can help prevent discussions and choices from becoming relative and subjective.

Of course, in any unit of study, but particularly one on global literature on controversial topics, great sensitivity and civility needs to be assured for a positive learning environment. Misunderstandings, communication difficulties, and differences of opinion should be expected and discussed with students prior to their occurrence. Again, several multicultural education and anti-racist resources can help teachers feel more comfortable in designing and implementing powerful, exciting, relevant, and possibly controversial global literature units in their English/Language Arts classrooms.

Finding, choosing, and organizing literary and nonliterary material and ensuring a positive, culturally responsive learning environment are critical, but of course, they represent just the beginning. A unit or course on global literature requires more than a supportive environment and more than just a wider and diverse selection of reading materials; we believe it requires a new perspective: a new way of reading.

COSMOPOLITAN READING

Global literature is not just about books, per se, but about an approach: what we are calling **cosmopolitan reading**. We believe this approach or stance can be brought to bear on all literature, but it seems particularly important in a unit on global literature for young adult readers.

Cosmopolitanism is a term with a long history that dates back to the ancient Greeks; it reappears in the works of the Enlightenment philosophers of the 18th century, and then it returns in the discourse of our own times. In its modern iteration, there are multiple definitions. Among other possibilities, a cosmopolitan might refer to a city dweller or to a world citizen. Cosmopolitanism might refer to a political position or philosophy. For some of you, "cosmopolitan" is a particular women's magazine or a famous cocktail.

Individuals become citizens of the world when they adopt a global mindset.

In what we are naming as cosmopolitan reading, cosmopolitanism refers to a critical perspective that frames self and other in relation to the world rather than, or in addition, to the nation. Part of this reframing, by necessity, involves extending the obligations of self to others beyond local and national borders and beyond national citizenship (Appiah, 2006; Banks, 2004; Nussbaum, 1999). Such a global reframing of the self is the result of a stronger local and global interface that finds many of us, and certainly many of our students, immersed in social and cultural diversity and difference, and where increasingly "21st-century life and identities are ethically and culturally simultaneously global and local" (Beck, 2002, p. 36; see also Apple, Kenway, & Singh, 2005). Students who develop or maintain contacts internationally as well as in their school or neighborhood using the Internet are certainly living out lives and identities that may be local and global. What students wear, what they listen to, where and what they eat, and where they may work or live now and in the future may reflect a global or cosmopolitan trajectory.

The intense interface of the local and global is a result of **globalization**, that is, by the extensive movement or flow of information, ideas, images, capital, and people across increasingly permeable political borders as a result of economic and technological change (Castells, 2004; Luke & Carrington, 2001). The speed, durability, flexibility, and mutability of networks and flows are effecting every aspect of local and national communities, albeit unevenly.

In the case of migration, James Banks (2004) noted that "worldwide immigration/ migration is increasing diversity . . . . Migration within and across nation-states is a worldwide phenomenon. However, never before in history has the movement of diverse racial, cultural, ethnic, religious, and linguistic groups within and across nation-states been so extensive, so rapid, or raised such complex questions about citizenship, human rights, democracy and education" (p. 132). In addition, for those with access, technological advancement has made worldwide communication, and the movement of ideas and images, easy and immediate. Thus, it is possible to gain instant access to the world community and its conditions, as well as to form and maintain global identities, attachments, commitments, and allegiances in both our work lives and our personal lives.

Individuals by choice or necessity become citizens of the world with a global mindset. In an ideal world, such "citizens may be more likely to make decisions and take actions in the global interests that will benefit mankind" (Banks, 2004, p. 134). Indeed, the underlying ethos of cosmopolitanism promises ways of living together in conditions of social and political difference . . . to understand our social and ethical responsibilities in the context of unexpected or perplexing diversity that exists within and beyond our borders (Appiah, 2006).

Although a cosmopolitan reading or perspective may be increasingly important for all of us, we would argue that for adolescents in the 21st century, it is absolutely critical and absolutely necessary. Although we cannot predict precisely what their lives will look like, we do know that they will be living in conditions that will be quite different from many of us.

We know now the following:

- Because of technology, the world of the 21st-century adolescent is much more globally interdependent and interconnected. There is and will be much more immediate virtual contact with communities beyond the local and national context.
- Because of globalization and the extensive migration and immigration of populations across the planet, adolescents now and in the future will be in direct contact with increasingly diverse populations in their local contexts or will be represented in the migrating and immigrating.
- Because immigrants and established minority populations are increasing in diversity among adolescents, new and established migrating groups along with indigenous populations more than ever need to work together to expand and deepen and enrich democratic life and the sensibilities it will require.

- Because of the mobility of people and capital, and the domination of capitalism, work and economic life patterns may be more dynamic and certainly more international in scope, and economic life will be more interdependent.
- Because the world continues to be plagued by poverty, inequality, injustice, violence, terrorism, and oppression, and because the nations of the world are increasingly interdependent and interconnected, solutions now and in the future will require global solutions. As citizens now and in the future, adolescents will be contending with these problems.
- Ecological issues and other issues related to the natural world will also require global cooperation. Adolescents will be facing difficult ecological dilemmas now and in the future and will need international cooperation.

Certainly global warming will require creative, courageous, and integrated efforts from the local, national, and global community.

This is our rationale for including global literature and cosmopolitan reading in this book and in our teaching lives; please add to it as you see fit. If global literature and cosmopolitanism reading are viewed as critical and necessary in these times for ourselves and particularly for our students, then the question remains: What does the articulation of this perspective look like in relation to the teaching of global literature to young adults?

LITERARY ORIENTATION AND PEDAGOGICAL STRATEGIES

As stated in the section on cosmopolitan reading, "cosmopolitanism" refers to a critical perspective that names and frames self and other in relation to the world rather than or in addition to the nation. In this work, we emphasize inquiry concerning social and cultural difference and diversity from a global perspective in efforts to increase global awareness and develop sensibilities suitable for global citizenship.

In these cosmopolitan/global times, culture, cultural difference, and identity are not fixed but are dynamic as individuals and groups fashion themselves a new in response to changing conditions and influences. Cosmopolitan readings work to increase knowledge and understanding of dynamic local and global cultures, as well as cultural identities, while acknowledging one's own cultural and geographical location(s), and so recognizing the limits of ever fully understanding others. It works against stereotyping and simplistic understandings of social and cultural issues and contexts. Although cosmopolitanism and the study of sociocultural difference could apply to any subject area, particularly social studies or civics, in the English/Language Arts classroom, it means organizing and structuring encounters with literature or text that allow for and encourages the reframing of the self and one's local/global cultural practices within a global frame.

In practical terms, a cosmopolitan reading focuses on the following three general sets of questions concerning any work:

1. *The World in the Text:* Questions concerning the nature and circumstances of the story and its context and its effect on the reader, for example, What is this narrative about? What surprised you about the setting and characters? What are the issues concerning cultural difference and diversity evident in this text or group of texts?

2. *The Text in the World:* Critical questions concerning text as a representation of the world and as an artifact in the world, for example, Who wrote this book and from what perspective? Who reads this text? Where was it published, and was it translated? How was it received locally and globally; that is, who would like or not like the text? How does it relate to other similar texts now and when it was written? How does the text work to support or challenge the dominant or conventional ways of understanding self and other in the world?

3. *The Text in the World of the Adolescent:* Questions concerning the effects/ relevance of this text on the immediate life, the cultural identities, and the identifications lived out locally/globally for teens, for example, What are the implications of this text for local adolescents? What critical actions might they take in light of their reading? What other reading would they like now to do?

Although it is possible that these foci might be approached through any of the general orientations toward the study of literature described in Chapter 3 (cultural heritage, personal or reader response, and cultural criticism), reader response and cultural criticism seem most appropriate. We list possible ideas and activities for you to consider and, if implemented, to customize for use in your particular context.

POSSIBILITIES FOR PRIOR READING ACTIVITIES

For students and teachers to engage deeply in the literature and other texts in the unit, let alone the overall theme or question framing their work, means attending to the local and global context: the local context in which the work is read and the context in which the work is set. The connections between the two are critical to creating an experience wherein the unit of study is not as viewed as a long travelogue in which the reader becomes a traveler studying another culture but as an engaged and deeply implicated participant, inside not outside the experience. In research, we call this position a participant-observer. Implicating the reader is an ongoing process, but initially it might mean beginning with students' local lives, identities, and communities, as well as their connections to the global community. Earlier, Activity 12.1 asked readers to trace their international experiences and connections experienced in their everyday lives (the food they eat, clothes they wear, and music they listen to). This activity might be a good way for students to begin to highlight the global, and to explore and reflect local lives and identities within a global frame.

In the case of the unit on "Adolescent Lives in Times of War and Conflict," teachers might begin with, and over the course of the unit return to, local teens and their knowledge and experience of the war in Iraq and the conflict in Afghanistan. It may mean beginning with listing possible effects of war on American adolescents. It might mean finding and analyzing military recruitment materials, ads on television, and news reports of the war; working with the social studies teacher to provide background on the war; and collecting local stories about the war and families. It will mean considering how the Middle East is represented positively and negatively in the local population and in the local culture (restaurants, fashion, and architecture). It might mean tracing the effects of war across family generations.

Reading global young adult literature helps students to understand the complex nature of cultural, national, regional, and global identifications.

Although the unit might start with the local, in any global literature unit, the local *in the global* needs to be developed to support reading and inquiry in the unit. Expanding out to the global through the study of texts will require knowledge, openness, and courage.

Thus, the specific context of the literary work or text to be read and studied will need to be attended to, as it is in any literature lesson. Background information begins with what knowledge individuals bring to the unit about war and how war stories are narrated, and in this case with what they know about the setting and circumstances of the literature they will be reading. This knowledge can be developed through supplementary reading, films, websites, personal contacts, and interviews and presentations from the pertinent community members and organizations.

QUESTIONS AND ACTIVITIES ARISING IN THE READING OF CORE TEXTS

Three sets of questions were listed in this chapter. Considering the unit on war, this framework might be articulated as follows:

The World in the Text: Groups or individual students work to develop understanding of a chosen text or narrative (see Chapter 3 for ideas) such that they can share the story, review its contents, and dramatize important selections to other students as part of a larger depiction of the war experiences of adolescents from various groups of students who are reading different works (e.g., literature circles). Comprehending the world in the text is the key to this activity.

The Text in the World: Students might contact, online or in print, the writer of the text, the adolescent featured in the work, or other readers of the text for their comments and thoughts about the work. Students might want to explore reviews of the texts and other information on authors' and publishers' websites. Students might want to develop comparisons with between the text and other narratives, and other genre forms on a similar topic/theme.

The Text in the World of the Adolescent: Students might want to reflect on what the readings across the unit mean in relation to their own direct and indirect experiences of war and conflict. They might be encouraged to consider their commitments and sacrifices during times of conflict and war. They may wish to write their own reviews of the pieces read, create a collage of quotes from the fictional and/or real-life teenagers they have read, or in some dramatic or artistic form represent the experience they have had in the unit and present it to an audience wider than their classmates. Such an activity could serve as a culminating event for the unit.

In working through the texts and the activities in the unit, James Banks, among others, has suggested that schools should help students to understand how cultural, national, regional, and global identifications are interrelated, complex, and evolving. Each student should be encouraged to examine critically his or her identifications and commitments and to understand the complex ways in which they are interrelated and constructed (Banks, 2004). In the case of this unit, students could explore how adolescence and adolescent life, its identity, and affiliations are changed, intensified, subverted, and obliterated in the context of local and global warfare as well as across borders.

MULTIMEDIA TEXT SET

In this text set, teacher Mark Fielding chose books and resources that explored the issue of refugees in different locations. He wanted students to understand that refugees are found in every part of the world and that this problem is not tied to a particular place. Moreover, he chose books that would allow students to understand the point of view of the main characters. In his words,

> I chose *Brothers in Hope: The Story of the Lost Boys of Sudan (Williams, 2005)* and *The Colour of Home (Hoffman, 2002)*. Both of these explore the subject from the point of view of children around the same ages of my students. Additionally, *The Colour of Home* deals with an experience that many of my students are familiar with, which is the experience of being a new student at a new school in a new place.

Picture Books:

1. Cha, D. (1996). *Dia's story cloth*. New York, NY: Lee & Low Books.

I selected this picture book because it explores the issue of refugees in another locale, Laos and Thailand. I really like the idea of students being able to see that the issue of being a refugee extends to many parts of the world, and that the hardship and difficult experiences are unfortunately common threads throughout. This book also has a very unique way of depicting the events with pictures from a story cloth. I thought this would be an interesting way to show students how illustration does not have to simply be a literal picture of the text.

2. Williams, M. (2005). *Brothers in hope: The story of the Lost Boys of Sudan*. New York, NY: Lee & Low Books.

I selected this picture book because it again explores the experiences of refugees in another location in the world. Additionally, it focuses on refugees that are around the ages of the students at my school, as the Lost Boys range from 8 to 15 years old. The sheer amount of refugees, the extreme difficulty of their experiences, and the resettlement of some of the boys in America make for extremely engaging topics to discuss with students.

3. Hoffman, M. (2002). *The colour of home*. New York, NY: Penguin.

This book explores the issue of refugees from Somalia but from a different perspective. In this story, Hassan is telling his experience as a newly resettled refugee in England and his difficulty adapting to his new home in England. For many of my students, changing schools and homes is something they have experienced, as well as the fear that comes with change. I thought this would be an excellent book to both explore the theme of refugees and connect it to my students' own experiences.

MULTIMEDIA SOURCES

1. Website of the United Nations High Commissioner for Refugees: www
   .unhcr.org/cgi-bin/texis/vtx/home

I chose this because I think students' first reaction to exploring the issue of refugees will be "What is being done to help them?" I want to show students that there are people who care and are trying to provide assistance to refugees, but unfortunately they cannot extend help to everyone.

2. Website for the Jewish Council for Racial Equality:

www.jcore.org.uk/what.php

   This is a website for an organization that promotes education about justice and equality for children, as well as provides practical support to refugees seeking asylum. I think it is an interesting resource because it shows one group of people, defined by their religion, proclaiming their belief that race and religion should have no bearing on a person's individual rights. I think it could lead into an interesting discussion about coexistence of different peoples.

SUMMARY

We believe the study of high-quality, high-interest global young adult literature taught from a cosmopolitan perspective will help in the development of students who are knowledgeable about, sensitive to, and comfortable with social and cultural difference and diversity locally, nationally, and globally and who will seek more just, equitable, compassionate, and democratic communities.

DISCUSSION QUESTIONS

1. What is the distinction between multicultural and global young adult literature? Provide examples.

2. How does global young adult literature encompass the international community from a variety of perspectives? Are there perspectives that are not represented?

3. How does cosmopolitan theory as it relates to the exploration of global texts provide students with a critical perspective?

4. What are the elements of global young adult literature? Which of the various strategies for exploring the genre with students would you want to try? Why?

KEY TERMS

Cosmopolitanism   250

Cosmopolitan Reading   250

Globalization   250

Global Literature   241

SMALL-GROUP ACTIVITY: CREATING AND DEVELOPING A UNIT

This is, of course, is only the beginning of a "unit on Adolescent Lives in Times of War and Conflict." In light of the students you teach or anticipate teaching, how would you customize this unit or another unit, what kinds of reading materials would you use, and what kind of activities might be possible? What kind of resistance might you anticipate? What kind of benefits might there be? Discuss with your classmates and/or colleagues.

RECOMMENDED READINGS

Carey-Webb, A. (2001). *Literature & lives: A response-based cultural studies approach to teaching English.* Urbana, IL: National Council of Teachers of English.

   This excellent resource offers teachers a critical perspective for engaging students in vibrant discussion.

Hadaway, N. L., & McKenna, M. J. (Eds.). (2007). *Breaking boundaries with global literature: Celebrating diversity in K-12 classrooms.* Newark, DE: International Reading Association.

   This edited volume includes lists of global literature and resources.

WEBSITES ON GLOBAL LITERATURE

Notable Books for a Global Society from the Children's Literature and Reading Special Interest Group of the International Reading Association: www.tcnj.edu/~childlit/proj/nbgs

JOURNALS ON YOUNG ADULT LITERATURE

The Alan Review
Dragon Lode

RECOMMENDED YOUNG ADULT LITERATURE FEATURED IN THIS CHAPTER

Al-Windawi, T. (2004). *Thura's diary: A young girl's life in war-torn Baghdad.* New York, NY: Penguin.

This account traces the onset of war in Baghdad from the perspective of an Iraqi citizen, Thura, a 19-year-old college student. Ultimately, she flees the city for the United States and a chance to continue her college studies. Her diary traces this journey away from the bombings and strife in her homeland.

Alexie, S. (2007). *The absolutely true diary of a part-time Indian.* New York, NY: Little, Brown.

Junior, the main character, leaves his friends in the struggling Spokane, Washington, reservation high school to attend a high-powered town school. This commute off the reservation angers Junior's friends and creates powerful inner conflicts as Junior experiences firsthand the radical differences in material resources in the two settings.

Alvarez, J. (2002). *Before we were free.* New York, NY: Knopf Books for Young Readers.

In the Dominican Republic, 12-year-old Anita de la Torre's family opposes a violent dictatorship and Anita must flee her country, leaving everything familiar behind.

Barakat, I. (2007). *Tasting the sky: A Palestinian childhood.* New York, NY: Melanie Kroupa Books.

Written as a memoir of a Palestinian refugee from the Six-Day War that concluded in 1967, resulting in the Israeli occupation of the West Bank and the Gaza Strip, this first hand account takes the reader into the heart of the Middle East conflict.

Ellis, D. (2001). *The breadwinner.* Toronto, Ontario, Canada: Groundwood.

The first of three books chronicling the war in Afghanistan, this novel follows a young teenaged girl, Parvana, as she and her family prepare to flee war-torn Kabul. Two other novels trace her journey out of her home country (*Parvana's Journey*, 2002, and *Mud City*, 2003).

Ellis, D. (2002). *Parvana's journey.* Toronto, Ontario, Canada: Groundwood.

Ellis, D. (2003). *Mud city.* Toronto, Ontario, Canada: Groundwood.

Ellis, D. (2004). *Three wishes: Palestinian and Israeli children speak.* Toronto, Ontario, Canada: Groundwood.

This is a very compelling collection of the voices of Palestinian and Israeli youth with their proposals for peace in the region. The 110-page book includes historical information, photos of the region, and biographical sketches of each of the young writers.

Frank, A. (1952/1995). *Diary of a young girl: The definitive edition*. New York, NY: Doubleday.

This crucial account is now part of any unit on the Holocaust, and it is clearly part of the literary canon. Newer accounts of youth in war zones like Deborah Ellis's trilogy also offer an insider's view of struggle and survival in war-torn nations.

Hosseini, K. (2003). *The kite runner*. New York, NY: Riverhead Books.

Myers, W. D. (2008). *Sunrise over Fallujah*. New York, NY: Scholastic.

The war in Iraq is seen from the perspective of a young African American soldier from Harlem working with the local people as part of a Civilian Affairs unit. The contradictions and doublespeak that cover the real purpose of this unit's operation weighs heavily on Robin Perry, the main character.

Naidoo, B. (2001). *The other side of truth*. New York, NY: HarperCollins.

This novel is located initially in Lagos, Nigeria, where Sade's father is a well-known journalist protesting the military coup. He is the target of an assassin who inadvertently kills Sade's mother and the family must flee illegally to London, England, where Sade and her brother are victims of racism and bullying. Sade is resourceful and a survivor, using the media to help her cause.

Reedy, T. (2011). *Words in the dust*. New York, NY: Arthur Levine Books.

In post-Taliban Afghanistan, Zulaikha learns to write poetry as a salve for everything she has gone through, but other challenges loom in her village.

Rifa'i, A., & Ainbinder, I. O. (2003). *We just want to live here*. New York, NY: St. Martin's Griffin.

Following a summer peace camp, two teenage girls carry on a conversation about their respective lives in Palestine and Israel. They correspond through letter writing and create alternatives to feeling trapped in their respective countries.

Ryan, P. M. (2000). *Esperanza rising*. New York, NY: Scholastic.

Set in a Mexican farm labor camp outside Bakersfield, California, this novel chronicles a young Latina girl's life during the Great Depression. The story is based on the author's maternal grandmother who left a rich life in Mexico to immigrate to the United States and work in a San Joaquin Valley labor camp. As historical fiction, the novel can be paired with nonfiction accounts in history to illuminate the grassroots experiences of Mexican immigrant workers during the Great Depression.

Satrapi, M. (2003). *Persepolis: The story of childhood*. New York, NY: Pantheon Books.

This graphic novel is a powerful autobiography of a young girl growing up in Tehran, Iran, during the Islamic revolution of 1979. It can be read and discussed alongside other young adult novels dealing with war issues.

Satrapi, M. (2004). *Persepollis 2: A story of return*. New York, NY: Pantheon Books.

In this sequel, Marjane returns to Iran after graduation, studies art at the university, and falls in love. Her struggles in fundamentalist Iran haunt her in this powerful graphic novel.

Spiegelman, A. (1986). *Maus I*: A *survivor's tale: My father bleeds history*. New York, NY: Pantheon.

Spiegelman, A. (1992). *Maus II: A survivor's tale: And here my troubles began*. New York, NY: Pantheon.

Vladek's tortured relationship with his aging father frames these comic pages.

Wiesel, E. (1982). *Night*. New York, NY: Bantam Books.

This Holocaust novel is centered in a Nazi German concentration camp with dark images and despair a constant.

Yang, G. L. (2007). *American-born Chinese*. New York, NY: First Second.

This popular graphic novel features three parallel stories and themes of struggling to fit in.

REFERENCES

Appiah, K. A. (2006). *Cosmopolitanism: Ethics in a world of strangers*. New York, NY: W.W. Norton.

Apple, M., Kenway, J., & Singh, M. (2005). *Globalizing education: Policies, pedagogies, & politics*. New York, NY: Peter Lang.

Banks, J. (2004). *Diversity, and citizenship education: Global perspectives*. San Francisco, CA: John Wiley & Sons.

Bean, T. W., Readence, J. E., & Baldwin, R. S. (2011). *Content area literacy: An integrated approach* (10th ed.). Dubuque, IA: Kendall/Hunt.

Beck, U. (2002). The cosmopolitan society and its enemies. *Theory, Culture, and Society, 19*(1–2), 17–44.

Castells, M. (1996). *Rise of the network society*. Cambridge, UK: Blackwell.

Hadaway, N. L., & McKenna, M.J. (Eds.). (2007). *Breaking boundaries with global literature: Celebrating diversity in K–12 classrooms*. Newark, DE: International Reading Association.

Luke, A., & Carrington, V. (2002). Curriculum, ethics, metanarrative: Teaching and learning beyond the nation. *Curriculum Perspectives 22*, (1), 49–55.

Nussbaum, M. (1999). Patriotism and cosmopolitanism. In M. Nussbaum & J. Cohen (Eds.), *For the love of country: Debating the limits of patriotism* (pp. 2–17). Cambridge, MA: Beacon Press.

Qureshi, K. S. (2006). Beyond mirrored worlds: Teaching world literature to challenge students' perception of "other." *English Journal, 96*(2), 34–40.

Reese, J. D. (2002). Learning for understanding: The role of world literature. *English Journal, 91*(5), 63–69.

PART III

Critical Issues in Young Adult Literature

Chapter 13

Boys Books/Girls Books? Gender and Sexuality in Young Adult Literature

Issues and concerns over the effects of gender on educational opportunities has been part of the conversation in literacy education for a long time. During the 1970s and 1980s, the concern was with girls and the representation of female authors as well as with the scope of women's perspectives and experiences offered in the literary fare provided to students in their school studies. This concern has not abated. In several recent texts, authors continue to press teachers to broaden the range of literature offered in their classes to include more women authors and stories, asking for literature that provides new and more complex narrative scripts concerning gender, in particular, ones that tie gender together with race, class, and other social constructions of identity (see, for example, Latrobe & Drury, 2009; Schmidt, 2011; Sprague & Keeling, 2007, 2009). Additionally, there are efforts to encourage teachers to include gender as a category of analysis in their literary lessons: to consider how femininity and masculinity is represented and functions in any narrative, how assumptions about gender affects our reading of any text, and to challenge conventional storylines about gender identity (Latrobe & Drury, 2009).

More recently, this conversation about gender and literacy has dramatically turned to boys and their underachievement in English/Language Arts. That girls read better than boys is part of popular consciousness, and certainly evidence suggests that some boys, particularly minority boys, may not be well served by the literacy curriculum, despite the preponderance of male characters and male authors in canonical school texts (Brozo, 2007; Brozo &

Gaskins, 2007). Both nationally and internationally, girls are outperforming boys in reading. The National Assessment of Educational Progress (NAEP) reports that 8th-grade girls consistently outscored males in reading and writing (Department of Education National Center for Education Statistics, 2009; Watson, Kehler, & Martino, 2010) and have consistently outperformed boys for the last 15 years (Moore, 2007; Sprague & Keeling, 2009, p. 187). A similar gendered pattern of literacy achievement also appears in results from international tests (e.g. PIRLS, PISA; Organisation for Economic Co-operation and Development [OECD], 2001, 2007; Mullis, Martin, Gonzales, & Kennedy, 2003). In addition, American data from the NAEP reveal a persistent and substantial gap between minority boys and the reading scores of their White counterparts (Department of Education National Center for Education Statistics, 2009; Moore, 2007; Tatum, 2005). Considering social class, race, ethnicity, and language background in addition to gender, and considering that not *all* boys underachieve or *all* girls overachieve, the question becomes exactly which boys (and which girls) are underachieving in literacy (Watson et al., 2010). Despite the importance of this question, and in the midst of considerable controversy, boys have been labeled by some as "the newly disadvantaged" (Farris, Werderich, Nelson, & Fuhler, 2009; Foster, Kimmel, & Skelton, 2001), and there has been a flood of conflicting ideas concerning how best to explain and address boys' literacy underachievement (for a discussion of this controversy, see Watson et al., 2010; also Mills, Martino, & Lingard, 2004).

The emerging concern with boys' literacy and the ongoing concerns about girls and their literacy education means that gender continues to feature strongly in the research literature as well as in classrooms.

Learning Objectives

- Understand the role that gender plays in the classroom in regard to differences in selecting personally relevant, culturally responsive young adult literature for all students.

- Consider and be able to discuss how perspectives on gender have influenced educational practice.

- Develop an understanding of the role played by sexual identity and heteronormativity in literature and the approaches to teaching young adult literature.

- Know a variety of in-class and out-of-class strategies for creating a democratic approach to young adult literature for all students.

Biological Essentialism: *Separate, Equal, and Homogeneous: Boys Books/ Girls Books*

One common way in which gender can be considered is as an effect of biology, and therefore, it is largely predetermined and immutable. In this case, gender and sex are considered synonymous. From this perspective, anatomy determines ones gender. All boys and all girls would be the essentially the same. Individuals who do not behave in ways consistent with others of their sex/gender assignment (based on anatomy) would be considered "odd" or abnormal, and perhaps a biological abnormality would be suspected. Working within this particular framework means accommodating for gender differences, which in turn means an English/Language Arts teacher would make a clear distinction between boys and girls, their pedagogy, and reading materials. Bookshelves might be labeled for boys or for girls. All girls and all boys would find the books designated for them appealing, and if they did not, then it would indicate something wrong with the individual and/or with the categorization of the book.

Sex Role Socialization: *Gender/Sex as Separate Cultural and Learned: Boys Books/Girls Books with a Purpose*

A second way in which gender is understood is through the idea of sex role socialization. Sex role socialization also begins with the assumption that biology determines sexual difference, but it explains the various and changing roles that men and women have assumed over time and across cultures by positing that children learn gender/sex roles and behavior by observing and modeling the adults in their world. Along with the adults in their world, the social and cultural institutions in children's lives (e.g., media, pop culture, schools, church, law, etc.) help maintain and enforce appropriate gender behavior. These cultural forces and institutions are responsible for narrowing the options offered individuals by creating narrow and rigid gender stereotypes and expectations.

In the literature, classroom teachers who believe in challenging gendered expectations and stereotypes would emphasize the need to ensure that both male and female students are exposed to a wider range of gender roles and circumstances in the literature read in class. Thus, there might be still be "boys" books and "girls" books, but in each case, these books would serve the purpose of expanding and challenging gender stereotypes, and rigid gender socialization.

There are significant problems with both these theories and the way they get articulated into classroom practice. Biological essentialism seems very rigid and easily renders pathological anyone who does not adhere to the conventional notions of what constitutes appropriate male and female behavior in any context—in the English/Language Arts classroom, those who do not conform to the convention and traditional notions of gender identity and the English/Language Arts gendered reading interests and abilities, and pedagogical practices. In addition, sex role socialization with its emphasis on social and cultural environment does not explain differences among those who grow up in the same environment, for example, in the same family. Moreover, both biological essentialism and sex role socialization renders an individual passive in the face of biological and social forces, passively modeling the behavior of adults or reacting to hormones, rather than as actively constructing themselves as gendered beings within the myriad of possibilities. However, many teens actively fashion an identity or indenties in the social circumstances and with the cultural resources available. In both of these theories, gender identity is considered fixed: an end product of socialization and biology, which does not account for the contradictions and shifts that occur in anyone's lifetime. Poststructuralism is an alternative theory that might better account for the struggles of adolescents as they fashion themselves as gendered beings in a changing world of many social contexts.

Poststructural theory: *Variable, Multiple, and Negotiated Masculinities and Femininities: Readings of Boys and Girls Books that Affirm and/or Challenge Dominant Scripts of Femininity and Masculinity*

Poststructuralism suggests that individuals actively position themselves with and against the various discursive and material practices available in any context that name and promote particular versions of masculinities and femininities. Gender is, thus, not a product of physical anatomy or of socialization but negotiated within the social and historical meanings given gender in any given context. Different discursive contexts have differing scripts concerning gender, which shifts the way an individual is positioned and/or can position themselves.

The more powerful or dominant a version of gender identity is, the more commonsensical it may seem, and therefore, the more difficult it is to challenge. For the English/Language Arts teacher who wants students to assess critically how gender identity is named in any text as a means to open up and challenge rigid and narrow assumptions about gender identity while increasing opportunity and assuring equity, the focus is not on books per se but on the readings of masculinity and femininity used in any narrative and reinforced (or not) by teachers' words and actions. All canonical or contemporary books or texts, print or otherwise, are sources that students can analyze for their portrayal of particular understanding and assumptions about femininity and masculinity.

Students need to be exposed to a wide range of gender roles and circumstances in literature.

In-Class Pedagogy

Using young adult literature incorporating both self-selected and relevant topics read by students individually, in small groups, or in literature circles is, of course, only the beginning. As discussed throughout this text, teachers need to provide readers with activities and discussion that support their reading and comprehension. But to ensure a focus on gender, Ms. Moffitt considered and reworked some of the following ideas for her class.

Media Study: *Study of Gender Assumptions and Social Expectations*
As an introduction to the topic of gender and after providing some examples, teachers might have students in small groups list and discuss the gendered expectations and assumptions society places on adolescents. Teachers may begin with media images and representations for critical assessment (for examples and a starting point for conversations about media constructions of gender, see these websites among many others: www.genderads.com, www.media lit.org/about_cml.html, and www.media-awareness.ca).

Over the course of a week have students collect actual verbal, print, and media examples of gendered social expectations, ideals, and assumptions about female and male teens to share with the class.

Literature Circles

Literature circles are a popular way of structuring in-class reading and pedagogy. In small groups, a book is selected and read according to a schedule worked out between the teacher and the group. In class/group assignments discussion/activities based on questions, specific to the text, and general questions such as those suggested by Sprague and Keeling (2007, p. 29) may be helpful in guiding a critical reflection of the text:

a. What role or expectations does society (family, friends, peers, media, school, and church) have for the main character?
b. Do these expectations match what the main character values and beliefs about herself/himself and the world?
c. What does my society expect of me? When do I and don't I conform?
d. Other questions might include

    i. How is femininity and masculinity portrayed in this novel? What role does it play in the development of the plot? Is this similar in plot or character to other texts you've read?

ii. Does this book reinforce or challenge your views or society's views of gender behavior and expectations?

In addition, the group completes in-class reading activities assigned by the teacher and a culminating assignment designed by the group presented to the class to promote the themes in the novel. Such culminating assignments may be multimodal in nature and include the transmediation of the book into iMovies, musical scores, dramatic interpretations of key scenes, or artistic renderings, to name a few possibilities. The use of multimedia text sets as demonstrated throughout this book might also offer a way for student to expand their ideas and "continue the conversation" begun in their discussion groups. Thus, the typical "literature circle" becomes a vehicle for not only comprehension and discussion but also creative collaboration.

Out-of-Class Pedagogy

To support in-school reading especially in the area of young adult literature, out-of-school activities can be encouraged and promoted to help improve students reading.

Forming Electronic Book Clubs

William G. Brozo, among others, suggests forming electronic or face-to-face after-school or summer book clubs as a means of engaging boys in young adult literature out of class to support in-class literacy engagement and achievement (Brozo, 2007). In his experience and research in a middle school book club with struggling male readers, teachers found some success; however, Brozo suggested ensuring a strong match between members' reading interests and what is read for the book club. He noted whatever their interest, humorous books were always welcomed. Brozo also indicated that responses to the books could take various multimodal forms in the book club, not just more school-like print assignments.

Likewise, after-school or summer school book clubs work as well. (See Activity 13.2.) Sprague and Keeling (2007, 2009) suggested that girls-only groups might better serve to develop girls' voices and discussion, but much depends on the group and the circumstances. However, this practice should be purposeful, perhaps as a means of providing a "safe" place for girls to develop a voice, especially around sensitive issues of gender. Perhaps more usefully, and to avoid essentializing gender roles, book clubs might be denoted by topic or genre of interest (i.e., science fiction, fantasy, graphic novels, and autobiographies).

ACTIVITY 13.2: Other Ideas for In- and Out-of-School Projects and Activities

Directions: In small groups, list and discuss other in- and out-of-school and community projects and events that would help promote the reading of young adult literature in same- and mixed-gender groups. How would you determine the construction of the groups?

SEXUAL IDENTITY/ORIENTATION

As sensitive and challenging as it might be to address gender issues and stereotypes in the English/Language Arts classroom, sexual identity and sexual orientation remain perhaps the most difficult topic in the English/Language Arts classroom. We include it in this chapter because it is difficult to talk about gender and the dominant social scripts about femininity and masculinity without running headlong into issues of sexual orientation, especially because reinforcing and underscoring dominant versions of appropriate feminine and masculine behavior are often assumptions about heterosexuality and homosexuality. Heterosexuality, for example, is tightly aligned with conventional notions of masculinity; thus, to "be a man" is aligned with a desire for women. Other reasons why English teachers might want to include some consideration of sexual identity in their curriculum include the knowledge that a portion of the student population and the general population are themselves sexual minorities and have been underserved by schools (Charles, 2010; Kumashiro, 2002; McCready, 2004; Vaught, 2005). Moreover, gay teens are more likely to suffer harassment in and outside of school (Human Rights Watch, 2001). In a democracy, acknowledging and challenging bias and inequality in text and in life is critical to American ideals, and understanding that popular (and indeed literary) culture is replete with texts and performances that highlight sexual identity is not to marginalize students inadvertently or promote bias even further. Perhaps one way to begin discussions around adolescent sexual identity with students is to hear the voices of GLBTQ teens themselves. In *The Shared Heart: Portraits and Stories Celebrating Lesbian, Gay, and Bisexual Young People* (Mastoon, 2001), 40 lesbian, gay, and bisexual teens share their thoughts and experiences about family, friends, culture, and coming out. It offers a moving collection of photographs and personal narratives that speaks to the struggles and soul-searching transformation of their own lives, families, and communities. Activity 13.3 provides an opportunity for you to peruse the text and discuss how this collection as well as your own experiences might influence how you approach gender and sexual identity and orientation in your classroom.

ACTIVITY 13.3: Personal Reflection and Discussion

Directions: Obtain a copy of *The Shared Heart* and peruse it with a partner. How can you use the narratives and photographs in the collection to explore issues of gender and sexual orientation? If you live in a community where such issues are difficult to discuss, are there ways to ensure that GLBTQ teens have access to literature that reflects their experiences?

HETERONORMATIVITY

Adult literature can challenge commonly held beliefs about gender and sexual identities.

Heteronormativity means a way of being in the world that relies on the belief that heterosexuality is normal, which implicitly positions homosexuality and bisexuality as abnormal and, thus, inferior. It is often much more subtle than homophobia, which is the more obvious hatred of homosexuals and homosexual behavior. Rather than a focus on GLBTQ-themed literature, a focus on heteronormativity means drawing attention to how social and discursive practices reinforce the idea that heterosexuality is normal and/or assumed with the effect that homosexuality is rendered invisible and aberrant. It is a collection of practices and institutions that legitimize and privilege heterosexuality and heterosexual relationships as fundamental and "natural" within society.

According to Mollie V. Blackburn and Jill M. Smith (2010), among others (see Berry, Jay, & Lynn, 2010; Dixson & Rousseau, 2006; Kumashiro, 2002), nearly every school in the United States is heteronormative; that is, they are foundationally based on the concept that heterosexuality is normal and homosexuality is abnormal. Most high school freshmen, for example, read Shakespeare's *Romeo and Juliet,* a text where heterosexual love, sex, and marriage are centrally positioned, rather than, say, the young adult novel *Know Not Why* (Johnson, 2010) where the protagonist, Howie, goes to work in a craft store ostensibly to "get" girls and ends up falling for co-worker Arthur instead. With the canonical text, a teacher might name and teach *Romeo and Juliet* as a story of adolescent romance, in which she assumes students will identify with either Romeo or Juliet along the lines of established sexual identities. Such naming and assumptions demonstrate heteronormativity; in this case, an adult (teacher) enforces heteronormativity—an enforcement that requires adolescents to read a text focusing on a heterosexual couple and to identify with those characters as heterosexuals—is one that presents only one option, that of an unchangeable binary: You are either Romeo or Juliet, boy attracted to girl, or girl attracted to boy. By comparison, the characters in *Know Not Why* are not bound to the same binary—in fact, Howie's sexual identity is in flux.

However explored, adding a focus on heteronormativity allows attention to GLBTQ issues both in novels such as *Know Not Why* as well as in canonical texts. Making visible and, thus, challenging how the naming and reinforcement of heteronormativity makes it possible for students to question commonly held assumptions and beliefs about gender and sexual identities contributes to the promotion of a more just, equitable, compassionate, and democratic society (Moje, 2007; Wickens, 2009).

SUMMARY

In this chapter, we discussed issues related to gender and sexual orientation and identity. Although of a sensitive and potentially provocative nature, the exclusion of these topics when addressing young adult literature may further exclude GLBTQ adolescents from full participation in schools, while further perpetuating a rigid definition of what constitutes appropriate gender roles both in literature and in life.

DISCUSSION QUESTIONS

1. What role does gender plays in the classroom in regard to selecting personally relevant, culturally responsive young adult literature for all students?

2. How have perspectives on gender influenced educational practice?

3. What role does sexual identity and heteronormativity play in literature and approaches to teaching young adult literature? How will you handle these issues in your current or future classroom?

4. What in-class and out-of-class strategies for creating a democratic approach to young adult literature will you use for your students?

KEY TERMS

Biological Essentialism   269

Heteronormativity   274

Poststructural theory   270

Sex Role Socialization   269

SMALL-GROUP ACTIVITY: LOVE BITES

Directions: In small groups, outline a unit titled "Love Bites," which highlights gender and sexual identity in relation to romance as depicted in the vampire romance and other young adult fiction as well as in canonical texts, for example, Shakespeare's *Romeo and Juliet*. What texts, activities, and questions regarding femininity and masculinity would be central to such a unit?

RECOMMENDED READINGS

American Association of University Women (AAUW). (2008). *Where the girls are: The facts about gender equity in education.* Washington, DC: AAUW Educational Foundations.

Appleton, D. (2009). The social construction of gender: A lens of one's own. In D. Appleton (Ed.), *Critical encounters in high school English* (pp. 65–83). New York, NY: Teachers College Press.

Bean, T. W., & Harper, H. (2007). Reading men differently: Alternative portrayals of masculinity in contemporary young adult literature. *Reading Psychology, 28,* 11–30.

Blackburn, M. V., & Smith, J. M. (2010). Moving beyond the inclusion of LGBT-themed literature in English Language Arts classrooms: Interrogating heteronormativity and exploring intersectionality. *Journal of Adolescent & Adult Literacy, 53* (8), 625–634.

Brozo, B. (2002). *To be a boy, to be a reader. Engaging teen and preteen boys in active literacy.* Newark, DE: International Reading Association.

Brozo, B., & Gaskins, C. (2007). Engaging texts and literacy practices for adolescent boys. In K. Woods & E. Blanton (Eds.), *Literacy instruction for adolescents: Research-based practice* (pp. 170–187). New York, NY: Guilford.

Brozo, B. (2007). Helping boys find entry points to lifelong reading: Book clubs, and other strategies for struggling adolescent males. In J. Lewis & G. Moorman (Eds.), *Adolescent literacy instruction: Policy and promising practices for adolescents: Research-based practice* (pp. 304–318). Newark, DE: International Reading Association.

Cherland, M. (2009). Harry's girls: Harry Potter and the discourse of gender. *Journal of Adolescent and Adult Literacy, 52* (4), 273–282.

Davies, B. (1989). *Frogs and snails and feminist tales: Preschool children and gender.* Sydney, Australia: Allen & Unwin.

Pinar, W. (1998). *Queer theory in education.* Mahwah, NJ: Lawrence Erlbaum.

Smith, M., & Wilhelm, J. (2002). *"Reading don't fix no Chevys": Literacy in the lives of young men.* Portsmouth, NH: Heinemann.

Sprague, M., & Keeling, K. (2007). *Discovering their voices: Engaging adolescent girls with young adult literature.* Newark, DE: International Reading Association.

Tatum, A. W. (2005). *Teaching reading to black adolescent males: Closing the achievement gap.* Portland, ME: Steinhouse.

Wickens, C. (2009). Social spaces, hierarchies, and regulations in LGBTQ young adult fiction. In K. Leander & D. Rowe (Eds.), *58th yearbook of the National Reading Conference* (pp. 348–361). Old Creek, WI: National Reading Conference.

RECOMMENDED YOUNG ADULT LITERATURE FEATURED IN THIS CHAPTER

Alexie, S. (2007). *The absolutely true story of a part-time Indian.* New York, NY: Little, Brown.

Budding cartoonist Junior transfers from his troubled school on the Spokane Indian Reservation to an all-White farm school where the only other Indian is the school mascot.

Anderson, L. (2002). *Fever: 1793.* New York, NY: Aladdin.

This is the story of Mattie, a girl living in 18th-century Philadelphia, who nurses the ill during a yellow fever epidemic and alone runs her family's business. This story is based on actual historical events.

Anderson, L. (2003). *Speak.* New York, NY: Penguin.

Melinda displays the classic signs of depression after being raped at a high school party. Over the course of the novel, she comes to speak about her trauma and confronts her rapist.

Anderson, L. (2009). *Winter girls.* New York, NY: Viking.

An 18-year-old girl named Lia comes to terms with the death of her friend from anorexia as she struggles with the same disorder.

Anthony, J., & Corral, R. (2011). *Chopsticks.* New York, NY: Razorbill.

After losing her mother, Glory withdraws into her piano prodigy world, subsequently going into a deep, downward spiral, only able to play "Chopsticks" endlessly. In a multi-modal combination of photos and pictures, and words, the author takes the reader into Glory's conflicted psyche.

de la Pena, M. (2008). *Mexican Whiteboy*. New York, NY: Delacorte Press.

Sixteen-year-old Danny struggles with his identity while spending the summer with his cousin and new friends in the baseball fields and back alleys of San Diego County, California.

Emond, S. (2011). *Winter town*. New York, NY: Little, Brown.

Golding, W. (1967). *Lord of the flies*. New York, NY: Penguin Putnam.

Johnson, H. (2010). *Know not why* [Kindle book]. Retrieved from http://www.amazon.com/Know-Not-Why-Novel-ebook/dp/B007ZVX57M

Littman, S. D. (2011). *Want to go private?* New York, NY: Scholastic Press.

Mastoon, A. (2001). *The shared heart: Portraits and stories celebrating lesbian, gay, and bisexual young people*. New York, NY: HarperCollins.

Naylor, P. R. (2001). *Alice on the outside*. New York, NY: Simon Pulse.

A story of 14-year-old Alice's attempts to learn about sex in her relation with boys and with a girl, Lori. It is a book commonly challenged.

Peters, J. (2003). *Keeping you a secret*. New York, NY: Little, Brown.

As she begins a very tough last semester of high school, Holland finds herself puzzled by her future and intrigued by a transfer student, Cece, who wants to start a Lesigay club at school.

Peters, J. (2003). *Luna*. New York, NY: Little, Brown.

A sister discovers and struggles to come to terms with her brother's transgendered identity.

Spinelli, J. (2002). *Stargirl*. New York, NY: Knopf.

This book is the story of an unconventional girl, Susan Caraway, who tries but fails to conform to the status quo at her school and is shunned by her peers and ultimately her boyfriend, Leo, who realizes too late what he has lost.

RECOMMENDED WEBSITES

www.genderads.com/Gender_Ads.com.html
www. media lit.org/about_cml.html
www.media-awareness.ca
www.tenreads.com
www.ala.org/yalsa
www.edb.texas.edu/resources/books4teens
www.guysread.com

REFERENCES

Berry, R. T., Jay, M., & Lynn, M. (2010, January 1). Introduction: Thoughts and ideas on the intersectionality of identity. *The Journal of Educational Foundations*.

Blackburn, M., & Smith, J. M. (2010). Moving beyond the inclusion of LGBT-themed literature in English Language Arts classrooms: Interrogating heteronormativity and exploring intersectionality. *Journal of Adolescent & Adult Literacy, 53*(8), 625–634.

Brozo, B. (2007). Helping boys find entry points to lifelong reading: Book clubs, and other strategies for struggling adolescent males. In J. Lewis & G. Moorman (Eds.), *Adolescent literacy instruction: Policy and promising practices for adolescents: Research-based practice* (pp. 304–318). Newark, DE: International Reading Association.

Brozo, B., & Gaskins, C. (2007). Engaging texts and literacy practices for adolescent boys. In K. Woods & E. Blanton (Eds.), *Literacy instruction for adolescents: Research-based practice* (pp. 170–187). New York, NY: Guilford.

Burke, J. (2008). *The English teacher's companion: A complete guide to classroom, curriculum, and the profession* (3rd ed.). Portsmouth, NH: Heinemann.

Charles, C. E. (2010). Complicating hetero-femininities: Young women, sexualities and "girl power" at school. *International Journal of Qualitative Studies in Education 23*(1), 33–47.

Dixson, A. D., & Rousseau, C. K. (2006). And we are still not saved: Critical race theory in education ten years later. In A. D. Dixson & C. K. Rousseau (Eds.), *Critical race theory in education: All God's children got a song* (pp. 31–56). New York, NY: Routledge.

Department of Education National Center for Education Statistics. (2009). *The Nation's Report Card* (NCES 2010451). Washington, DC: U.S. Government Printing Office.

Farris, P., Werderich, D., Nelson, P., & Fuhler, C. (2009). Male call: Fifth-grade boys' reading preferences. *The Reading Teacher, 63*(3), 180–188.

Foster, V., Kimmel, M., & Skeleton, C. (2001). What about the boys? An overview of the debates. In W. Martino & B. Meyenn (Eds.), *What about the boys? Issues of masculinity in schools* (pp. 1–27). Buckingham, England: Open University Press.

Human Rights Watch. (2001). *Hatred in the hallways: Violence and discrimination against lesbian, gay, bisexual, and transgendered students in U.S. schools*. New York, NY: Human Rights Watch.

Kumashiro, K. K. (2002). *Troubling education: Queer activism and antioppressive pedagogy*. New York, NY: Routledge Falmer.

Latrobe, K. H., & Drury, J. (2009). Critical approaches to young adult literature. New York: Neal-Schuman.

McCready, L. (2004). Understanding the marginalization of gay and gender nonconforming Black male students. *Theory Into Practice, 43*(2), 136–143.

Mills, M., Martino, W., & Lingard, B. (2004). Attracting, recruiting, and retaining male teachers: Policy issues in a male teacher debate. *British Journal of Sociology of Education, 25*(3), 355–371.

Moje, E. (2007). Developing socially just subject-matter instruction: A review of the literature on disciplinary literacy teaching. *Review of Research in Education, 31*, 1–44.

Moore, D. (2007). Advocating reading instruction in middle and high school classrooms. In K. Woods & E. Blanton (Eds.), *Literacy instruction for adolescents: Research-based practice* (pp. 13–37). New York, NY: Guilford.

Mullis, I. V. S., Martin, M. O., Gonzalez, E. J., & Kennedy, A. (2003). *PIRLS 2001 International Report: IE's study of reading achievement in primary schools in 35 countries*. Chestnut Hill, MA: Boston College.

National Council of Teachers of English: Guidelines for gender-balanced curriculum in English grades 7–12 (p. 1). Available from: www.ncte.org

Organisation for Economic Co-operation and Development. (2001). *Knowledge and kills for life: Pisa, 2000*. Paris, France: Author.

Organisation for Economic Co-operation and Development. (2007). *Pisa, 2006: Science competencies for tomorrow's world; executive summary*. Paris, France.

Schmidt, S. J. (2011). Who lives on the other side of that boundary: A model of geographic thinking. *Social Education, 75*, (5), 250–255.

Sprague, M., & Keeling, K. (2007). *Discovering their voices: Engaging adolescent girls with young adult literature*. Newark, DE: International Reading Association.

Sprague, M., & Keeling, K. (2009). Paying attention to girls' literacy needs. In K. Woods & E. Blanton (Eds.), *Literacy instruction for adolescents: Research-based practice* (pp. 187–209). New York, NY: Guilford.

Tatum, A. W. (2005). *Teaching reading to black adolescent males: Closing the achievement gap*. Portland, ME: Steinhouse.

Vaught, S. (2005). The talented tenth: Gay Black boys and the racial politics of Southern schooling. *Journal of Gay and Lesbian Issues in Education, 2*(2), 5–26.

Watson, A., Kehler, M., & Martino, W. (2010). The problem of boys' literacy underachievement: Raising some questions. *Journal of Adolescent and Adult Literacy, 53* (5), 356–361.

Wickens, C. (2009). Social spaces, hierarchies, and regulations in LGBTQ young adult fiction. In K. Leander & D. Rowe (Eds.), *58th yearbook of the National Reading Conference* (pp. 348–361). Old Creek, WI: National Reading Conference.

Chapter 14

Young Adult Literature and Critical Content Area Literacy

In this chapter, we consider the role of young adult literature in enriching critical content area engagement and comprehension. Briefly defined, **content area literacy** refers to the level of reading and writing necessary to read, comprehend, and react to instructional material in the disciplines (Bean, Readence, & Baldwin, 2011). Young adult literature has much to offer across print-laden disciplines including English, social studies, science, and other content areas. Each of these fields has particular and unique discourse forms that inform thinking like a scientist, historian, literature expert, and so on (Moje, 2008). While we do not attempt to cover every discipline, recommended readings and other resources are offered to extend your thinking around this topic.

Learning Objectives

- Understand the ways in which young adult literature may be used to increase critical content area comprehension and engagement.

- Consider and be able to discuss how **critical content area literacy** differs from traditional notions of content area literacy.

- Develop an understanding of how approaches such as deliberative process and critical literacy questions facilitate cross-content collaborations.

- Know a variety of strategies for using young adult literature and content area texts in a complementary manner.

Vignette: Mr. Theodore Jackson's High School English Class

Mr. Jackson teaches in an advanced technology academy charter school where his students plan careers in business and industry. They are uninterested in literature classes and gravitate toward their preferred technology courses. Mr. Jackson has an uphill battle to convince his students of the value of reading. Young adult novels, nonfiction magazines, and online selections enrich his efforts to engage students in critical content area literacy discussions.

Mr. Jackson created a unit on *cloud computing* to entice these students into critically reading and discussing nonfiction and fiction in his English classroom. *Cloud computing* refers to the use of remote servers that store huge amounts of clients' data on the Internet (Zomaya, 2010). Thus, one's contact lists and a host of other material including notes and reports are available from any computer or mobile device. Companies like Amazon and Google exemplify cloud computing with vast information resources available to users at the click of a mouse. Although that is the upside of cloud computing, Mr. Jackson wants his students to think critically about points that University of Sydney professor and Centre for Distributed and High Performance Computing scholar Albert Zomaya raise. In addition, they have been on *Wired* magazine's blog website, Cloudline (http://wired.com/cloudline) where distinguished engineers and scholars comment on cloud computing issues. Mr. Jackson has students discuss the blog postings and articles in small groups in terms of any problems that Zomaya mentions, and they then participate in a whole-group discussion where they must support a positive or negative stance about cloud computing based on drawing roles out of a hat.

Mr. Jackson: Let's start with those of you who have been charged with supporting a negative view of cloud computing. What are some of the problems that Professor Zomaya raises, and do you buy his argument?

S1:   The servers use huge amounts of electricity, which could further increase global warming conditions.

S2:   He includes calculations that show that the heat produced by Intel processors has been increasing and could eventually exceed that of the surface of the sun.

S3:   And that vast heat could interfere with server performance, reducing cloud computing's efficiency.

Mr. Jackson: These are good points, and there's also the issue of cyber security with remote systems handling all our data storage.

S1:   Right. I read a *Wired* magazine interview with George Dyson who actually grew up around Princeton University where his father, Freeman Dyson, worked on the first fully random access memory computer, MANIAC (Kelly, 2012). It was pretty primitive compared with digital devices now.

S3:   Yeah, I thought the coolest thing Dyson said in that interview was about the way computers learn and create their own instructions. Here, I have it in my backpack, and what he said was: "This space can't be supervised. As the digital universe expands, so does this wild, undomesticated side" (Kelly, 2012, p. 122).

Mr. Jackson: Okay, so cloud computing isn't all rosy and perfect, and you've done a nice job critiquing its downside. What I would like you to do now is select a young adult e-novel that deals with computer hacking or some other aspect of the digital universe. Based on your reading of the novel you select, I would like you to construct a multimedia project (e.g., PowerPoint, video clip, and YouTube clip) to share with the rest of the class. I will give you the grading rubric for it, and for our next class, you can locate a young adult novel. Here are a few examples to get you started.

Young Adult Fiction

1.   Jinks, C. (2009). *The genius wars*. Boston, MA: Houghton Mifflin Harcourt.
     Cyber-espionage and action-packed scenes drive this series. Other books in the series can be found online (www.catherinejinks.com).

2.   Wasserman, R. (2007). *Hacking Harvard*. New York, NY: Simon Pulse.
A bet, the goal of this high-tech ruse is to get a high-school deadbeat into Harvard University.

Young Adult Nonfiction

1.   Jacobs, T. (2010). *Teen cyberbullying investigated: Where do your rights end and consequences begin?* Minneapolis, MN: Free Spirit.
     This book explores threats to teens including harassing e-mails, texts, and so on. It offers examples of court cases and related decisions, along with tips to avoid cyberbullying.

HOW TO GET STARTED WITH CRITICAL CONTENT AREA LITERACY

Although content area literacy has been around for some time now, centered largely on learning concepts in the disciplines, critical content area literacy adds another important dimension for the development of a democratic citizenry. Critical literacy asks readers to consider carefully positions and stances in any text in terms of who has power and voice (Bean et al., 2011; Stevens & Bean, 2007). Thus, in the vignette considering cloud computing, multiple viewpoints about the good and potentially bad features of cloud computing can be explored and discussed. Various stakeholder positions can be evaluated with an eye toward who stands to benefit from a phenomenon like cloud computing (e.g., major companies like Amazon and Google).

While content area literacy is centered largely on learning concepts in the disciplines, critical content area literacy adds democratic dimensions.

English and social studies teachers often team up in collaborative arrangements where their students read and discuss texts that offer poignant problems. Social studies scholars have called for an increasing emphasis on deliberation and discussion (Baildon & Damico, 2011; Damico & Baildon, 2011). Walter Parker (2003) offered a carefully designed process for engaging students in critical content area literacy. The following steps are first outlined, and then in Activity 14.1 (see page 287), you will have a chance to put these steps into play around a compelling issue (e.g., immigration) and related young adult readings.

The deliberative process that Parker has developed involves the following:

1. Having students explore the issue under consideration (e.g., immigration)

2. Having each group break into pairs

3. Having each pair take up a different position on the issue and do further reading to support its position

4. Having each pair present its argument to another pair

5. Having each pair reverse perspectives to take up the opposing view

6. Having each pair recombine into a group of four and seek consensus on the issue (or, agree to disagree)

Case 14.1 provides an opportunity for you to view this deliberative process with the young adult novel *A So-Called Vacation* (Gonzalez, 2009). In this coming-of-age novel, two high school brothers, Gabriel and Gustavo, leave their Texas home with their father for a summer in California doing field work. Although they are native-born Texans and are less than thrilled about this trip, their dad was an immigrant worker as a kid and he feels this will be an important growth experience for Gabriel and Gustavo. They live in a migrant camp shack with no electricity or running water, experience racial discrimination directed toward recent immigrants, and begin to appreciate their dad's journey as an immigrant.

CASE 14.1: Javier Hernandez's Classroom

This case is set in a rural high school in the San Joaquin Valley, California, where Spanish is the first language and agricultural work in the grape and lettuce fields thrives. The social studies teacher, Mr. Javier Hernandez, is part of a cooperative project aimed at helping struggling readers read and critically discuss literature that engages their interest.

A So-Called Vacation, with its controversial premise involving two high school students in a forced summer of migrant labor and life in a migrant camp, lends itself to deliberation and critique. Mr. Hernandez has divided the class into pairs with each pair having to defend one of the two positions: (a) The dad's idea to take his two sons to work in a migrant camp was a good idea, or (b) the dad's idea to take his two sons to work in a migrant camp was a bad idea. Consistent with Parker's (2003) deliberative process, we can observe both groups initially arguing their assigned position and then having to flip positions and argue the other side's point of view.

Team 1:
(position a)
We think this kind of summer would be hard but important for these brothers to appreciate the struggles of immigrant workers. Reading about it helps, but actually doing the work, living in the rough conditions in the camp, that made it real.

Our moms and dads were in the migrant camps, and it made them tough and able to handle prejudice and job discrimination. The brothers prefer hip hop to the Spanish rhythms embraced by their father. But, they also realize that "their world was but one generation removed from his" (p. 164). So, we think this was a mind-expanding way to spend their summer, and others should do this to really understand the problems immigrant families face in the United States.

Team 2:
(position b)
We can appreciate your point of view, but we talked it over and we really feel that this is like some summer camp experience. The brothers and dad get to go home to their plush life. The migrant works in the agricultural camps don't have that option. So, we really think this story is just that, a story, not real.

Mr. Hernandez:
Okay, if you were going to find some agreement in these two positions, what would that be?

Team 2:
We think it makes for a good story but not something that could really happen. Lawyers would be all over this because of liability issues with the two brothers working in an adult labor camp.

Team 1:
Okay, we can see that would be an issue, but we still think some type of experience like this one helps privileged youth see the other side of life and maybe respect hard work.

Team 2:
Right. This novel exposes us to a life that maybe some of our parents lived, but we are really lucky to be the next generation, out of the camps and getting educated.

CRITICAL LITERACY PRACTICES AND YOUNG ADULT LITERATURE

Critical literacy challenges the neutrality of texts. Critical content area comprehension requires close and multiple readings of important passages.

Parker's (2003) deliberative process is one of many you can use to engage your students' in critical content area literacy practices. Critical literacy views texts as anything but neutral. The narrative world of novels can be deconstructed through critical questions about gender, race, and class. The following questions provide a critical framework for close reading and discussion (Bean et al. & Baldwin, 2011):

- Who has a voice (or power) in this novel?
- Who does not have a voice (or power) in this novel?
- What race, class, and gender issues are highlighted?
- What ideologies are in play that shape this text?
- How could this novel be shaped differently?

Each of these questions gets at gaps and silences in a novel, but this level of critical content area comprehension requires close reading and rereading of important passages. Dennis Sumara (2002) likened this careful reading to participating in an anthropological dig:

> I have come to think of the experience of developing a deep relationship with a literary text as a focal practice—an interpretive event that occurs when one becomes committed to the making of something that provokes attention to detail, requires the development of interpretation and production skills, and sustains attention, energy and interest. (p. 150)

Activity 14.1 asks you to create a critical content literacy lesson based on the popular series and film that began with *The Hunger Games* (Collins, 2008). In this futuristic novel, North America has been reduced to ruins. A central capital rules over the 12 outlying districts by forcing one boy and one girl between the ages of 12 and 18 to go to the annual Hunger Games where they fight to the death on live television. The main character is 16-year-old Katniss Everdeen, and she must participate in the games.

Following the model from Mr. Hernandez's class where students analyzed the experience requiring the two boys to spend the summer in a migrant worker camp with their dad, we can explore a similar experience in *The Hunger Games* that requires exile and battle far from home. This activity is centered on an integrated English and social studies unit and related lessons comparing and contrasting conquering and colonizing societies that reward physical prowess and survival (e.g., the Vikings).

ACTIVITY 14.1: Professional Reflection and Discussion

Directions: Using the young adult novel and film, *The Hunger Games*, create a multimedia text set that includes novels, plays, and films from other cultures in history where a battle to the death is required for survival. Classic public domain short stories like *The Lady or the Tiger?* (Stockton, 1882) follow a similar plot. Gladiator battles and contemporary Ultimate Fighting competitions, whereas they do not require a battle to the death, parallel the intense competition obvious in *The Hunger Games*. Using the multimedia text set you created, develop a series of critical literacy questions aimed at deconstructing the plot and events in the reading selection.

SUMMARY

This chapter introduced critical content area literacy and demonstrated its application in a social studies classroom with struggling readers. Walter Parker's deliberative process for critically discussing young adult literature was illustrated, along with critical literacy questions aimed at engaging students in close, critical reading of young adult literature selections.

DISCUSSION QUESTIONS

1. How can young adult literature be used to increase critical content area comprehension and engagement?

2. How does critical content area literacy differ from traditional notions of content area literacy? What are the strengths of this approach?

3. Consider your current or future classroom. How will you use approaches such as deliberative process and critical literacy questions to facilitate cross-content collaborations among students and other teachers?

4. Which strategies for using young adult literature and content area texts will you be the most likely to try? What other strategies might also be appropriate?

KEY TERMS

Content Area Literacy   281   Critical Content Area Literacy   281

SMALL-GROUP ACTIVITY: CREATE A CRITICAL LITERACY LESSON

Now that you have a sense of how critical content area literacy lessons can be developed, identify a young adult novel from the recommended young adult literature list provided for this chapter and create a critical literacy lesson. Share and conduct a trial run of the lesson with your small group.

RECOMMENDED READINGS

Baildon, M., & Damico, J. S. (2011). *Social studies as new literacies in a global society: Relational cosmopolitanism in the classroom*. New York, NY: Routledge.

   The authors created a critical web reader resource teachers can use to create questions students can use to critically interrogate website content (see Recommended Websites section). In addition, other critical literacy lesson examples are offered for conventional print texts.

Bean, T. W., Readence, J. E., & Baldwin, R. S. (2011). *Content area literacy: An integrated approach* (10th ed.). Dubuque, IA: Kendall/Hunt.

   This text includes sections on critical literacy, as well as examples of how to guide students' critical reading and discussion of young adult literature (see Chapter 7).

Damico, J. S., & Baildon, M. (2011). Content literacy for the 21st century: Excavation, elevation, and relational cosmopolitanism in the classroom. *Journal of Adolescent & Adult Literacy, 55* (3), 232–243.

   These authors offer examples of applying critical literacy practices to social studies content, and their text (see Baildon & Damico, 2011) includes additional examples.

RECOMMENDED YOUNG ADULT LITERATURE FEATURED IN THIS CHAPTER

Collins, S. (2008). *The hunger games*. New York, NY: Scholastic.

   In this futuristic novel, North America has been reduced to ruins. A central capitol rules over the 12 outlying districts by forcing one boy and one girl between the ages of 12 and 18 to go to the annual Hunger Games where they fight to the death on live television.

Curtis, C. P. (2002). *Bud, not Buddy*. Austin, TX: Holt, Rinehart & Winston.

   Set in Depression-era Michigan, a young boy sets out to locate his missing father living in harsh conditions. This novel earned a Newberry Award and captures life in the Depression era.

Gonzalez, G. (2009). *A so-called vacation*. Houston, TX: Pinata Books.

In this coming-of-age novel, two high school brothers, Gabriel and Gustavo, leave their Texas home with their father for a summer in California doing field work. Although they are native-born Texans, and less than thrilled about this trip, their dad was an immigrant worker as a kid and he feels this will be an important growth experience for Gabriel and Gustavo.

Myers, W. D. (2002). *Bad boy: A memoir*. New York, NY: Amistad.

Acclaimed young adult author Walter Dean Myers offers a vivid picture of his childhood growing up in Harlem during the 1940s.

RECOMMENDED WEBSITES

Films

The American Library Association Young Adult Library Services Association. Each year this organization offers a list of "Fabulous films for Young Adults": www.ala.org/yalsa

Critical Literacy Lesson Planning

The Critical Web Reader: cwr.indiana.edu/

This set of tools (Baildon & Damico, 2011) allows the reader to take any website and use a series of questions to critique and write about the website. The site offers students four interpretive lenses to frame their critique: (a) a descriptive lens to help students gauge the reliability of a particular website, (b) an academic lens to critique and examine claims and warrants, (c) a critical lens to gauge gaps and silences on a website (who has a voice, who has been left out), and (d) a reflexive lens so that readers can examine their own beliefs and biases in relation to the website.

ReadWriteThink lesson plans: www.readwritethink.org/lessons/

This website offers an array of English model lessons and discussion resources to foster close and critical reading of narratives. For example, see Shea's (2010) lesson plan, Exploring Language and Identity: Amy Tan's "Mother Tongue" and Beyond for grades 9–12. Retrieved from http://www.readwritethink.org/classroom-resources/lesson-plans/exploring -language-identity-mother-910.html

REFERENCES

Baildon, M., & Damico, J. S. (2011). *Social studies as new literacies in a global society: Relational cosmopolitanism in the classroom*. New York, NY: Routledge.

Bean, T. W., Readence, J. E., & Baldwin, R. S. (2011). *Content area literacy: An integrated approach* (10th ed.). Dubuque, IA: Kendall/Hunt.

Damico, J. S., & Baildon, M. (2011). Content literacy for the 21st century: Excavation, elevation, and relational cosmopolitanism in the classroom. *Journal of Adolescent & Adult Literacy*, 55(3), 232–243.

Jacobs, T. (2010). *Teen cyberbullying investigated: Where do your rights end and consequences begin?* Minneapolis, MN: Free Spirit.

Jinks, C. (2009). *The genius wars*. Boston, MA: Houghton Mifflin Harcourt.

Kelly, K. (2012). The hacker historian. *Wired*, 20(3), 94–122.

Moje, E. B. (2008). Foregrounding the disciplines in secondary literacy teaching and learning: A call for change. *Journal of Adolescent & Adult Literacy*, 52, 96–107.

Parker, W. (2003). *Teaching democracy: Unity and diversity in public life*. New York, NY: Teachers College Press.

Stevens, L. P., & Bean, T. W. (2007). *Critical literacy: Context, research, and practice in the K-12 classroom*. Thousand Oaks, CA: Sage.

Stockton, F. (1882). The lady or the tiger? *The Century Magazine*. Retrieved from http://www.eastoftheweb.com/short-stories/UBooks/LadyTige.shtml

Sumara, D. J. (2002). *Why reading literature in school still matters: Imagination, interpretation, insight*. Mahwah, NJ: Lawrence Erlbaum.

Wasserman, R. (2007). *Hacking Harvard*. New York, NY: Simon Pulse.

Zomaya, A. Y. (2010). *Cloud computing & green IT*. Sydney, Australia: The University of Sydney. Retrieved from http://sydney.edu.au/distributed_computing/themes/cloud.shtml

Chapter 15

Censorship and Young Adult Literature

"It can hardly be argued that either students or teachers shed their constitutional rights of speech or expression at the schoolhouse gate. . . . In our system, students may not be regarded as closed-circuit recipients of only that which the State chooses to communicate."

Supreme Court Justice Abe Fortas, in *Tinker v. Des Moines Community School District* (1969)

Because contemporary young adult fiction with its focus on adolescent issues and realities may address gender and sexual identity, it may be prone to censorship challenges. In some communities, parents and others can find this sex and sexuality in school literature highly objectionable and wish it removed; for example, Laurie Halse Anderson's (2003) *Speak* is an award-winning young adult novel that describes the experiences of a 16-year-old girl after she was raped at a party. The rape scene is not described graphically, but some parents and others may still not be happy with it as a choice of school reading material. In fact, to date, *Speak* remains one of the most consistently challenged books in the United States (www.ala.org).

Fenice B. Boyd and Nancy M. Bailey (2009) reminded us that while any parent has the right to determine what he or she finds appropriate for his or her child to read or view, no one parent has the right to demand that a classroom, school, or community not read a particular text. Indeed, the First Amendment guarantees protection of citizens from just such actions. Yet, censorship is an issue all teachers, and certainly all teachers of English, will more than likely face. It is important that teachers know their school and district's policies and procedures for book selection and for dealing with parental objections and complaints about book and course content. Teachers, as professionals, need to defend their textual and pedagogical choices to students, parents, and administrators, as well as to the community at large. For support, teachers can look to the American Librarian Association's "Freedom to Read" initiative, among many other sources. The use of award-winning, highly recommended contemporary novels are often easier to defend; yet there might also exist the danger of selecting such novels because of their perceived "safety" rather than for the topics they address or the relevance of them to the lives of students and the issues they face.

Activity 15.1 provides an opportunity to discuss censorship from multiple perspectives.

Learning Objectives

- Understand the ways in which censorship impacts freedom of speech as well as classroom practice.

- Consider and be able to discuss various rationales for including censored or challenged young adult literature in the classroom.

- Develop an understanding of how young adult literature may be challenged or censored.

- Know a variety of strategies and resources for defending the right to read a wide variety of texts in the classroom.

Vignette: Mr. Dorian's 10th-Grade Honors Class

Mr. Dorian paced nervously outside of his high school's library. Inside, a hearing involving parents, school, and district administrators and other community stakeholders was taking place that would determine to a great extent his autonomy as a teacher and his ability to teach from a critical perspective. As one of the 10th-grade English teachers, he was generally well respected by parents and students alike for his innovative and challenging honors classes, but not today. Several parents of his 10th-grade honor's class were challenging his use of Jonathan Foer's novel *Extremely Loud and Incredibly Close* (2005), which tells the story of Oskar Schell, whose father perished in the 9/11 World Trade Center attacks.

Although the novel did include descriptions of the violence of the terrorist attacks as well as some profanity, Mr. Dorian had carefully read the novel and had decided that it would be appropriate for his students given its topic and themes of loss, redemption, sorrow, and hope against the backdrop of a national tragedy. Despite being critically acclaimed, the parents did not want their children reading a book that described the attacks of 9/11 so vividly, nor did they approve of some of the language in the text. The fact that one of the parents had lost a family member in the attacks made a school-based issue into a community controversy, with vocal proponents on both sides. Mr. Dorian was now caught up in a maelstrom that threatened not only his credibility as a teacher but also his membership in the small, tight-knit community. Although none of the parents had read the novel and were basing their opinions solely on their impressions of the recently released film, Mr. Dorian feared that the competent, yet inexperienced, new administrator might yield to community pressure to ban the book and reassign Mr. Dorian away from the honor's section.

ACTIVITY 15.1: Professional Reflection and Discussion

Directions: In small groups, discuss censorship from the perspective of parents, teachers, administrators, and adolescents. Are there, or should there be, limits to the power of each group in determining classroom content for all? If you were in Mr. Dorian's place, what might your argument be?

THE ROAD TO CENSORSHIP—PAVED WITH GOOD INTENTIONS?

Despite the good intentions of parents or groups who aim to "protect" children and adolescents from texts that they find inappropriate, the banning of books remains a serious threat to all stakeholders involved, even for those who seek the ban in the first place. Reading should enable all people to read not only the words but also the world around them (Freire, 1991). Educators would do well to remember that "censorship is about restriction and control of intellectual development, and the danger when educators fail to investigate what censorship truly means . . . is that people will merely 'shrug off' the removal of books from libraries and classrooms and fail to see the challenges of books as a violation of First Amendment rights" (Boyd & Bailey, 2009, p. 675). Although procedures must be followed in the United States when challenging or seeking to ban a book, the most common means of "banning" a book is simply not to make it available to students. For example, during the height of the popularity of the *Harry Potter* books by J. K. Rowling, an elementary school in Florida came under scrutiny when the principal made the decision simply to not purchase anymore of the series for the school library. "It was because of the witchcraft themes," Principal Joan Bookman said. "We just knew that we probably had some parents who wouldn't want their children to read these books" (Gazella, 2000, para. 3). Principal Bookman was not alone in her decision. Nationwide,

Censorship and banning books violates both civil and human rights.

the books sparked controversy in some school districts where some parents and religious groups thought the witchcraft collided with their Christian beliefs. In some schools and districts, teachers were forbidden even to discuss the books in class.

More recently, Stephanie Meyer's *Twilight* series has sparked fierce debate over what counts as "appropriate" literature for students and who gets to make that decision. The *Twilight* books chronicle the story of a 17-year-old American girl named Isabella "Bella" Swan and her romantic, but perilous, relationship with a vampire named Edward Cullen. Often compared with J. K. Rowling for both the success of her books and the controversy surrounding them, Meyer's work has been the topic of contentious debate over whether the novels should be allowed in schools.

In San Capistrano, California, the books were banned briefly from middle school libraries when the literacy coordinator for the district decided that they contained subject material that was too mature for students at the middle school level. An e-mail was sent that instructed librarians to remove all books by Meyer from their collections and send them to the district office, where they were to be redistributed to the district's high school libraries. Although the decision to ban the books was reversed four days later by district officials, the event still speaks to the ease with which controversial novels can be banned based on individual opinion. In the following section, we explore some of the titles and reasons books in 2011 (Doyle, 2011) were challenged or banned according to the American Library Association (ALA). As you read through this selection of books, think about your own (or future) classroom library. Which would you include? Are there any you might exclude? How do you decide?

1. Alexie, S. (2007). *The absolutely true diary of a part-time Indian*. New York, NY: Little, Brown.

Banned in the Stockton, Missouri School District (in 2010) because of violence, language, and some sexual content. Retained in the Helena, Montana School District (in 2011) despite a parent's objection that the book contained "obscene, vulgar and pornographic language." This *New York Times* bestseller won the National Book Award in 2007 in the "Young People's Literature" category, and it is on many recommended book lists.

2. Brashares, A. (2007). *Forever in blue, the fourth summer of the sisterhood*. New York, NY: Dell Laurel-Leaf.

This book was challenged at the Theisen Middle School in Fond du Lac, Wisconsin (in 2010), by a parent who believed that the book has inappropriate subject matter for children. "Some (of the characters in the book) are sexually active, and alcohol is part of their recreation."

3. Chopin, K. (1899). *The awakening*. New York, NY: Herbert S. Stone.

This book was challenged at the Oconee County, Georgia Library (in 2011) because the cover of the book—a novel about a woman whose desires run against the family structure of the 1890s—shows a painting of a woman's bare chest, which upset the patron. The novel was first published in 1899.

4. Collins, S. (2010). *The hunger games*. New York, NY: Scholastic.

This book was challenged and presented to the Goffstown, New Hampshire school board (in 2010) by a parent claiming that it gave her 11-year-old nightmares and could numb other students to the effects of violence.

5. Frank, A. (1952/1995). *Diary of a young girl: The definitive edition*. New York, NY: Doubleday.

This book was challenged at the Culpeper County, Virginia public schools (in 2010) by a parent requesting that her daughter not be required to read the book aloud. Initially, it was reported that officials decided to stop assigning a version of Anne Frank's diary, one of the most enduring symbols of the atrocities of the Nazi regime, because of the complaint that the book includes sexual material and homosexual themes. The director of instruction announced the edition published on the 50th anniversary of Frank's death in a concentration camp will not be used in the future even though the school system did not follow its own policy for handling complaints. The remarks set off a hailstorm of criticism online and brought international attention to the 7,600-student school system in rural Virginia. The superintendent said, however, that the book will remain a part of English classes, although it may be taught at a different grade level.

6. Ehrenreich, B. (2001). *Nickel and dimed: On (not) getting by in America*. New York, NY: Henry Holt.

This text was challenged at the Easton, Pennsylvania, School District (in 2010) but retained despite a parent's claim the book promotes "economic fallacies" and socialist ideas, as well as advocating the use of illegal drugs and belittling Christians. Removed from the Bedford, New Hampshire, School District's required Personal Finance course (in 2010) after two parents complained about the "book's profanity, offensive references to Christianity, and biased portrayal of capitalism." The nonfiction account is about Ehrenreich's struggles to make a living on multiple minimum-wage jobs in America. A checklist has been proposed that Bedford school officials would use to rate books and other instructional materials.

7. Saavedra, D., & Madaras, L. (1983). *What's happening to my body? Book for boys: A growing-up guide for parents & sons*. New York, NY: Newmarket Press.

This book was banned from 21 school libraries in Buda, Texas (in 2011), after a parent's complaint. The book includes definitions of rape, incest, sexual assault, and intercourse.

8. Sonnie, A. (2000). *Revolutionary voices: A multicultural queer youth anthology*. Los Angeles, CA: Alyson Books.

Banned by the Rancocas Valley Board of Education from the Mount Holly, New Jersey, high school library shelves (in 2010) after a local conservative group expressed concern that the book was too graphic and obscene. The local group, part of the 9/12 Project, a nationwide government watchdog network launched by the talk-radio and television personality Glenn Beck, called for the banning of three books, all dealing with teenage sexuality and issues of homosexuality. The two other titles challenged but retained were *Love and Sex: Ten Stories of Truth* edited by Michael Cart and *The Full Spectrum: A New Generation of Writing about Gay, Lesbian, Bisexual, Transgender, Questioning, and Other Identities*, edited by David Levithan and Billy Merrell. *Revolutionary Voices*, however, was removed from the Burlington County, New Jersey, public library (in 2010) after a member of Glenn Beck's 9/12 Project complained about Sonnie's book. Named as one of the best adult books for high school students by *School Library Journal* in 2001, the book was called "pervasively vulgar, obscene, and inappropriate."

A QUESTION OF RIGHTS

Even more than a violation of American civil rights and liberties, censorship and the negation of intellectual freedom that the previously mentioned challenged or banned books entail speaks to a violation of the principles of free expression as described in the Universal Declaration of Human Rights (UDHR) adopted by the United Nations General Assembly in 1948. Intellectual freedom is defined by the ALA as "the right of every individual to both seek and receive information from all points of view without restriction." Similarly, the UDHR in Article 19 affirmed that "Everyone has the right to freedom of opinion and expression; this right includes freedom to hold opinions without interference and to seek, receive, and impart information and ideas through any media and regardless of frontier." One of the most important aspects or being able to impart and receive information afforded by freedom of expression is the ability to challenge injustice or voice opinions that provide a counter-narrative to a dominant discourse (Falk-Ross & Caplan, 2008). Likewise, the most insidious danger of censorship is the silencing of voices that speak back to repression or call attention to hegemonic practice. Thus, the danger of "shrugging off" the removal of a few books deemed questionable or offensive by a particular group is no less than negating the human right of freedom of expression for all involved.

STANDING UP TO CENSORSHIP

In the Introduction to *Places I Never Wanted to Be: Original Stories by Censored Writers* (2001), author Judy Blume described her own oft-fought battles with the censorship of her own novels for adolescents. In reflecting on her struggles and the opposition her books faced for including topics encountered adolescents including bullying and sexual maturity, Blume wrote.

> What I worry about most is the loss to young people. If no one speaks out for them, if they don't speak out for themselves, all they'll get for required reading will be the most bland books available. Instead of finding the information they need at the library, instead of finding novels that illuminate life, they will find only those materials to which nobody could possibly object. . . . In this age of censorship I mourn the loss of books that will never be written, I mourn the voices that will be silenced—writers' voices, teachers' voices, students' voices—and all because of fear. How many have resorted to self-censorship? How many are saying to themselves, "Nope . . . can't write about that."

Book banning prevents access to multiple voices and perspectives on issues and events.

Young adult author Chris Crutcher, one of the most frequently banned authors, speaks out against censorship in a YouTube clip (www .chriscruther.com/censorship.html).

In addition, public librarians can be great allies in the effort to make a broad range of material available to students interested in critically and realistically examining issues ranging from relationships, immigration, identity, and so on.

So what can we all do to combat censorship when it is encountered? The National Coalition Against Censorship offers a resource guide and toolkit including protest letter templates along with steps for activism for students, teachers, schools, and parents. In addition, the National Council of Teachers of English (NCTE) includes extensive website resources for challenging censorship with a rationale and example cases. The NCTE resources are annotated at the end of this chapter along with a small group activity aimed at further exploring ways to challenge censorship in your classroom.

Some initial steps recommended by the National Coalition Against Censorship are outlined as follows.

For Teachers and Administrators

- *Be prepared*. Teachers and educators should be familiar with the school's policies and procedures for dealing with book challenges and should be prepared to follow the procedures.
- *Key messages about school curricula*. If responding to a challenge, focus on three key points:

  1. School curricula reflect a spectrum of social and political views and experiences.

  2. School curricula are chosen by professional educators familiar with students' educational needs and abilities.

  3. In many cases, parents' concerns can be addressed by requesting an alternative assignment.

Fielding Complaints

1. Encourage parents to raise any concerns they may have about their children's education.

2. Explain the three key points listed above.

3. Be prepared to articulate the educational rationale for reading the book in question.

4. Be prepared to discuss the school's policies and procedures for challenging books, and provide forms or written instructions, if available.

Let others know. Notify parents, students, colleagues, and other interested parties if a formal complaint process is initiated.

For Parents and Students

- *School board meetings*. You may have the opportunity to share your opinions in an "open forum" part of a school board meeting. Prepare your comments in advance in writing, and be clear and concise. Share personal stories, and be prepared to quote teachers, parents, or children about what the book has meant to them.

- *Writing letters*. Write a letter to the school principal, superintendent, and school board, urging them to follow a thorough review process to deal with a complaint, and to retain the book in the curriculum. Emphasize the importance of protecting the freedom to read and the educational value of the book as a whole. You may also want to write a letter to the editor of your local newspaper or contact your local radio station.

Organize! Create a local anti-censorship coalition. For tips on activism and organizing opposition to censorship, visit www.ncac.org/organize-locally and www.ncac.org/fight-censorship (retrieved on April 20, 2012, from judyblume .com/censorship/toolkit.php).

Teachers and educators should be familiar with policies and procedures for dealing with censorship.

Classroom Vignette Revisited—Mr. Dorian

After a particularly emotional call for the removal of *Extremely Loud and Incredibly Close* from the curriculum by one community member, the review board adjourned to make its decision. Thanks to Mr. Dorian's advanced preparation and knowledge of district policies, as well as his activism in encouraging many stakeholders to read the novel prior to the hearing, he was successful in both retaining his position and the book in his curriculum—but it had been close. In compromise, he agreed to permit students to complete an alternative assignment if their parents' requested it. For their part, Mr. Dorian's students decided to form an anti-censorship club that would read the most frequently banned and challenged books in the United States.

SUMMARY

In this chapter, we examined censorship and the impact it has on both civil and human rights. Although historically there have been instances of mass censorship and repression, most frequently in this country, the censorship of young adult literature seeks to violate the freedom of many for the ideology of the few. Yet for teachers, the balance between defending the freedom of expression against the potential for professional endangerment is tenuous indeed. It is crucial for teachers to be prepared to face censorship and to be familiar with the resources available should a book they are using be challenged or banned.

DISCUSSION QUESTIONS

1. In what ways does censorship impact freedom of speech as well as classroom practice?

2. Consider your current or future classroom. What rationales could you use for including censored or challenged young adult literature in your classroom?

3. How does young adult literature come to be challenged or censored?

4. What are some strategies and resources for defending the right to read widely in the classroom?

KEY TERMS

Censorship   291

SMALL-GROUP ACTIVITY: EXAMINE READINGS AIMED AT COUNTERING CENSORSHIP

In teams of two or more, examine the following recommended readings and NCTE websites and discuss how you might use these resources in lesson and unit planning with young adult literature. The rationales for using challenged books and example lesson plans offer an extensive array of resources for teachers.

RECOMMENDED READINGS

American Library Association. (2011). *Banned and challenged books*. Retrieved from http://www.ala.org/advocacy/banned

Boyd, F. B., & Bailey, N. M. (2009). Censorship in three metaphors. *Journal of Adolescent & Adult Literacy*, 52, 653–661. doi: 10.1598/JAAL.52.8.1

RECOMMENDED YOUNG ADULT LITERATURE FEATURED IN THIS CHAPTER

Anderson, L. H. (2003). *Speak*. New York, NY: Penguin Books.

Laurie Halse Anderson's award-winning novel centers on the first-person voice of Melinda Sordino. Melinda is alienated by her peers after busting an end-of-summer party. Her sarcastic humor covers the real trauma of that party that she has to eventually face.

Cart, M. (2001). *Love and sex: Ten stories of truth*. New York, NY: Simon Pulse.

Ten award-winning authors candidly explore the intricacies of love and sexuality with a combination of humor, pathos, and honesty.

Foer, J. (2005). *Extremely loud and incredibly close*. New York, NY: Houghton Mifflin.

Oskar Schell is an inventor on a mission to find a mysterious key that belonged to his father, tragically killed in the World Trade Center bombing. Oskar invents devices to keep people safe as he journeys throughout New York City on his quest, meeting a host of interesting characters.

Levithan, D., & Merrell, B. (2006). *The full spectrum: A new generation of writing about gay, lesbian, bisexual, transgender, questioning, and other identities*. New York, NY: Knopf.

This collection features poems, essays, and stories about young adults' identity and sexuality encompassing gay, lesbian, bisexual, straight, transitioning, and questioning characters.

RECOMMENDED WEBSITES

Chris Crutcher on Censorship: www.chriscrutcher.com/censorship.html

This acclaimed young adult author is one of the most frequently banned authors with edgy, driving books that feature complex and realistic young adult characters.

The site includes book synopsis material and interviews with the author.

National Council of Teachers of English Anti-Censorship Center: www.ncte.org/action/anti-censorship

This excellent website offers five additional sites aimed at developing rationales for teaching challenged books and combating censorship including censorship of nonprint materials. Additional sites include the following:

Guideline on The Students' Right to Read:

www.ncte.org/positions/statements/righttoreadguideline

Rationales for Teaching Challenged Books:

www.ncte.org/actions/anti-censorship/rationales

This section provides a step-by-step approach to developing a rationale or justification for book selection and reading in the classroom.

Guidelines for Dealing with Censorship of Nonprint and Multimedia Materials:

www.ncte.org/positions/statements/censorshipofnonprint

This website is especially important given the proliferation of online reading materials including music videos and other multimedia distributed online. The website discusses direct and indirect censorship issues including teacher self-censoring material to avoid controversy, which then limits students' opportunities to critique and discuss controversial issues.

The underlying principles in all of these NCTE documents are centered on developing a critically conscious citizenry that respects and understands cultural difference. For example, Principle 5 states that

> In order to succeed in a global society, students need to understand cultures beyond their own. Nonprint and multimedia materials can expand students' access to a variety of cultural products and perspectives. Students must develop a respect for other cultures and the ability to analyze the ways the mainstream media shape their perceptions of those cultures. (p. 2)

This site provides 11 explicit guidelines for dealing with censorship of nonprint and multimedia materials in schools.

REFERENCES

American Library Association. (2011). *Banned and challenged books.* Retrieved from http://www.ala.org/advocacy/banned

Blume, J. (2001). *Places I never wanted to be: Original stories by censored writers.* New York, NY: Scholastic. Retrieved April 14, 2012 from http://judyblume.com/censorship/places4.php).

Boyd, F. B., & Bailey, N. M. (2009), Censorship in three metaphors. *Journal of Adolescent & Adult Literacy, 52,* 653–661. doi: 10.1598/JAAL.52.8.1

Doyle, R. P. (2011) *Books challenged or banned 2010–2011.* Chicago, IL: American Library Association.

Falk-Ross, F., & Caplan, J. (2008). The challenge of censorship. In *Reading today* (p. 20). Newark, DE: International Reading Association

Freire, P. (1991). The importance of the act of reading. In B. M. Power & R. Hubbard (Eds.), *Literacy in progress* (pp. 21–26). Portsmouth, NH: Heinemann Educational Books.

Gazella, K. (2000, January 28). School shelves orders for new Harry Potter books. *St. Petersburg Times.* Retrieved from http://www.sptimes.com/News/012800/Hillsborough/School_shelves_orders.shtml

Tinker v. Des Moines Community School District, 393 U.S. 503 (1969).

ONLINE LITERATURE CIRCLES

Literature circles (Daniels, 2002) have been used in numerous classrooms to engage students in small-group discussion of their self-selected young adult novels. This approach is not without problems related to group members' level of participation (Bowers-Campbell, 2011). Although the benefits literature circles provide in terms of increased comprehension, higher level thinking, and deep reading are some of the established features of literature circles, these benefits all depend on group cohesion. Joy Bowers-Campbell (2011) studied the impact of online virtual literature circles with teachers in a summer class to evaluate moving novel literature circles into this format. Students' posts demonstrated group cohesion, piggybacking on each others' ideas, and generally demonstrating interest and engagement. These students made personal connections to the novels and discussed sensitive topics including child abuse and racism (Bowers-Campbell, 2011).

You can use a variety of social media websites (e.g., we routinely engage our students in novel discussion using Ning.com as a closed website for our classes) to establish an online community for literature circle discussions. For example, numerous fanfiction websites offer forums for students to discuss anime, manga, cartoon, and other forms (e.g., see http://fanfiction-directory.com). Readers in small groups or, in this case, online social media participants can discuss a young adult novel in terms of the characters, conflict in the story, and how they, as readers, relate personally to events in the novel. The general steps involved in online literature circles include the following (Bean et al., 2011; Bowers-Campbell, 2011):

- Students self-select young adult novels related to a theme (e.g., immigration).
- In online postings, they make personal connections to events in the novel.
- Students explore how their particular novel connects to other novels in the group, as well as to other texts and media.
- Students use these initial postings to expand the discussion to include larger issues such as racism and prejudice.

Responding to discussion in a virtual online literature circle overcomes some of the group dynamic problems mentioned earlier. Working with the school librarian and ensuring students have access to a rich collection of young adult literature (e.g., see the short story collection by Donald Gallo on immigration) is crucial for this approach.

SOCIAL MEDIA AND BOOK DISCUSSION

Social media and social networking via websites like Ning.com and numerous blog (WebLog) websites as well as websites that mimic Facebook (e.g., Edmodo) "engage us through personal relationships, cognitive interest, escape and stimulation, and a sense of serving the greater good" (Hayes, 2012, p. 28).

Several social media websites offer professional resources via blogs and discussion forums (Hayes, 2012). For example, the National Council of Teachers of English (NCTE) has a connected community website (http://ncte .connectedcommunity.org/home).

Well-known English educator Jim Burke has a Ning website with forum discussions and video clip support (http://englishcompanion .ning.com).

The widely used Twitter website provides a way to stay abreast of favorite young adult authors (https://twitter.com).

In addition, Twitter chats (e.g., #engchat) and chat archives address teaching topics of interest (www.engchat.org).

The Teachers Teaching Teachers website offers live chats and video support (http://teacherteachingteachers.org).

As you consult these and other websites mentioned throughout the book, you are likely to find a rich and expanding wealth of digital resources to support your teaching of young adult literature.

"Technology is a tsunami of change that will continue to influence the nature of young adult literature" (Bean, Readence, & Baldwin, 2011, p. 18).

SUMMARY

This chapter discussed electronic books (e-books) and their growing influence on the availability and access to a fantastic array of young adult literature. In addition, the increasing use of social media websites offering online book discussion platforms was introduced with a particular focus on closed websites where your students can post their comments (e.g., Ning.com).

DISCUSSION QUESTIONS

1. In what ways has technology impacted the teaching and reading of young adult literature?

2. What role will technology play in enhancing or altering more traditional literacy classroom practices in your current or future classroom?

3. How do various forms of technology increase engagement and relevancy for adolescent readers?

4. What are some of the strategies for using technology you will employ to engage and teach adolescent readers?

KEY TERMS

Electronic Books   304

SMALL-GROUP ACTIVITY: READING AND DISCUSSING A SHORT STORY ON IMMIGRATION

Directions: Using one of the Donald Gallo short stories on immigration and Ning.com, read and discuss the story in your small group. How did this discussion compare with ones you have had in class? What are the advantages and disadvantages of a social media website to discuss a young adult novel?

RECOMMEND READINGS

Bean, T. W. (2010). *Multimodal learning for the 21st century adolescent*. Huntington Beach, CA: Shell Education.

Chapter 3 includes additional teaching strategies (e.g., talking drawings and polar opposites) to engage students in multimodal responses to texts.

Bowers-Campbell, J. (2011). Take it out of class: Exploring virtual literature circles. *Journal of Adolescent & Adult Literacy, 54*(8), 557–567.

This article offers a comprehensive look at three online literature circle discussions with categories for organizing responses to young adult literature. In addition, the author conducted a study to validate the impact of online literature circle discussion.

Daniels, H. (2002). *Literature circles: Voice and choice in book clubs & reading groups* (2nd ed.). York, ME: Stenhouse.

This classic in designing various literature circle response approaches is a valuable mainstay that can support online discussion, in addition to more traditional print-based, face-to-face modes.

RECOMMENDED YOUNG ADULT LITERATURE FEATURED IN THIS CHAPTER

Carman, P. *Skeleton creek* [series]. New York, NY: Scholastic.

Scholastics *Skeleton Creek* online mystery series by Patrick Carman mixes diary and video media, along with a blog offering readers a chance to solve and converse about these exciting stories with Ryan writing in his diary and Sarah capturing their adventures on videocam. The series can be found online (www.scholastic.com/skeletoncreek/books/index .htm).

Collins, S. (2008). *The hunger games.* New York, NY: Scholastic.

This hugely popular dystopian novel and related Hollywood film have captured adolescent readers' interest.

Conifer, D. (2012). *eBully* [Kindle book]. Retrieved from http://www.amazon.com/eBully-ebook/dp/ B001PBFEL8

Set in a middle school, this novel challenges simplistic thinking about cyberbullying and the harassment and stalking laws that allow it to happen.

Lerangis, P. (2012). *The dead of night (the 39 clues: Cahills vs. Vespers).* New York, NY: Scholastic.

This story features the kidnapping of 11-year-old Atticus and the cliffhanger plotting that captures readers' interest. Each book comes with six game cards that unlock clues to rescuing Atticus. A companion website and message board offer additional ways of collaborating to locate the 39 clues hidden around the world. The series can be found on the *39 Clues* website (www.the39clues.com) or on the Amazon.com website for the Kindle.

Littman, S. D. (2011). *Want to go private?* New York, NY: Scholastic.

This novel explores the dark side of the Internet where online predators prey on teens in closed social media websites.

Sawyer, A. (2012). *Notes to self* [Kindle book]. Retrieved from http://www.amazon.com/Notes-to-Self-ebook/dp/B006AY9UGK

Accidents and a traumatic brain injury are at the center of this novel and main character Robin's journey to rebuild her life and memories.

Valentino, A. *The Amanda project* [series]. New York, NY: HarperTeen.

The Amanda Project aimed at girl teen readers provides a weekly online mystery format with the opportunity to write stories and artwork for the series. This visually engaging, interactive website includes a main character whose identity morphs and changes each week. The website offers readers a zine and interactive resources for discussion. This series can be found at *The Amanda Project* website (www.theamandaproject.com/).

RECOMMENDED WEBSITES

Internet Safety

http://wantogoprivate.com
http://chezteen.com

REFERENCES

Bean, T. W. (2010). *Multimodal learning for the 21st century adolescent*. Huntington Beach, CA: Shell.

Bean, T. W., & O'Brien, D. (2012). Past and future directions in content area literacy: A conversation between two experts. *Journal of Adolescent & Adult Literacy, 56*(3).

Bean, T. W., Readence, J. E., & Baldwin, R. S. (2011). *Content area literacy: An integrated approach* (10th ed.). Dubuque, IA: Kendall/Hunt.

Bowers-Campbell, J. (2011). Take it out of class: Exploring virtual literature circles. *Journal of Adolescent & Adult Literacy, 54*(8), 557–567.

Daniels, H. (2002*). Literature circles: Voice and choice in book clubs & reading groups* (2nd ed.). York, ME: Stenhouse.

Hayes, S. (2012). Lessons from a lurker. *The Council Chronicle, 21*(3), 28–29.

Moyer, J. E. (2011). Digital literacies: What does it really mean to "read" a text? *Journal of Adolescent & Adult Literacy, 55*(3), 253–256.

GLOSSARY

Autobiography: The story of a person's life written by that person.

Bibliotherapy: A term coined in 1929 by psychiatrist Dr. G. O. Ireland to refer to his use of books as a cathartic treatment for his patients' mental health therapy. Interest in this work continues today but remains controversial.

BIC: This acronym refers to a basic level of second language learning competency: basic interpersonal conversation. This level is usually acquired after one to two years of exposure to the target second language.

Biographical Essay: An essay about true events in a person's life.

Biography: The story of a person's life written by another author.

Biological Essentialism: A theory that posits gender as an effect of biology and, therefore, largely predetermined and immutable. In this case, gender and sex are considered synonymous. From this perspective, anatomy determines ones gender. All boys and all girls would be basically the same in their behavior.

Body Biography: A tracing of a full-sized human body with collage-like images placed into the interior of the tracing that depict a particular character and events in a novel, short story, poem, or nonfiction text.

CALP: This acronym refers to an advanced level of second language learning: cognitive academic language proficiency. This stage of second language acquisition includes the knowledge and use of complex academic language and concepts.

Censorship: Challenges to students' right to read particular texts, view or listen to material, and have access to multiple points of view on controversial topics.

Content Area Literacy: The literacy practices related to subject area fields including English, social studies, science, mathematics, and the arts.

Cosmopolitanism: Occurs as a result of globalization and refers to the framing of self and other in relation to the world rather than to the nation. Part of this reframing, by necessity, involves extending the obligations of self to others beyond local and national borders, beyond national citizenship.

Cosmopolitan Reading: Is a perspective to the teaching of literature that encourages students to cross local and national borders in their reading to experience, aesthetically and intellectually, the widest range of experiences and perspectives possible, and to reread and reconsider local and national literature in relation to the global literature they have read.

Creativity: The creation of unusual or novel productions.

Critical Content Area Literacy: Views all texts as anything but neutral and explores power relationships in texts from a critical stance.

Critical Literacy: Active questioning of the stance found within, behind, and among texts with an eye toward how a book positions the reader and silences or privileges some characters but not others.

Cultural Criticism Orientation: Cultural criticism is an amalgamation of various forms of literary criticism: feminism, deconstruction, poststructuralism, Marxism, postcolonialism, among others. It begins from the premise that no texts, literary or otherwise, are politically neutral. All texts offer particular and interested readings of the world.

Cultural Heritage Orientation: Works on the literacy canon are considered to be the best writing a culture has produced. They are works that have stood the test of time and will have continuing universal appeal. According to cultural heritage, such writing offers unique and profound renderings of the human condition worthy of close, intense study.

Dinner Party: This strategy is a dramatic enactment of a particular part of scene in a novel. The notion is as follows: How would this dialogue look if you could invite char-

acters from the novel home with you for a dinner party?

Dystopian Science Fiction Novels: These novels trouble utopian views of the future by offering readers seriously flawed fictional societies.

Electronic Books (e-books): Complete works of fiction and nonfiction that have been digitized for reading on a computer or portable e-book reader.

English Language Learners (ELLs): Refers to students whose first language (L1) is not English.

E-zines: A handmade publication that is centered on the unique interest of its creator. Often made with scissors and glue, these publications satirize, critique, or entertain the reader based on a variety of contemporary topics. An e-zine may use desktop publishing software.

Fanfiction: Original works of fiction based on popular media including television, movies, books, music, and video games.

Fanzines: Often devoted to following the careers of bands or actors and actresses, these publications are created by adolescents using either handmade materials or computer-based applications. They may include travel diaries or accounts and blogs. See "*E-zines*" and "*Zines*" definitions.

Fantasy: This genre takes the reader on fantastic journeys where magic prevails, creatures of all kinds talk and have magical powers, and anything is possible.

Genre: A way of classifying texts into recognizable categories including biographies, novels, comedies, satires, tragedies, short stories, and so on. Films may also be categorized in this fashion (e.g., documentaries, cartoons, romance, and so on).

Giftedness: Ideal cognitive development that leads to actualized or potential mastery of a domain (or domains).

GLBTQ: This shorthand acronym refers to gay, lesbian, bisexual, transgender/transsexual, and queer.

Global Literature: Works that are focused on the experience of social and cultural difference and diversity, locally, nationally, and most importantly globally. It is a category that includes minority, indigenous, and other literature that highlights local or national culture, communities, and regions in addition to historical and contemporary works from the international community, that is, from other countries, other regions, or specific global populations.

Globalization: The extensive movement or flow of information, ideas, images, capital, and people across increasingly permeable political borders as a result of economic and technological change.

Graphic Novels: These comic book based stories and nonfiction accounts range from 100 to 200 pages and deal with novel-length topics. Illustrations and comic book-like panels appeal to a variety of readers.

Heteronormativity: Means a way of being in the world that relies on the belief that heterosexuality is normal, which implicitly positions homosexuality and bisexuality as abnormal and, thus, inferior.

High-Interest, Low-Vocabulary Books: High–Low books feature vocabulary in the 3rd- to 4th-grade range and interests likely to be appealing to adolescent readers including sports, horror, science fiction, romance, nonfiction, and other popular genres.

Historical Fiction: This genre reconstructs the past both materially and emotionally, showing the impact that major social and cultural events had on the lives of people at a particular place and time.

Homophobia: The hatred and fear of homosexuals and homosexual behavior.

Horror: Overlaps with gothic literature and its ancient tradition depicting the trials of characters who sell their souls to the devil for material gain. These are engaging stories set in foreboding places that hold the potential to scare the reader.

Humor: Writing that amuses and pokes fun at life's foibles.

Intertextuality: Meanings constructed when reading and interpreting a text but mediated by meanings from other texts such as books, CDs, DVDs, conversations, art work, movies, and so on. (Additional Definition)—Making connections across genres, multimedia, and using background knowledge to interpret the often surreal images and allusions in postmodern picture books and novels.

Literary Canon: These novels are generally thought of as "the classics" and include well-established authors like William Steinbeck and others. Young adult literature can be paired with canonical selections including Shakespeare and other well-established authors.

Literature Circles: A collaborative approach to instruction that integrates the reading of a book with discussion of characters, themes, and how the reader relates to the story.

Manga: Based on Japanese drawings, manga feature comic-book-like characters in visual panels, often battling evil forces. Written in sequential series, manga and its animated cousin, anime, enjoys a significant teen and adult following.

Memoir: A reflection on one's life with roots in autobiography.

New Literacies: A broadening of what counts as text and literacies to include multimedia of all kinds, especially film, streaming video, and podcasts.

New Times: This term takes into account adolescents' literacies in and out of school with an emphasis on both print and nonprint media connected to global contexts.

Nonfiction: Prose writing about real people and true experiences.

Poetry: Literature in verse with powerful images that shed light on taken-for-granted experiences.

Poststructural theory: Poststructuralism suggests that individuals actively position themselves with and against the various discursive and material practices available in any context that name and promote particular versions of masculinities and femininities. Gender is thus not a product of physical anatomy or of socialization but negotiated within the social and historical meanings given gender in any given context.

Postmodern Elements: These include multiple meta-fictive elements like nonlinear plots, self-referential writing and illustrations, narrators who step out of the story to directly address the reader, multiple narrators, mixing genres, surreal art and images, font shifts, and mixed settings.

Postmodern Picture Books: Trouble the traditional sandwich structure of the story to bend time, space, and other features in order to make a point. They are potentially confusing to readers, requiring some teacher scaffolding and rereading.

Postmodernism: A movement in architecture, film, art, music, and literature aimed at breaking away from conventional forms from the modernist period. (Additional Definition)—A philosophical movement that generally distrusts and deconstructs simple views of events, sometimes called grand narratives (e.g., voyages of discovery).

Reader Response Orientation: From this perspective, there can be multiple readings of any text by an individual reader and certainly by groups of readers. The differences in their readings will be a result of their personal histories and contemporary experiences.

Realistic Fiction: This genre features young adult main characters facing issues that adolescent readers can identify with, and contemporary realistic fiction often includes multiple viewpoints, imagery, flashbacks, and time shifts.

Romance Novels: Explore young adults' quest for love and friendship amid sometimes overly simplistic views of gender and socioeconomic status.

Rubric: A concrete description of the qualities and criteria expected in a piece of writing. These descriptive scoring statements are generally tied to numeric values depicting high-quality or low-quality performance (e.g., earning a 1 on a 4-point rubric would equate to poor quality performance).

Science Fiction: Generally characterized by the inclusion of science, technology and invention, futuristic elements, time travel, and other captivating and fluid dimensions.

Sex Role Socialization: A theory of gender identity that begins with the assumption that biology determines sexual difference but explains the various and changing roles that men and women have assumed over time and across cultures by positing that children learn gender/sex roles and behavior by observing and modeling the adults in their world. Along with the adults in their world, the social and cultural institutions in children's lives, e.g., the media, pop culture, schools, church, the law, and so on, maintain and enforce appropriate gender behavior.

Short Stories: A brief work of prose fiction with a tightly wound plot and the rapid onset of conflict, characters, setting, point of view, and theme.

Street Literature: Set in gritty urban scenes where poverty and personal struggle for survival and identity collide, these primarily African American female authors feature characters who are strong and resistant. They actively seek to move ahead and leave abusive relationships with domineering male characters.

Struggling/Striving Readers: This is a highly diverse category that may include ELL students, students struggling with academic reading, students whose interests depart from school reading tasks, and students reading at least two or more grades below their current year in school.

Thematic Unit: A series of lessons developed around a theme and often in collaboration with other teachers in a core team (e.g., English, science, and social studies) or in more informal teams of two teachers in related subject areas (e.g., English and social studies).

Web Quest: An inquiry-oriented activity in which some or all of the information acquired from the activity comes directly from the student's interaction with the Internet. The teacher can construct a Web Quest using one of the online templates available or other software (e.g., Inspiration).

Young Adult Literature: Literacy works (usually fiction but not always) intended for readers between the ages of 12 and 18.

Young Adult Mysteries: Introduce challenging problems, puzzles, or elements of suspense where the protagonist is an adolescent able to unravel the mystery.

Zines: Generally handmade and created to offer a counterpoint and social critique of mainstream issues including homophobia, excess dieting, environmental issues, and community political consciousness. Zines create a unique space for creative writing and for sharing ideas and opinions.

AUTHOR INDEX

Subject Index

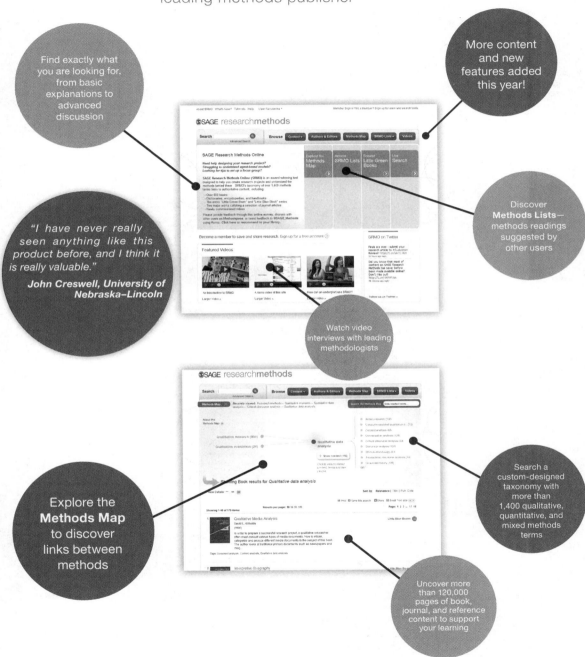